Philosophy and the End of Sacrifice

equinox

SHEFFIELD UK BRISTOL CT

The Study of Religion in a Global Context

Series Editors:

Tim Jensen
Executive Editor
University of Southern Denmark

Morny Joy
Series Editor
University of Calgary

Katja Triplett
Managing Editor
University of Göttingen

The series, published in association with the International Association for the History of Religions, encourages work that is innovative in the study of religions, whether of an empirical, theoretical or methodological nature. This includes multi- or inter-disciplinary studies involving anthropology, philosophy, psychology, sociology and political studies. Volumes will examine the continuing influence of postcolonial, decolonial and intercultural dynamics, as well as contemporary responses from intersectional studies. They will also address the relevance and application of more recent approaches such as cognitivist, as well as ones concerned with aesthetic culture – art, architecture, media, performance and sound.

Philosophy and the End of Sacrifice
Disengaging Ritual in Ancient India, Greece and Beyond

Edited by
Peter Jackson and Anna-Pya Sjödin

Published by Equinox Publishing Ltd.

UK: Office 415, The Workstation, 15 Paternoster Row, Sheffield, South Yorkshire S1 2BX
USA: ISD, 70 Enterprise Drive, Bristol, CT 06010

www.equinoxpub.com

First published 2016

British Library Cataloguing-in-Publication Data

A catalogue record for this book is available from the British Library.

ISBN-13 978 1 78179 124 0 (hardback)
978 1 78179 125 7 (paperback)

Library of Congress Cataloging-in-Publication Data

Philosophy and the end of sacrifice : disengaging ritual in ancient India, Greece and beyond / edited by Peter Jackson and Anna-Pya Sjödin.
pages cm. — (The study of religion in a global context)
Includes bibliographical references and index.
ISBN 978-1-78179-124-0 (hardback)
ISBN 978-1-78179-125-7 (paperback)
1. Sacrifice—India. 2. Rites and ceremonies—India—History.
3. Sacrifice—Greece. 4. Rites and ceremonies—Greece—History.
5. Sacrifice—History of doctrines. I. Jackson, Peter, 1971 - editor.
II. Sjödin, Anna-Pya, 1972 - editor.
BL1236.76.S23P45 2015
203'.4--dc23

2015010614

Edited and typeset by Queenston Publishing, Hamilton, Canada

Printed by Lightning Source Inc. (La Vergne, TN), Lightning Source UK Ltd. (Milton Keynes), Lightning Source AU Pty. (Scoresby, Victoria).

Contents

Introduction

Peter Jackson and Anna-Pya Sjödin

This volume addresses the means and ends of sacrificial speculation. It examines recurrent philosophical modes of thought – especially in Ancient India and Greece – and considers the commonalities of their historical provenance. Scholars have long observed, yet without presenting any transcultural *grand theory* on the matter, that sacrifice seems to end with, or perhaps more accurately, to continue *as* philosophy, in both Ancient India and Greece. How are we to understand this important transformation that so profoundly changed the way we think of religion, and philosophy as opposed to religion? Some of the complex topics inviting closer examination in this regard are the interiorization of ritual, ascetism and self-sacrifice, sacrifice and cosmogony, the figure of the philosopher-sage, transformations and technologies of the self, analogical reasoning, the philosophy of ritual, vegetarianism, and metempsychosis.

In 2004, historian of religions Guy Stroumsa provided a lucid and innovative exposition of these matters in a series of lectures at the Collège de France. First published in French in 2005, the lectures appeared in English a few years later under the title *The End of Sacrifice: Religious Transformations in Late Antiquity*. The study delineates the gradual emergence of a so called "communitarian religion," which enhanced soteriological aims in favour of earlier forms of civic religiosity sustained through the practice of blood sacrifice. The current collection of papers owes a great deal to Stroumsa's original statement, not least his elaboration of the interplay between philosophical and sacrificial discourses in Late Antiquity. Can a similar development be discerned elsewhere, and what are we to make of the disengaging contrast between religious and philosophical discourses that seems to emerge as a consequence of that development? These challenging questions were to form points of departure for a research colloquium on *Philosophy and the End of Sacrifice*, which took place in Stockholm, Sweden, in the fall of 2011. Hosted by the Department of Philosophy at Södertörn University, Stockholm, and the Department of the History of Religions at Stockholm University, the two-day colloquium was attended by a small group of Indologists, Historians of Religions, and Philosophers, all of whom presented drafts of the papers collected in this volume. We wish to express our gratitude to the Wenner-Gren Foundations and to Axel and Margaret Ax:son Johnson foundation for generously funding the colloquium. We also wish to direct our warmest thanks to editors Tim Jensen, Morny Joy, and Katja Triplet for accepting this collection of papers as the first volume in the series *The Study of Religion in a Global Context.*

Writing to his wife Marcella around 200 CE, the Neoplatonist Porphyry dwells on the role of philosophy as the sublimation and interiorization of sacrifice. He compares the sacred duties of a priest with the superior duties of the philosopher. The latter's duties are transformed into mental acts inside the temple of the mind, performed in front of a living statue, and purified by knowledge rather than being defiled by the useless offerings of food:

> Reason tells us that the Divine is present everywhere and in all men, but that only the mind of the wise man is sanctified as its temple, and God is best honoured by him who knows Him best. And this must naturally be the wise man alone, who in wisdom must honour the Divine, and in wisdom adorn for it a temple in his thought, honouring it with a living statue, the mind moulded in His image [...] Now God is not in need of any one, and the wise man is in need of God alone. For no one could become good and noble, unless he knew the goodness and beauty which proceed from the Deity. Nor is any man unhappy, unless he has fitted up his soul as a dwelling- place for evil spirits. To a wise man God gives the authority of a god. And a man is purified by the knowledge of God, and issuing from God, he follows after righteousness.[1]

This passage aptly illustrates an ancient theme that has haunted philosophy, despite its occasional neglect in contemporary scholarship: the meaning and efficacy of sacrifice. It is also a passage indicative of religious transformations in Late Antiquity. These would forever change the global religious landscape, culminating in the rise of the – to borrow Hans G. Kippenberg's designation – "Middle Eastern religions of salvation" (*Vorderasiatischen Erlösungsreligionen*).[2]

Before providing an outline of the present volume, we need to clarify some of the historical circumstances in which philosophy and sacrifice emerge as interdependent human propensities. In so far as this connectedness can be convincingly explained, a whole sequence of secondary reconsiderations could be expected to follow in its wake. One such reconsideration involves the historicity of academic exploration as a whole, for it cannot be neglected that philosophy has played a foundational part in determining a sense of truth and reality beyond the premature bounds of immediate judgement.

The early development of Greek philosophy is often conceived as a gradual detachment of human reason from the bonds of religion. Religion, in this context, is represented as a container of prescriptive yet irrational notions (myths, omens, superstitions, etc.). For this reason, attempts at tracing the origin of Greek philosophy are still characteristically informed by the notion that the first philosophically valid statements were formally restricted to, and ultimately obstructed by, a discourse permeated by myth and epic.[3] According to this view, the delusion of myth defines the essence of religion (the inferior yet imputed "theory") from which the philosopher seeks to detach himself by means of inference and pure reason. Representing the tension between early philosophy and religion in these terms is anachronistic. In other words: it is a misrepresentation nurtured by specific historical circumstances.

In contemporary Western society, religion is often understood as a system of beliefs underlying various ritual and scriptural enactments. Religion is therefore held to be sustained by faith to the same extent as this faith is considered universally valid by its adherents. Despite its tenacity and occasional accuracy, this biased outlook depends on a gradual transformation of religion in Late Antiquity, a process that began to exert a pervasive historical impact through the adoption of Christianity as the *vera religio* of the Roman Empire.

Religion in pre-Christian Antiquity was principally a civic concern defined by the practice of public worship, not so much a matter of personal faith. Besides clothing, language, laws, and other ethnic characteristics, religion was a matter of participation and loyalty in relation to a specific community. It was a mode of behaviour that neither had to interfere with the personal quest for truth and salvation nor pose a threat to the political interests of other communities. The practice of animal sacrifice was a distinctive feature of civic religion usually involving eating and feasting. Hence, it was particularly suited to the reinforcement of solidarity and shared abundance within the community.

Alongside the mainstays of civic religion, however, currents of spiritual and philosophical inquiry had long flourished. Less grounded in place and ethnicity, these currents instead revolved around the teaching of mythical or historical "sages" (such as Orpheus or Pythagoras), emphasized the transformation of the self, and thrived within networks of free association and initiation. While not necessarily in opposition to the religious duties of civic life, they provided platforms for spiritual guidance that had never been a main concern of civic religion. The fact that some members of the Pythagorean order – the virtual prototype of a philosophical society, emerging in the 6th century BC – abstained from eating meat is an early indication that philosophy was considered incompatible with the practice of animal sacrifice. At the same time, however, the Pythagorean way of life was highly ritualized and required adherence to a set of orally transmitted doctrines (so-called *akousmata* or "heard things"). Isocrates even believed that Pythagoras had brought philosophy to the Greeks as a partial result of his careful attention to sacrificial rites among the Egyptians.[4]

The suspicion thus arises that it was not religion as such, at least not in the contemporary sense of the term, that constituted the antithesis of early philosophy. Rather, it was those aspects of public worship that merely served the interests of the civic community. Since animal sacrifice constituted the hallmark of public worship, it is not surprising that it was considered incompatible with the esoteric teaching of philosophy. Furthermore, the practice of prayer and animal sacrifice in public space could be construed as a mischievous satisfaction of appetite and desire that perverted the virtues of philosophy. It was apparently this notion of sacrifice that led Aristotles' successor Theophrastus (c. 370-c. 287 BC) to feel such admiration for the Jewish practice of *holokaustos* ("burnt whole," "burnt-offering"). The Jews, a people of philosophers, are said not to feast on the sacrifices, but to burn them whole and to fast for the intervening days. During this time they converse with each other about the deity and observe the stars at night. While they were the first to institute sacrifices, they did it by compulsion and not from eagerness.[5]

These examples seem to indicate that musings on the meaning of sacrifice were a crucial element in the inception of Greek philosophy. But besides simply orienting itself beyond the bounded space of civic religion, philosophy also implied a theoretical continuation and interiorization of sacrifice. It is probably not a coincidence that similar notions characterized some of the decentralized religious movements that flourished in Late Antiquity. One of these was eventually to recapture the domain of public worship, thus causing an inversion of the original polarities (sacred/profane, public/private) that enabled its development as a cosmopolitan quest for truth and transformation: Christianity.[6]

These issues should invite serious reconsideration of the tension and interrelationship between religion and philosophy before the rise of Christianity. They might also encourage us to reconsider the conception of philosophy as a quintessentially Greek phenomenon. A closer examination of the sacrificial instigation of philosophy, or the philosophical continuation of sacrifice, is an undertaking that seems to require comparison. It is from India, not from Greek Antiquity, that the earliest and most apparent examples of this notion derive. Furthemore, the tenets of Greek and Indian philosophy need not have evolved completely independent of each other. The Greek familiarity with the so-called "naked sages" (*gumnosophistai*) of India and the Orphic/Pythagorean notion of metempsychosis may have foregrounded earlier stages of mutual influence. Notwithstanding the notion of such direct or indirect influences, comparisons between these complex quantities could still prove fruitful.[7]

The exegesis, interiorization, and critical discourse on sacrifice was crucial to the emergence of Hindu, Buddhist, Jain, and Materialist vocations and schools of philosophy. The meaning and efficacy of Vedic sacrifice had already been hotly debated, as it were, within its own ritual framework. This is clearly exemplified by the complex sacrificial speculations and esoteric teachings encountered in the Brāhmaṇas and the Upaniṣads from the first millennium BC. Despite its obvious dissimilarity to public worship in the Greek city-states, Vedic worship was also a communal concern bound to a mutual agreement between guilds of ritual specialists (members of priestly families) and chieftains (members of a warrior aristocracy). The latter were the sponsors who increased their renown through the staging of expensive animal sacrifices. While hard to grasp in its detail, the tendency to move beyond the social and soteriological premises of this unwieldy sacrificial economy was accompanied by new techniques of interrogation and personal transformation. Such new techniques, whether focused on pure reasoning or asceticism, all reverberated with the notion that the principles of ritual causality were necessary keys to salvation and enlightenment. An early instance of this practice, linked to a general development within the Brāhmaṇic tradition, was the so-called "daily sacrifice of the breath" (or *prāṇāgnihotra).* The textual realization of this practice bears a striking resemblance to the simile employed by Porphyry in his *Letter to Marcella.* This is demonstrated here by an excerpt from the *Vaikhānasasmārtasūtra* (II.18):

> The self-luminous *ātman* is the sacrificer; the intellect is the house-wife; the heart-lotus is the vedi [i.e. the sacrificial altar]; the hairs of the body are the *darbha*-blades; the *prāṇa* (out- breathing) is the *gārhapatya* [housholder]; the *āpana* (in-breathing) is the *āhavanīya* [sacrificial fire] [–] The organs of sense, the tongue etc., are the sacrificial vessels; the objects of sense, the taste etc., are the sacrificial substances. Its aim (or "fruit") is the insight into the meaning of the syllable *om* (viz. the Bráhman). Therefore, in this way he should as sole priest, having formulated the "Sacrifice of the Self," with the mantra: "Thou art the underlayer of nectar," besprinkle the food; touch it with the hymn to the food.[8]

As Stephanie Jamison points out in her contribution to the present volume, readers should be dissuaded from equating this form of analogical reasoning with the transformation of sacrifice into a purely mental act, especially as the *prāṇāgnihotra* is also seen to involve eating a meal. Sacrifice and the contemplation of sacrifice are certainly not mutually exclusive undertakings. Still, the notion that actions performed on the ritual ground can be inoculated into the mundane works of the sacrificer's own life and body is a necessary precondition for a means of living that no longer perceives the necessity to appease the gods with physical offerings.

Irrespective of one's disciplinary leanings, it is difficult to disregard the resemblances between the excerpts from the *Vaikhānasasmārtasūtra* and Porphyry's *Letter to Marcella* as expressions of analogous historical and cognitive exigencies. This being the case, further attention to the preconditions of such resemblances might throw unexpected light on our own scholarly modes of historicizing and philosophizing, on who we are and why we think the way we do.

The first section of the volume, "Historical and Comparative Approaches to Ritual Thought in Ancient India and Archaic Greece," is devoted to changes in religious behaviour and the place of sacrifice in early Indian intellectual history. Instead of searching for origins and closures, the individual contributions rather attempt to map changes, and sometimes to catalogue the complexity in thinking and acting that comes to light in the early Indian material. What becomes clear then, instead of a simple one-way causality between thought and performance, is an ongoing transformation mediated by both intellectual activity and ritual reflexivity. Beginnings and ends in this sense never actually take place as clearly definable moments in time. The precarious act of historical and/or logical comparison can of course not be disregarded in this connection, because the terminology underlying one's research is always confronted with the general problem of translation.

Stephanie Jamison's contribution undertakes to think along with sacrifice and its performative and intellectual expressions. She thus challenges the view of interiorization as the resultant idea of an end of sacrifice as exterior performance. By clarifying these aspects Jamison points to instances of ritual speculation, for example the famous hymn of *Puruṣa*, the cosmic man, and the theme of interiorizing ritual in the earliest Vedic texts. The changes depicted apparently have more to do with what she labels "ritual inflation" rather than with the "death of ritual." By describing the complex activity of equating and substituting the cosmic and the mundane, in both the early and later Vedic texts, she emphasizes the centrality of sacrifice within Indian intellectual endeavours, both past and present.

Clemens Cavallin's text takes as its point of departure the theme of interiorized ritual and its relation to changes in religious and ritual practices in early India, especially the tendency to shift focus towards the person or human being. He argues that such interiorizations of ritual practice and discourse need to be placed in a larger comparative context that is based on a theoretical model of ritualization and forms of interiorization. Cavallin employs a notion of abstract action, as formulated by Caroline Humphrey and James Laidlaw in their analysis of the Jain *puja* (1994). He develops a theory of the relationship between the abstraction of meaning (concepts) and of action (ritual acts) as they are connected to the religious principles of sacralization and personification.

Gerald James Larson's paper discusses five principal questions posed in relation to the topic of the "end of sacrifice" and the emerging concept of "religion" in the Late Antiquity. The first two questions concern the use of the concepts of "religion," "philosophy" and "theology," and the apparent absence of their counterparts in the early Indian material. By outlining important notions in Indian thinking, Larson stresses the extent to which the worldviews between Mediterranean Europe and the Indian subcontinent differ. The third question concerns the possible naming of a second axial age that occurred around the first centuries CE in both of these cultural spheres. This could be postulated at least in terms of far-reaching changes taking place within their respective intellectual discourses. The two last points of discussion concern the need for rethinking and rectifying Jaspers' notion of a first axial age and his notions of "religion," "philosophy," and "theology."

Anna-Pya Sjödin addresses the conceptualization of agency in *Bṛhadāraṇyakopaniṣad* by outlining the metaphors used in this text to capture notions of sacrificial and epistemological agency. At the same time as this Upaṇiṣadic text elaborates the then-emerging ideas of self (*ātman*) and the consequences of knowing that self, it also carries impressions of discussions and speculations that were formulated within a culture of sacrificial ritual. Traces of the Upaṇiṣadic expressions are then shown to have a structural continuity in later systematic philosophy, a continuity expressed mostly in terms of epistemological agency and formulated within a discourse on the self as the acting and knowing subject.

The final contribution to the first section also functions as a prelude to the next section. Peter Jackson compares early Greek and Indic examples of a sacrificial ideology. Its dynamics seem to result from these two similar sacrificial institutions, both of which were based on the contract between patrons and ritual specialists. He thereby attempts to emphasize the tension between a civic religiosity, celebrating and seeking to consolidate an existing community, and a sectarian religiosity seeking emancipation from the civic community. The latter mode of religiosity was characterized by voluntary ordeals of initiation and asceticism in a quest for values of a purportedly stable nature (truth, immortality, salvation, and so on).

The themes forming the backbone of the book's midsection, "Ritual Thought in Late Antiquity," are all grounded in textual sources from Late Antiquity, such as the *Corpus Hermeticum*, the Nag Hammadi texts, and the letters of Paul. As will become clear, however, they also point in quite different directions, both spatial and temporal, by evoking ancient Egyptian material (Jørgen Podemann Sørensen and Christian Bull), ethnographic *comparanda* (Sørensen), and 20th century philosophy (Hans Ruin).

While Guy Stroumsa gave us the original stimulus to prepare this book, we are happy that he has agreed to revisit the crucial issues of his monograph in a newly written piece. Besides rehearsing and developing some already familiar topics, Stroumsa takes the opportunity to critically ponder the recent scholarly revitalization of Karl Jaspers' concept of an Axial Age (*Achsenzeit*). This trend is particularly visible in the late Robert Bellah's ambitious delineation of the early development of the world's religious traditions in *Religion in Human Evolution: From the Paleolithic to the Axial Age* (2011).

Jørgen Podemann Sørensen explores how sacrifice, in its capacity as a necessary subspecies of ritual, has informed both modern theories of religion, and the speculative responses of its indigenous performers. He does this by instigating a specific sacrificial logic. He compares the ethnographically documented bear ceremonialism among the Ainu of Hokkaido with the ancient Egyptian sacrifice of the goddess Maat. These examples serve to bring the radicalized Hermetic idea of spiritual sacrifice into the broader context of sacrificial speculation. He thereby demonstrates how the radicalized idea of sacrifice always depends on its more traditional mode, even when the latter may appear to have come to an end.

In a similar vein to Sørensen, and likewise proceeding from the *Corpus Hermeticum*, Christian Bull follows a recent scholarly development in the evaluation of the Hermetic treatises as appendages of a *real* cultic community. Bull insists on rectifying the notion of the Hermetic spiritual and spoken excercises as dismissals of material sacrifice. Unlike the intentions of traditional Graeco-Roman animal sacrifice to increase the prosperity of land and lineage, the concept of material sacrifice in ancient Egypt was distinctly tied to a concept of piety and cosmic order. This notion responds well with the ideals of both Jewish and Hermetic communities in Late Antiquity.

Jögen Magnusson opens his case with a summary of the scholarly controversies surrounding the concept of "Gnosticism" in the wake of the discovery of the Nag Hammadi codices in 1945. He then proceeds to compare the understanding of Gnostic mythology in a recent addition to the data set, the so-called *Gospel of Judas* (first made publicly accessible in 2006), as well as in one of the most studied texts in the Nag Hammadi corpus, the so-called *Gospel of Truth*. Magnusson identifies important points of dissent in the two treatises that provide different, yet distinctively Gnostic views regarding the sacrificial death of Jesus.

Against the backdrop of anti-pagan Christian imperial policies during the 4th century, Hans Ruin draws attention to the core of the Christian canon: the letters of Paul. While taking its lead from Stroumsa's overall interpretative scheme concerning the transformation and internalization of sacrifice during and after the time of Christ, as essentially a transformation within Jewish culture itself, the analysis differs when it comes to the specific role and meaning of the Pauline letters. These canonical documents for Christianity, notably *Romans*, *Hebrews*, and *First Corinthians*, are interpreted as decisive expressions of precisely this inner critical transformation of Jewish spiritual culture in the direction of an internalized sacrifice. They also became the cornerstone for the emergence of a new "sacrificial subjectivity." The analysis critically engages with Hegel's understanding of Christianity, and also revokes Foucualt's and Hadot's work on the ancient culture of care for the self. Finally it acknowledges the work of Derrida, thus building a bridge to the last section of the book.

The sole contribution to the last section, "Repercussions of Sacrifice in Western Philosophy," closes the historical circuit by addressing the continuation of sacrificial themes in contemporary continental philosophy. Marcia Sá Cavalcante Schuback's point of departure is the relation between philosophy and sacrifice in Jean-Luc Nancy's readings of the philosophy of sacrifice as proposed by Georges Bataille in the 1940s. In showing how Bataille's philosophy of sacrifice accomplishes rather than overcomes the philosophical sacrifice of the singular for the sake of the universal, Nancy argues for a suspension of the philosophical concept of sacrifice and addresses the idea of an open offering of singular finite being. In question here is not the end of sacrifice, nor the sacrifice for ends, but the unsacrificeable finite offering of existence.

It is our hope that this volume will spur scholars within different branches of the humanities to further scrutinize the issues addressed by its individual contributors. How are we to understand the ritual frameworks within which philosophical propensities seem to emerge, again and again, both as reactions *against* and incorporations *of* that same ritual framework? What were the historical conditions of that development, and to what extent are we justified in theorizing their raisons d'être without losing sight of the local contingencies? Today, students of religion are sometimes reluctant to undertake cross-cultural comparative approaches, because the recurrent themes (or matrices) informing such approaches are thought to obscure the uniqueness of each data set. Nevertheless, it is easy to imagine the impoverished understanding of human culture that will eventually result from the avoidance of comparative studies.

We need to keep in mind that a rethinking of the historical connectedness of philosophy and sacrifice may eventually shed new light on the stature and historicity of the contemporary academic subject, unveiling its philosophical beginnings as a locus of interior ritual exercise and exegesis. It is especially against this background that the particularities treated in this collection seem to foreshadow a more general concern in the present, namely the role of critical scholarship and its potential impact on a society running a constant risk of becoming ignorant of itself and its own past.

Notes

1. Zimmern 1896:§12
2. Kippenberg 1991
3. The following statement by H.-G. Gadamer, 1996: 130, is characteristic of this view: "[...] *die von Homer und Hesiod ausgehende große epische Überlieferung,* [*hat*] *trotz ihrer mythischen und erzählenden Form, philosophischen Wert* [...] *Daß zwischen episch-religiöser Sicht und begrifflichem Denken ein enger zusammenhang bestehen kann, liegt auf der Hand. Zu einer Zäsur gelangen wir erst bei Platon, und zwar dann, wenn es als besonders kennzeichendes Merkmal seiner Vorgänger hinstellt, daß sie Märchen erzählt haben.*"
4. *Busiris*, 28.
5. Theophrastus is quoted in Porphyry's *On Abstinence* 2,26. The passage is discussed in Stroumsa 2009: 60.
6. Stroumsa 2009: 90–91.
7. As indicated by Philostratus' *The Life of Apollonius of Tyana* (3,19), it was a common belief in Late Antiquity that the sages of India (*hoi brakhmânes* [Sanskrit *brāhmaṇas*]) had transmitted the doctrine of metempsychosis to the Egyptians, from whom Pythagoras had learned it and transmitted it to the Greeks.
8. Caland 1927: 2.18

References

Caland, Willem. 1927. The Domestic Rules of the Vaikhānasa School belonging to the Black Yajurveda. Calcutta: Asiatic Society of Bengal.

Gadamer, Hans-Georg. 1996. *Der Anfang der Philosophie*. Stuttgart: Reclam Philipp Jun.

Humphrey, Caroline and James Laidlaw. 1994. *The Archetypal Actions of Ritual: A Theory of Ritual Illustrated by the Jain Rite of Worship*. Oxford: Clarendon Press.

Kippenberg, Hans G. 1991. *Die vorderasiatischen Erlösungsreligionen in ihrem Zusammenhang mit der antiken Stadtherrschaft*. Frankfurt am Main: Suhrkamp Verlag.

Stroumsa Guy. 2009. *The End of Sacrifice: Religious Transformations in Late Antiquity*. Chicago, IL: Chicago University Press.

Zimmern Alice. 1896. *Porphyry. The Philosopher to his Wife Marcella*. London: G. Redway.

HISTORICAL AND COMPARATIVE APPROACHES TO RITUAL THOUGHT IN ANCIENT INDIA AND ARCHAIC GREECE

1

The Principle of Equivalence and the Interiorization of Ritual: The "End" of Ritual?

Stephanie W. Jamison

I will preface this paper with a few admissions. First, I am a philologist, not a philosopher, and philosophical thinking is one of the major blind spots in my mental makeup. Moreover (or, perhaps, therefore), much of what I will say today write is well known to Vedicists, and I claim no novelty for it. I can only hope that it may be fresher for those of you outside Indology.

Let me begin with three Upaniṣadic passages. All of these passages are quite famous and quite rich and can serve as points of departure for many different approaches to the question. The first is the beginning of the Bṛhad Āraṇyaka Upaniṣad, considered by most to be the oldest of the Upaniṣads. It concerns the horse that is elaborately sacrificed and dismembered at the end of the famous year-long royal ritual, the Aśvamedha. Here and throughout the translations are based on Olivelle 1998, with a few amendments of my own.

> The head of the sacrificial horse is really the dawn – its eye is the sun; its breath is the wind; and its gaping mouth is the fire common to all men. The body of the sacrificial horse is the year – its back is the sky; its abdomen is the intermediate region; its underbelly is the earth; its flanks are the quarters; its ribs are the intermediate quarters; its limbs are the seasons; its joints are the months and fortnights; its feet are the days and nights; its bones are the stars; its flesh is the clouds; its stomach contents are the sand; its intestines are the rivers; its liver and

Keywords: Brāhmaṇa texts, Bṛhad Āraṇyaka Upaniṣad, sacrifice, *bandhu*

> lungs are the hills; its body hairs are the plants and trees; its forequarter is the rising sun; and its hindquarter is the setting sun. When it yawns, lightning flashes; when it shakes itself, it thunders; and when it urinates, it rains. Its neighing is speech itself. (BĀU I.1)

The next two are found nearby each other, likewise in the BĀU. Both of them compare a woman to elements in the ritual and sexual intercourse to sacrifice. In the first, the focus is entirely on the ritual fire:

> Fire is really a woman. The kindling wood is her vulva; the smoke is her pubic hair; the flame is her vagina. When one penetrates her, those are the coals; the sparks are the climax. In that very fire the gods pour semen as an oblation; from that offering a man comes into being. (BĀU VI.2.13)

In the second passage the woman is likened to the place of sacrifice and her parts to sacrificial equipment, of which the sacred fire is only one element:

> Her vulva is the sunken altar (*vedi*); the sacred grass is her pubic hair; the skin there is the double-sided soma-press; her labia minora are the fire in the middle. (BĀU VI.4.3)

These three passages have a lot in common, but they also differ from each other in important conceptual ways. In all of them something belonging to the ritual realm – the sacrificed horse, the sacred fire, the ritual ground – is equated with something outside the ritual. But the equation is not just a one-off thing: it involves a *structured set* of equivalences. The object being compared is broken down into its constituent parts, and each of those parts finds its counterpart in a part of the object to which the whole is being compared. These types of equivalences have a technical name – *bandhu* 'bond, connection' (a word of course cognate with English 'bind', etc.) – and also, if the etymology of Paul Thieme is accepted, the term *upaniṣad* itself, which, though it comes to be the name of a class of texts, originally meant 'equivalence' or 'substitution'. It is almost impossible to convey to people outside of Vedic studies how dominated the texts of the Middle and Late Vedic periods are by this mode of expression – to the point, sometimes, of tedium.[1]

Let us take a closer look at the equivalences in the passages under discussion. In the first, the parts of the sacrificed horse, down to the contents of its stomach, are compared to cosmic elements, both the physical constituents of the world (e.g., "its eye is the sun") and the divisions of time ("its limbs are the seasons"), and its actions are compared to events in the natural world ("When it urinates, it rains"). By contrast, the two passages concerning the woman offer two different systems of equivalences between a woman's body and the elements of the sacrifice; some of the same parts are involved, but because the overall object of comparison is different, those parts have different counterparts in the system. So, in the "fire" example, her pubic hair is smoke, whereas in the "sacrificial ground" example it is the sacred grass that is scattered on the place of sacrifice to provide a seat for the visiting gods. These examples homologize the sacrifice to human life in the mundane world.

The difference between the cosmic and the mundane system of equations is pervasive enough to be distinguished by technical terms: the cosmic level is called *adhidaivam* or *adhidevatam*, roughly "concerned with the divine," while the mundane is called *adhyātmam*, roughly "concerned with the person(al)." These two systems meet in and focus on the sacrifice, a controlled and orderly manmade system, as a way of modelling the complex web of relationships that obtain in the two other realms, which are not under human control. The level of the sacrifice is called *adhiyajñam* "relating to the sacrifice."

Let us note a few further features of the equations themselves. Some of the comparisons are quite obvious: even our dull modern mental apparatus can see the logical basis of "its eye is the sun." Some are imaginative, but still easily grasped: in the comparison of woman with fire "the sparks are the climax" strikes a universal chord. But some cannot be immediately decoded: why, for example, are the limbs of the sacrificial horse the seasons? It was critically important for a Vedic ritualist to understand the reasons behind the unobvious connections, and learning to apprehend the reasons, and to produce similarly opaque equations, obviously formed a major part of his education. Why did it matter? Why was this not simply a kind of parlor game? Because it is only by understanding the deep web of associations that attaches to ritual performance that a ritualist can unlock the real power of the sacrifice, on the one hand, and, on the other, harness the power of sacrifice in performing the mundane actions of daily life. The person who understands these things is characterized, monotonously regularly, as *yá evám̥ véda* (/*evám̥ vidvā́n*) "(one) who know thus." What happens when you "know thus" and when you don't is vividly spelled out in the continuation of the passage about the woman as the place of sacrifice.

> A man who, "knowing thus," engages in sexual intercourse obtains as great a world as a man who performs a Vājapeya sacrifice and appropriates to himself the merits of the women with whom he has sex. But a man who, "not knowing this," engages in sexual intercourse – the women themselves appropriate *his* merits. (BĀU VI.4.3 [cont'd])

So simply by having sex (and, note, with plural women, not woman) in normal life, the man who knows that sex is really, secretly, a ritual gets all the good of having performed quite an elaborate sacrifice, the Vājapeya, and, incidentally, scoops up the value of whatever good deeds his female partners have done. But ignorantly having sex gives the advantage to the women, who scoop up his good stuff in turn.

We will return later to the issue of "sacrificial inflation," whereby doing something pretty simple (and, in this case, one hopes pleasurable), like sex, is just as good as performing something lengthy, complicated, and expensive, like the Vājapeya. Right now I want to set out a little typology of the ways in which *bandhus* are configured. We have already noted the different levels of comparison – *adhidaivam*, like the horse = cosmos, and *adhyātmam*, like sex = fire ritual. In both types of examples given, we also noted the point-by-point comparison. The horse example is a stand-alone comparison, as is the second of the sex examples. But the first sex example (VI.2.13) is part of a series, where the ritual element, namely fire, along with its constituent parts, is homologized to one complex structure after another (VI.2.9–14): "yonder world" (i.e., heaven and the cosmos), the thunderstorm (Parjanya), "this world," and man himself. The woman comparison quoted is (almost) the last of the series. In all of them, the parts of fire are held constant: fire itself, kindling wood, smoke, flame, coals, and sparks. I'll give just one example:

> Fire is really the thunderstorm. Its kindling wood is the year; its smoke is the clouds; its flame is lightning; its coals are thunder; its sparks are hail. In that very fire the gods pour King Soma as an oblation; from that offering rain comes into being. (BĀU VI.2.10)

Such a series, with the same points of comparison in each entry, invites superimposition of all the entries one upon the other, producing an even more complex, multidimensional web. To take only one element – if the lightning is the flame of the thunderstorm and the vagina is the flame of the woman, one can go one step further and equate lightning and vagina. The other homologies to flame – the day for yonder world, the night for this world, and speech for man – can be added to this mix.

And there is more to be said about this example. The series is a totalizing one, providing a complete survey of the major parts of the universe: the three worlds – heaven, the "midspace" between heaven and earth, represented by the thunderstorm, which takes place there, and earth itself, with the two halves of humanity, man and woman. In other words, everything important on the *adhidaivam* and *adhyātmam* levels has a counterpart in the ritual fire, and the series ends with a climactic equation, about which I've withheld mention – of fire to fire itself. Each part is repeated, and each part is the same: the fire is the fire, the kindling wood is the kindling wood, etc. The final lesson is not homology, but identity.

One more thing: this series is not simply a list, ordered or unordered, for there is one element in the presentation that develops as each entry is added – that is the nature of the thing that the gods offer into the fire-substitute, and the thing that arises. We have seen that semen offered into the woman produces a man, and before that, that soma offered into the thunderstorm produces rain. The full sequence is "faith" (*śraddhā*), yielding soma, yielding rain, yielding semen, yielding a man. This man is then offered into the fire, in the final identity comparison. So, the various entries in the series are linked not merely by the superimpositional quality of shared homologies, but also by the progression and transformation of the sacrificial substance.

A final thing – the people "who know thus," who know this "Five Fire" doctrine (for so it is called in the literature), have the best outcome at their death. They go to the world of *brahman* and do not return. I do not want to linger on the contents of this doctrine, which has been amply treated by others; my point here is the intricate structure of the sequence, built up from simple homologies.

Another type of equational structure is the chain, where x = y, y = z, etc., and by standard logical procedure the beginning point, the end point, and all points in between can be interpreted as secretly identical. A BĀU example of this chaining is found in VI.4.1, where the essence or sap (*rasa*) of beings is the earth, that of the earth the waters, of the waters the plants, of the plants the flowers, of the flowers the fruits, of the fruits man, and of man semen. A chain always has the potential to be hierarchical, with each item on the list being a better or more distilled example of its predecessor – though it need not be.

Let me now state, or restate, the relevance of the preceding discussion to the topic that concerns us today. In the Vedic worldview the sacrifice is the realm that mediates between the cosmic and the personal and mundane, and thinking about the sacrifice and its constituent parts provides a conceptual structure by which to make sense of the uncontrollable complexities of the other two realms and to provide linkage between those two other realms. Moreover, on the one hand, seeing these connections brings the vast cosmic realm literally to earth: the whole of cosmic time and space and all the distant elements therein (sun, stars, etc.) are contained in the body of the sacrificed horse lying right there in front of us on the demarcated ritual ground. On the other, it infuses even the most trivial daily act with meaning, *if* you know that these actions are really ritual performances. The key in all of this is knowledge. This has been nicely formulated by Theodore Proferes in his 2007 book, *Vedic Ideals of Sovereignty and the Poetics of Power*, in discussing the symbolism of the ritual of royal unction:

> The underlying rationale for the rite of royal unction is that waters charged with solar fire confer upon the king the power to rule while simultaneously generating his solar body. The qualities of the sun ... can

> henceforth be applied equally to the king. Sovereignty is thus consistently linked to the natural elements.... The ritual symbolism of royal unction and its accompanying liturgical discourse draw upon these elements of the natural world to articulate a holistic vision of the interaction between human political authority and the powers of the cosmos, homologizing the waters and the clans on the one hand and the sun/fire and the king on the other. These elemental motifs employed by the poets present not a handy grab-bag of expressive tropes loosely related to sovereignty; they constitute *a systematic symbolic language capable of expressing the functional correlations between the processes of nature and the internal operations of human society.*[2] [my italics]

Now our topic here is, in part, the "interiorization" of ritual and, supposedly stemming from that, "the end" of ritual. So far I haven't said anything about either one. But, as far as I can tell from the blurb that accompanied my invitation to the colloquium, the presupposition of this colloquium is that reflection on the sacrifice leads, more or less inevitably, to the substitution of mental for physical rites, and ultimately to the rejection of rites altogether in favour of "pure" speculation, that is, philosophy. In what follows I will mildly dispute this presupposition, by claiming that a robust and continuing sacrificial tradition was necessary in the Indian context for the kinds of speculation we're talking about, and that, though there is certainly evidence for interior and mental rites, these were parallel to and, one might even say, parasitic on the standard physical performance of rituals (or at least on the theoretical existence of physical performance – about which I'll have more to say later). I should admit here that I am planning to overstate my case, and that a more traditional – and triumphalist – account of Vedic and Classical Indian intellectual history would claim that Vedic sacrifice gave way to the speculations about sacrifice in the Upaniṣads, which led to non-sacrifice-based intellectual speculation. And that in philosophical terms the Mīmāṃsā (or Pūrvamīmāṃsā 'Prior Inquiry'), with its emphasis on action, that is, sacrifice, led to the superior Uttaramāmīṃsā ("Later Inquiry') or Vedānta, which replaces action with knowledge. I find this too neat, but I recognize that there's some truth to this standard "progress" approach.

Part of my claim rests on the further assertion that, though the kind of speculation I've been talking about is generally associated with the Middle and Late Vedic periods, especially with the so-called Vedānta, the "end of the Veda," namely the Upaniṣads, from which I've drawn my examples so far, in fact this type of thinking is much older, going back to the oldest of our Vedic texts, the Rig Veda, and perhaps even to Indo-Iranian times. So, before talking further about interiorization and substitution in their well-known and full-blown forms, I want to spend some time teasing out evidence for reflection on the ritual in the earlier texts.

Let me briefly bring up the possibility that sacrificial homologies go back to Indo-Iranian and can be discerned in the earliest Old Iranian texts, the Gāthās attributed to Zarathustra. In an intriguing and unfortunately unpublished paper, Stanley Insler asserts that the Gāthās do not, as used to be claimed, represent Zarathustra's rejection of inherited Old Iranian sacrifice, nor do they, as is often now claimed, under the surface represent Indo-Iranian sacrificial business-as-usual. But that the abstract elements that the Gāthic poet ceaselessly deploys – Truth, Good Thinking, Rulership, etc. – actually correspond to physical elements of the natural world also employed in ritual. So, e.g., Truth corresponds to fire, Good Thinking to cattle and milk, Rulership to metal, and so forth. If he is correct (and the claim is bound to be controversial), thinking in homologies, and here with very abstract homologies, is an Indo-Iranian habit of mind, inherited by the Vedic people and elaborately developed by them. Let us now turn to the earliest evidence for them in Indic.

No treatment of Vedic sacrificial speculation can ignore the most famous early example of it, namely the Puruṣasūkta ("the hymn of Man") in the late Rig Veda (X.90). My apologies to those of you for whom it is mind-numbingly familiar, but it is a key text for our purposes. For we see in it in fully developed form much of what I've noted about the Upaniṣadic passages: the focus on the sacrifice as the mediating realm between the divine and the human, as well as the system of identifications that articulates the connections among these realms. There is also, quite prominently, a feature I have not mentioned about such speculations (though it is also quite common later): the notion that sacrifice is a creative act, that it literally *produces* the other realms, rather than simply reflecting them. In this 16-verse hymn, the gods sacrifice a man – a gigantic man, to be sure, but a man. Already this scenario connects the divine and the human via the sacrificial realm, but with a sort of twist, since the gods are otherwise generally the recipients of sacrifice, not its performers. The first verses of the hymn describe the vastness of the man to be sacrificed and his birth. In verse 5 we encounter a familiar trope, the *bandhus* of sacrifice itself:

> When, with the Man as oblation, the gods performed the sacrifice,
> spring was its melted butter, summer its kindling wood, autumn its oblation. (RV X.90.6)

Subsequent verses list what resulted from the sacrifice: the three divisions of animals, wild animals, domestic ones, and birds (vs. 8, also vs. 10) and, self-referentially, the verbal elements of sacrifice, metres and chants (vs. 9). And, more importantly, what things arose individually from the various parts of the sacrificed Man, in a system quite reminiscent of the sacrificed horse passage from the BĀU, including some of the same associations. On the one hand, elements of the cosmic and divine realm (what will later be called *adhidaivam*):

> The moon was born from his mind; from his eye the sun was born.
> From his mouth (the god) Indra and (the god) Fire [Agni]; from his breath (the god) Wind [Vāyu] was born.
> From his navel the midspace, from his head heaven took shape –
> from his feet the earth, from his ear the directions. In this way they arranged the worlds. (RV X.90.13-14)

But the *adhyātmam* or human realm is not neglected. In addition to the totality of animals already mentioned, the major divisions of human society, the *varṇas*, are a product of the sacrificed Man. The body parts from which the various societal segments arise impose an implicit hierarchy, in probably the most famous verse of this famous hymn:

> His mouth was made the Brahmin (priest), his two arms the Rājanya [=Kṣatriya] (warrior),
> his thighs the Vaiśya (producer). From his feet the Śūdra (servant) was born. (RV X.90.12)

In fact many scholars believe that this hymn was inserted into the late Rig Veda to provide a charter for the hierarchical *varṇa* system, of which there are few traces elsewhere in that text.

Thus, the hymn of Man depicts the whole universe in all its parts as a product of a primal sacrifice, and therefore the universe cannot be understood without reference to the sacrifice, for the relations among the elements now existing were determined by their sources and roles in the sacrifice.

Speculations inspired by the sacrifice are not rare in the Rig Veda. They are often numerological, taking off from the number of elements in the sacrifice (the three fires, the three soma-pressings, the two arms and ten fingers of the priest, etc.) and framed as riddles – often riddles whose solutions we moderns fail to see. I will just give you a flavor of some of the more enigmatic – this example from a hymn (X.114) far less famous (and far less comprehensible) than the hymn of Man. In its first verse it seems to connect ritual elements with cosmic ones, and assign knowledge of the whole to the gods:

> The two contiguous heats (i.e., probably heat sources, = ritual fire and sun / gharma pots or chant and melody) have pervaded the threefold (world) [/ Trivṛt Stoma]. Mātariśvan has come to enjoyment of the two.
> Seeking to acquire the milk of heaven, they have toiled: the gods know the ritual chant provided with melody. (RV X.114.1)

Similar knowledge is attributed to inspired and sage poets later in the hymn (vs. 5), in contrast to the "simple mind" of the 1st person speaker of the hymn (vs. 4), thus highlighting the theme of "who knows thus" and suggesting that one who knows is equal to the gods. This knowledge, explicitly about the sacrifice, is explicitly tested towards the end of the hymn:

> Who is the wise one who knows the yoking of the meters? Who has undertaken the holy speech?
> What champion do they call the eighth of the priests? Who indeed has discerned the two fallow bay horses of Indra? (RV X.114.9)

I'm sorry to say that the "wise one who knows" all that is not to be found on the earth today.

As is well known and often discussed, riddles are deeply serious verbal formulations in Vedic thought, because they capture the hidden connections among apparently independent entities – the *bandhus* in fact. The riddle is a kind of code, and there is much evidence that learning to solve and to produce riddles was an important part of a Vedic ritualist's intellectual education. One famous and very long Rigvedic hymn (I.164, with 52 verses) is popularly known as the "Riddle Hymn," though it is officially, as it were, dedicated to the All Gods and various individual divinities. Despite its length the hymn is not just a random collection of enigmas on various topics; it has been argued that it is a fairly systematic treatment of a particular Vedic ritual, the Pravargya, in which a special pot filled with milk and milk products is heated to overflowing.[3] The elements and procedures in this ritual, cryptically described, are identified with equally cryptically presented cosmic counterparts. Let us just sample the first verse:

> This Hotar-priest is gray and precious – his middle brother is ravenous and his third brother has melted butter on his back. There I saw the clanlord with his seven sons. (RV I.164.1)

As you see, it does indeed have the form of a classic riddle, lacking only the explicit "who am I?" at the end. The verse can be (and has been) interpreted on both the ritual and the cosmic levels. On the ritual level the three brothers are the three fires of solemn ritual: the Āhavanīya or offering fire, the Southern fire, and the Gārhapatya or householder's fire. The clanlord is the fire god Agni and/or the sacrificer, and the seven brothers are the officiating priests. In cosmic terms the three brothers are the sun, lightning, and fire; the clanlord is probably the sun (again) and the seven brothers the seven legendary seers (the Saptarṣi), who at least in later tradition are the seven stars of Ursa Major. Note that, as in the Upaniṣadic passages discussed above, the riddle doesn't present us with a single element to identify, but with a structured set: it is not enough to guess the identity of, say, the grey Hotar-priest; whatever we decide is the referent of that phrase must work as a "brother" to something ravenous and something covered with melted butter. The hymn continues in this vein for 51 more verses, each challenging the hearer to decode multiple related puzzles, but riddles of this type are not limited to this particular hymn.

Let us now turn to a different kind of cryptic speculation on the ritual, which may bring us closer to the notion of sacrificial substitution towards which we are tending. Vedic sacrifice is defined, in certain ways, by two deified ritual substances, the ritual fire, which is also the god Agni, and the ritual drink, which is also the god Soma, both of whom are the objects of intense intellectual reflection in the Rig Veda and later – we have just had a glimpse of this with regard to fire in the first verse of the riddle hymn. Both fire and soma are treated both as physical substances and as divinities, and furthermore they both have cosmic counterparts: as we just saw, the fire Agni can be identified with the sun; in the later tradition Soma is identified with the moon, though this is not really reflected in the Rig Veda, where Soma has more solar characteristics.

It is perhaps not surprising that Vedic poets and thinkers, adept at discerning the most unlikely connections between disparate things, should attempt to identify the two, fire and soma, which have almost opposite physical properties but are both central to the correct performance of the major Vedic rituals. One product of this identification project is, at least in my interpretation, RV V.44, which Geldner, the authoritiative RVic translator, calls "the hardest hymn in the RV" ("das schwierigste Lied des ṚV") and Oldenberg, an equally authoritative commentator, deems "mostly uncertain or hopeless" ("meist fraglich oder hoffnungslos"). I have no time here to defend my interpretation of the hymn as an elaborate double riddle, carried through 15 discouragingly opaque verses, but the mind-boggling challenge of this hymn would make sense if the poet is in fact wrestling to equate two ritual substances, two gods, and two sequences of ritual procedure through a whole hymn. And this equation must then be considered a meditation on the sacrifice itself – how are these two apparently very different features of the sacrifice ultimately, underlyingly, the same? I'll give a single sample of the hymn, though it's difficult to digest in this context. The scenario of this verse is that the poet's hymns are being chanted at the same time as two ritual actions are being performed: streams of melted butter are poured into the ritual fire and streams of water are mixed with the pressed soma. The words for both butter streams and waters are grammatically feminine, hence the phrase, the "twinned sisters," that refers to them both.

The underlying word for hymn is grammatically masculine, and these male hymns go seeking the females that represent the streams of butter and water. But the words "hymns," "butter offerings," and "waters" do not actually appear in the verse; the audience is expected to intuit the referents from their grammatical genders, the actions they perform, and the adjectives that qualify them. By the way, the final clause of the verse is essentially impenetrable, due to the word *krívi*, which may (or may not) be a pun on the word for poet *kaví*.

> These (hymns) of yours, easy to yoke, (go) forth on their course to seek the twinned sisters [=butter offerings / waters], strong through truth, that (go) downwards towards yonder one [=Agni / Soma],
>
> with reins easy to control, directing everything. Krivi [=Agni/Soma / the poet (<kavi)?] steals (their) names [=butter offerings / waters?] at their precipitous fall. (RV V.44.4)

This example of the identification and equation of ritual substances and activities is, essentially, theoretical and speculative – the product of a poet who is using the ritual as a starting point for an intellectual exercise and as a showcase for his verbal agility. I now want to turn to an example of a more practical nature, with a less rarified verbal aesthetic. This requires a bit of background. The rituals we've been discussing are what, in the classical ritual system of Middle Vedic times, are called śrauta rituals – "high" or "solemn" rituals that can only be undertaken by someone who is eligible to "establish fires" and has in fact done so (an *āhitāgni*). Probably only a small proportion of those eligible actually did so and participated in the *śrauta* system through their lifetimes. Technically speaking, *śrauta* rituals require three fires for their performance, and except for the daily offering of milk into the fire, the Agnihotra to which we will return, also a corps of priests representing different Vedas. Alongside this elaborate system of high ritual, there is a more or less parallel system of domestic or gṛhya rituals, which require only one fire and are simpler and less expensive. They are treated in separate ritual manuals. Presumably most of the twice-born Aryans performed at least some of the gṛhya rites, which include life-cycle rites like marriage. Although it's not certain that the distinction between these two systems was absolute and explicit in earlier Vedic, it is clear that different levels of ritual engagement existed and were perceived. Or, to put it more strongly, that certain habits and customs of domestic life were given a ritual gloss by homologizing them to the formal high rituals.

One of the finest early examples of this is found in the Atharva Veda, the second-oldest Sanskrit text. AV IX.6, entitled by its translator William Dwight Whitney as "Exalting the entertainment of guests," is a long prose hymn (62 sections roughly corresponding to verses in verse hymns) in which the various elements and procedures in the dispensing of hospitality, which are elaborately codified in the later Gṛhya Sūtras, are compared, point by point, to solemn ritual. The ceremony begins with the statement

> When the lord of guests looks upon his guests, he is really seeing a sacrifice to the gods. (AV IX.6.3)

Each separate attention to the guests is likened to a piece of sacrificial equipment or a ritual procedure. For example,

> When they fetch mattress and pillow, those are the "enclosing sticks." (10)
> The grains of rice and barley that are scattered out – those are the soma-shoots. (14)
> When the servers go forward with drinking-vessels in their hands, they are really the cup-bearing priests (*camasādhvaryu-*). (51)

As the hymn proceeds, it becomes clear that not only are the elements of hospitality and solemn ritual identified, but that offering hospitality is tantamount to performing such a ritual and brings the same rewards – if the host is one "who knows thus." The mode of expression will be familiar from the BĀU sex passage above.

> He who, knowing thus, pours out milk and presents it (to the guest) – he acquires as much as one who has performed a very successful Agniṣṭoma sacrifice. (40)

Subsequent provisions promise the merit equivalent to even greater sacrifices, if a knowing host gives his guest butter (41), honey (42), or meat (43).

In this remarkable hymn we see what we might call the sacralization of everyday life. The simple acts of giving food, drink, and a place to sit to a guest become ritual acts by being compared and indeed assimilated to the parts of a ritual, like the soma sacrifice, which is explicitly defined as *outside of* the everyday.

This kind of sacralization is systematized in later Vedic in the so-called *mahāyajñas* or "great sacrifices" required of a householder every day. There are five of them: the sacrifice to beings (*bhūta*), to men (*manuṣya*), to ancestors (*pitṛ*), to gods (*deva*), and to *brahma*. The sacrifice to *brahma* is the householder's personal study of the Veda, that to men is the reception of guests (such as we just examined) and the distribution of food to begging brahmins; the bare minimum for the rest involves offering a stick of wood in the fire for the gods, a pot of water for the ancestors, and some flowers or cooked food [*bali*] for the beings, all with appropriate verbal exclamations (see, e.g., BDS II.11.1–8; ŚB XI.5.6; HDS II.1.696ff., ŚGS III.1.etc.). These five sacrifices participate in the system of equations from the very beginning of their codification in several different ways. On the one hand, the sacrifices are superimposable upon each other and upon more elaborate rites. The Śatapatha Brāhmaṇa, an important Middle Vedic text, takes up each part of the *brahmayajña*, study of the Veda, and provides its counterpart in solemn ritual (ŚB XI.5.6–7), equating, for example, the study of the Rig Veda with milk offerings (XI.5.6.4), of the Yajur Veda with ghee offerings (5), etc. On the other, we see the kind of sacrificial inflation discussed previously, whereby something requiring less effort and expense comes to be equivalent to something greater. For the *mahāyajñas*, performing only part of the full sacrifice is tantamount to performing the whole thing. The "bare miminum" I just mentioned is deemed sufficient by a number of authoritative texts, such as BDS II.11.1–7, TĀr II.10. The stick of firewood, the cup of water, the pronouncing of the syllable *om* stands for the whole ritual. It is symbolically enough.

This is not simply a question of domestic practice; a similar kind of sacrificial inflation by equivalence was articulated for the various śrauta sacrifices. Again, a bit of background – one of the principles of organization of the system of śrauta rituals is frequency of performance, which generally correlates, not surprisingly, with complexity and expense. The simplest śrauta ritual is the daily Agnihotra, the offering of milk into the sacrificer's fire at the two twilights, dawn and dusk. Up the scale of elaboration is the Darśapūrṇamāsa, or New and Full Moon sacrifice occurring every two weeks; then the Four Monthly sacrifices (Caturmāsyāni). And crowning these are the great rituals like the Aśvamedha, which takes a year and whose performance is restricted to kings. Obviously the big payoffs in terms of merit acheived come from the big, long sacrifices, which most sacrificers couldn't afford and in many cases were prevented from performing. So a system of homologies developed whereby the performance of a sacrifice lower down the scale was tantamount to one higher up. See, for example, ŚB XI.2.5, which begins by claiming that the New and Full Moon sacrifice is the *original* or *normal* (*prākṛta*) Aśvamedha (XI.2.5.1, 4), so that when a man performs these simpler sacrifices he is really performing an Aśvamedha and therefore accrues whatever merit is attached to the latter, more elaborate sacrifice. In the same section it is also claimed that the Agnihotra is really an offering connected to the sacrificial horse of the Aśvamedha (XI.2.5.2), and the section ends (XI.2.5.6) with the happy conclusion that when "who knows thus" offers the Agnihotra and the New and Full Moon sacrifices through the year, for him an Aśvamedha is being offered every month. The Jaiminīya Brāhmaṇa goes even further (I.40): each part of the daily Agnihotra represents a different sacrifice, the New and Full Moon, the Four Monthly, the Animal Sacrifice, the Vājapeya, and the Aśvamedha.

Thus, just by pouring the milk into his fire every day the sacrificer in essence performs all these higher rites.

Although neither the "interiorization" of sacrifice nor its "end" is involved in these examples, we are getting close. We see in these theological discussions that sacrifice is conceptually fungible. A part can substitute for the whole, a simpler sacrifice for one more elaborate. All that's necessary is to know the exchange rates of this ritual currency. This type of economic calculation about the value of certain sacrifices and sacrificial acts arises from the same type of reasoning that produced the dispassionate meditations on the hidden connections (*bandhus*) among disparate elements, like the sacrificial horse passage with which we began, but the economic approach has practical consequences: it allows every Aryan (or every Aryan man) to participate in the sacrificial system and derive the tangible and intangible benefits that sacrifice is supposed to produce for its performer. It is almost the Vedic equivalent of a mutual fund, allowing even the small investor to take part in the economic markets.

This brings us to the Prāṇāgnihotra ("Breath Agnihotra"), the sacrificial example that was cited in the blurb about this colloquium as an example of the interiorization and critique of sacrifice – with a long citation from Caland's translation of the Vaikhānasasmārtasūtra exhibiting the same types of homologies we have been discussing ceaselessly (e.g., "the hairs of the body are the darbha[-grass] blades, the prāṇa breath is the Gārhapatya[-fire]..."). We have recently touched on the regular Agnihotra, the twice-daily offering of milk into the fire that is required of every śrauta sacrificer, that is, every man who has "established fires," and we have just seen that, by some twists of logic, this relatively humble ritual can be made equivalent to other, more exalted sacrifices. The Prāṇāgnihotra takes this one step further, though not really the step that is implied in the conference blurb. As was argued at length, and with some ill-temper, by Henk Bodewitz in his 1973 book, the Prāṇāgnihotra has nothing to do with "interiorization" of ritual or with a transcendence of sacrifice. Instead, using my terms, it represents the "sacralization of the mundane." Instead of offering an oblation of foodstuffs into the ritual fire, the sacrificer makes an offering, as it were, of foodstuffs into his own body. That is, he eats a meal. (For a description of the ritual see BDS II.12.) When a man "who knows thus" eats at morning and at evening, prefacing and finishing the actual eating with the recitation of mantras and performing certain prescribed actions during and after the meal, that meal, that eating, becomes the equivalent of an Agnihotra – offered not into the fire, but into "the breaths," that is the body, the life, of the sacrificer. This equivalence is bolstered by a long theological tradition of equating the fires that a śrauta sacrificer establishes with his own breaths, his very life. Therefore, feeding himself is the same as feeding his ritual fires. As Bodewitz repeatedly states, the procedure is neither interior nor mental, nor does it represent a rejection of ritual – quite the reverse: it makes the simple act of eating into a real sacrifice, by employing the verbal and physical behaviours of ritual – which are definitely exterior, not interior, behaviours – and by infusing an ordinary action necessary to daily life and generally undertaken without thought with the glamour and meaningful deliberateness of ritual activity.

Bodewitz also points to another version of the Agnihotra that really is mental and interior, namely, the Agnihotra that a traveller undertakes when he is away from home and thus separated from his fires (called the Pravāsāgnihotra). At the proper times of day he thinks his way through the Agnihotra that he would be perfoming physically at home. As P. V. Kane says in the *History of Dharma Śāstra* (II.2.1008), "When the householder is away alone it is his duty to perform all actions at the time of agnihotra and darśapūrṇamāsa (such as sipping water) which he can perform without his fires and to go mentally through the whole procedure." When he left home, he entrusted his fires to his wife, who is, as I've discussed at great length (Jamison 1996), an indivisible half of the ritual partnership, and appointed a priest to make the necessary offerings. So, simultaneous with the absent sacrificer's mental offering, the priest, his surrogate, is making the physical offerings, in the presence of the wife, who ensures the continuity of the established fires. (If both husband and wife go away without taking their fires, it's not enough to have a priest make the offerings. The relationship between the ritual couple and their fires has been broken, and when they return, they have to start over and re-establish the fires [in a ritual known as the Punarādheya "Re-establishment"] Kane 1974: II.1.683–84.) Though the traveller's ritual on the road is actually mental and interior, it doesn't represent a transformation or distillation of ritual into a higher, mental form, but rather symbolizes, by its shadowing of the actual ritual happening at home, the tyrannical necessity of sacrifice.

There is a place much earlier in the Vedic period that does seem to point to a mental Agnihotra that is presented, somewhat playfully, as superior to the physical kind. Rig Veda VIII.102, dedicated to the fire-god Agni, is, for most of its length, a standard praise of Agni, though laying particular stress on his role as kavi "poet" or "sage poet," but it ends with four verses in a light and self-deprecating tone. The poet claims to have neither of the barebones requisites for even a simple offering to Agni – a cow for the oblation and wood to feed his flames (vs. 19) – in other words, an Agnihotra, though not so called there. [The word does not occur in the Rig Veda.] All he has is "something like this" – namely the hymn he has just produced. This is clearly false modesty, and indeed the poet treats the standard wood and ghee rather slightingly in the next two verses (20–21). In the final appended verse (22, not part of a *tṛca* or "triad," in which the hymn is organized), he proudly pronounces that a man should kindle Agni with his mind (*agním índhāno mánasā*) and his vision (*dhī́-*) (not, the implication is, with mere wood and ghee), and indeed that he has just done so.

19. Because I have no cow, nor an axe in a wooden (tree),
I therefore bring just a thing like this to you.
20. When, Agni, we set any pieces of wood whatsoever in you,
enjoy them, youngest one.
21. What the little termite eats, what the ant creeps over,
let all that be ghee for you.
22. Kindling Agni with his mind, the mortal should follow his visionary thought.
I have kindled Agni with the dawning lights.

So, on the one hand, at the beginning of the Vedic period we find a moderately clear statement (nothing in the Rig Veda is *very* clear) in favour of the mental performance of a ritual, indeed the Agnihotra. But, on the other, it would be hasty and unwise to take this as evidence for a move towards the interiorization of the sacrifice. It rather bespeaks the underlying tension between the two major aspects of Vedic sacrifice: the verbal and the physical. Each of these aspects is absolutely essential for the successful ritual performance, and each is the province of different priests. Indeed, each Veda is associated with a different priestly office: the Rig Veda with the Hotar, the Invoker, but more especially in its origin with the poet; the Sāma Veda with the Udgātar or Singer; the Yajur Veda with the Adhvaryu, who performs the physical acts of offering. It is not hard to imagine that our Rigvedic poets, wordsmiths of great skill and daring, might feel a bit of intellectual superiority to the mere drudges who shuffle back and forth on the ritual ground pouring melted butter into the fire – a feeling that the poets almost never give vent to, as they ceaselessly praise the sacrificial *acts* of tending the fire, pressing the soma, and so forth. But this rare, light-hearted, and oblique acknowledgement of private scorn at the end of an otherwise orthodox praise hymn – and it's at the end of hymns that such asides get made, especially in the VIIIth Maṇḍala – should not mislead us into thinking that the poet thinks he can go at it alone. He knows that coordinating the full orchestral score of priestly personnel, ritual actions, and verbal accompaniments is absolutely necessary for the success of the sacrifice. It is not even chamber music, much less a solo turn.

There are many more directions this paper could go – and could have gone (I would especially have liked to further explore the role of language and sound associations) – for, as I hope I have shown, Vedic sacrifice is an endlessly fruitful subject for contemplation and speculation. "Good to think with" in the oft-repeated cliché. But I will stop here, simply repeating the major point I've been trying to make throughout – that there is no clear progression from sacrificing, to thinking about sacrifice, to transcending sacrifice. From the moment Vedic sacrifice appeared the sacrificers were thinking about it and organizing their speculations about cosmic and human matters with reference to sacrifice. And while they thought about it, they continued to sacrifice. In fact, sacrifice is necessary to the intellectual enterprise; it remains the standard, the benchmark, to which all other things are compared, and even when sacrifice is denigrated in such speculations, it still provides the universally accepted measure of value. In fact, the persistence of the minutest details of sacrifice as objects of intellectual investigation is quite amazing. The highly influential system of hermeneutics, Mīmāṃsā, whose methods of inquiry permeate most of the branches of Classical Indian intellectual exertion, began as a system for interpreting ritual texts, and questions about ritual minutiae provide the model for asking and answering questions even into the late medieval period, indeed until today. We must thus interpret the word "end" in the title of this colloquium in a different way: the "end" of Vedic sacrifice is thus not its finish, but its goal, and one of its goal has always been to provide those who think about it with a coherent and satisfying account of the structure and organization of the universe and of human life.

Notes

1. See Olivelle 1998: 24 n. 29, citing the secondary literature.
2. Proferes 2007: 113.
3. See Houben 2000.

Abbreviations

AV	Atharva Veda
BĀU	Bṛhadāraṇyaka Upaniṣad
BDS	Baudhāyana Dharma Sūtra
HDS	Hiraṇyakeśi Dharma Sūtra
JB	Jaiminīya Brāhmaṇa
RV	Rig Veda
ŚB	Śatapatha Brāhmaṇa
ŚGS	Śāṅkhāyana Gṛhya Sūtra
TĀr	Taittirīya Āraṇyaka

References

Bodewitz, H. W. 1973. *Jaiminīya Brāhmaṇa I, 1-65: Translation and Commentary with a Study of Agnihotra and Prāṇāgnihotra*. Leiden: Brill.

Houben, Jan E. M. 2000. "The Ritual Pragmatics of a Vedic Hymn: The 'Riddle Hymn' and the Pravargya Ritual." *Journal of the American Oriental Society* 120:499–536.

Jamison, Stephanie W. 1996. *Sacrificed Wife / Sacrificer's Wife: Women, Ritual, and Hospitality in Ancient India*. New York: Oxford University Press.

Kane, P.V. 1974. *History of Dharmaśāstra*, vol. II, pts. 1 and 2, 2nd ed. Poona: Bhandarkar Oriental Research Institute.

Olivelle, Patrick. 1998. *The Early Upaniṣads: Annotated Text and Translation*. New York: Oxford University Press.

Proferes, Theodore. 2007. *Vedic Ideals of Sovereignty and the Poetics of Power*. American Oriental Series v. 90. New Haven, CT: American Oriental Society.

About the author

Stephanie W. Jamison is Distinguished Professor of Asian Languages and Cultures and of Indo-European Studies, University of California, Los Angeles. Jamison was trained as a historical and Indo-European linguist (PhD Yale 1977), but for many years she has concentrated on Indo-Iranian, especially (Vedic) Sanskrit and Middle Indo-Aryan languages and textual materials. She works also on literature and poetics, religion and law, mythology and ritual, and gender studies in these languages, and also holds an interest in comparative mythology and poetics, especially with Greek materials. Jamison has recently published (with Joel P. Brereton) a new complete English translation of the *The Rigveda* (Oxford University Press, 2014).

2

Ritual Interiorization and Abstract Action

Clemens Cavallin

Introduction

The *Brāhmaṇa* texts bear witness to intense speculations on the practice of ritual - its meaning and correct performance. Ironically, there occurs in the detailed attention to the minutiae of the sacrificial acts a shift towards various forms of interiority, both mental and physical, that partly lie outside of the ritual arena. In this speculation, the notion of breath and the various forms of breath play an important part and the ontological question underlying the discourse is the essence or constitution of the human person and with it the cosmos; later in the Upaniṣads so elegantly summarized in the most famous of all Vedic correspondences: *tat tvam asi* (you are that). Whether this should be understood as an equation (monism) or a relation (dualism) has provided Indian philosophy with a basic opposition.

The Vedic texts give us fascinating glimpses into how a preoccupation with ritual details gradually developed into a search for the essence of the human person, while preserving its connection with practice through its soteriological interest. My thesis, *The Efficacy of Sacrifice*, focused on the relationship between the system of ritual correspondences in the *Brāhmaṇa* texts and this interior turn.[1] However, in order to give the phenomenon of ritual interiorization a fuller analysis, the Vedic material has to be set in relation to similar cases from other cultural contexts in a comparative venture that is based on to a general, theoretical understanding of ritualization. In my book *Ritualization and Human*

Keywords: ritualization, interiorization, semiosis, Veda

Interiority (published 2013), I set out a theoretical framework for such a project, and in the following I will present one central part of that work.

Abstract action

An interesting concept for the consideration of ritual interiorization discussed by Caroline Humphrey and James Laidlaw (1994) in their book *The Archetypal Actions of Ritual* is abstract action, a notion borrowed from Merleau-Ponty. The abstract quality of an action refers to that it is being performed disconnected from its context, that the action is more directed towards its own performance than outside goals.[2] A special world of reified actions is in this way created. The doing away with the ordinary context of an action, thus making it abstract, is something which also Paul Ricoeur has discussed, but then under the theme of analysing actions as texts. He pinpoints the severance of individual intention and text (action) as the basic feature of the objectification of discourse. When moving from discourse to text, a process of fixation occurs which entails that: "the author's intention and the meaning of the text cease to coincide."[3] The actual meaning of fixed discourse is then the worlds that it opens up, an almost unlimited spectrum of references. This is due to that the original context of discourse is lacking, simple ostentation is not possible as in the unfixed live oral discourse; furthermore, in a text, the dialogical partner is exchanged for a potentially unlimited audience. In extending this analysis of texts as fixed discourses to social action, a similar focus on action as disembedded occurs, the objectification of action. Humphrey and Laidlaw take up the same thread in regard to ritual action, turning our attention towards its detachment from individuality, and creation as a social object.

While it is helpful to treat actions as texts, as Ricoeur does, I would like to take this analogy along a somewhat different road. The text metaphor primarily highlights the withdrawal of action from individual intention, but this abstract quality of ritual action can also be connected with conceptual abstraction, that is, the movement from the specific to the general, for example, from the idea of the individual you, the reader, and, me, the writer, to the notion of a human being. In this process, most of the individual characteristics of you and me are taken away, and what remains is the idea of a "human being" that possesses some general qualities. The same process of abstraction takes place in the formulation of norms, for example, those governing the Vedic sacrifices.[4] A norm is intended, in order to be a norm and not simply a command, to cover a more or less wide spectrum of behaviour that takes place in different locations and at different times. The rules governing the Vedic Soma sacrifice, for example, have in common with the abstract notion of a "human being"' that they are general, that is, abstracted from the irrelevant features of specific contexts. When a human being tries to conform to a general rule this demands some creative work of application, similar to the interpretation of a text, but what characterizes ritual action is that it tries to be *like a* norm, that it strives to eliminate the individual idiosyncrasies of the ritual participants: One can, in a ritual context, be expected to walk like an illustration of the abstract concept of walking, a kind of walking which is more at home in a platonic world of ideas than in everyday reality. This abstract quality of ritual actions is often referred to as formality, which Bell characterizes as "the use of a more limited and rigidly organized set of expressions and gestures, a 'restricted code' of communication and behaviour."[5]

There is a close connection between stylized theatrical *dramatis personae* and the ritual person; they share this tendency of abstraction, of moving away from a particular context, a definite position in time and space, and striving towards an intersubjective world of abstract notions, social roles and norms: all of which, however, to a high degree are instantiated in a narrative form and guided by the principle of personification. The individual in submitting to ritual norms acts out abstract actions which are part of an intersubjective repertoire of ideal notions and narratives. Ritual practice is not merely pure action to which meanings are arbitrarily connected, but action raised to the level of meaning itself. This is, as indicated above, a matter of degree – an action can become increasingly abstract, that is, ritualized, in the sense of being governed by norms. However, this formation of action is, as argued by Humphrey and Laidlaw, not always and probably more seldom accomplished by explicit discursive instruction and instead mostly effectuated through habituation with the help of mimesis, developing an embodied ritual know-how through imitating; learning by doing.

While Humphrey and Laidlaw focus on the social constitution of action types such as the Jain puja and argue for the arbitrary connection between ritualized actions and meaning, they nevertheless open up for the connection between ritualized actions and individual meaning through their view of ritual acts as "apprehensible."[6] Ritual actions invite attempts at understanding and emotional response, which does not jeopardize the nature of the act which is independent of those individual mental states. That is, if not the meaning thus given starts to push the interpretation of ritual action in the direction of individual intentionality, as when the true meaning of sacrifice is seen as residing in the purpose and motives of the individual.

My focus on the "conceptually" abstract nature of the ritualization process is not meant to contradict the basic thesis of Humphrey and Laidlaw, but is a way to develop it; the actions are not merely stipulated as particular social forms of action, but the rule-following, more or less embodied or discursive in nature, is connected to a process of making the movements as abstract as possible, as not individual in character. This gives ritualized actions their peculiar formal character; they are meant to be instantiations of an archetype, so to speak, not expressions of individuality. This is, as I see it, very much in harmony with Humphrey and Laidlaw's line of arguing. The connection with conceptual abstraction, of seeing actions governed by ritual norms and concepts as instances of the same process, however, opens up for a closer connection between meaning and ritual action. The actions are conceptualized in that they are made to conform to an abstract scheme which can be internalized either through wordless instruction and imitation or by linguistic instruction.

Before continuing with this topic, I would like to remark that the focus on ritualization espoused by Bell, Humphrey and Laidlaw, combined with the notion of it having degrees, opens up for a very broad spectrum of domains for ritualization. The same process is active in military drills, religious ceremonies, golf and the automatization of movements in manufacturing. The actions are through a commitment to a set of abstract templates separated from the individual's intention: the focus is on correct performance. The difference which, nevertheless, makes it inappropriate to label all such actions as rituals is located in the higher level of instrumental rationality at work in the latter two examples. The formalization of action is then done in order to achieve certain empirical goals (hole-in-one or higher productivity) and there is no sense of sacrilege when these are changed, even though for the individual it can be difficult to break a settled habitus. The golf swing and the automatic movements of the worker in the factory are, therefore, not apprehensible in quite the same way as religious actions or civil rituals as the hauling of the flag. In these contexts, ritualized actions are parts of a symbolic world which is constituted by the abstract central notions, narratives and personalities of that particular culture or subculture. Not all ritualized actions are therefore rituals.

By the notion of apprehension, Humphrey and Laidlaw pave a way for the reconnection to their first purpose of studying the Jain puja, namely, symbolism. There is thus a possibility to link their theory with that put forward by the phenomenology of religion in the form presented by Mircea Eliade, even though their theory of ritual breaks with his basic idea of the inherent nature of symbolism in, for example, the snake as a lunar animal. They have by their separation of individual intention and ritual action made symbolism secondary to ritualization: instead of the other way around, when ritualization is a way to enact symbolical understandings. But, according to the development of the abstract nature of ritual action above, such a connection becomes once more intimate, though not the same as in the symbolism of Eliade. Sacredness becomes then, the elevation of a person or a thing to the abstract nature of the intersubjective cultural world. And in order to return to ordinary life a de-abstraction, with other words, desacralization or individualization, has to take place to effectuate its re-entrance into profane life. A thing, on the other hand, becomes sacred (abstract) not by acting, but by being reserved for ritual action, by being used only in a ritual way, and it becomes desacralized by lifting that restriction on its use. In this way, ritualization is the basis of sacredness and not sacredness of ritualization. Sacred carries the meaning of being set apart, abstracted from the contingent nature of everyday life, and instead being linked to a more perfect world. The sacred is in this way differentiated from the concept of the holy as it has been used within the phenomenology of religion; the holy refers to a higher degree of being (more permanent, independent of time and space, and saturated with power), which manifests itself in our finite world. Closely connected to the holy are the feelings it inspires in mortal men. Thus presented, the holy clearly presupposes the real existence of the supernatural, but in a strictly phenomenological sense, it refers to the manifestation of a more powerful form of being in the finite world. The manifestation, or hierophany, is a phenomenon of this world, but interpreted as a natural sign, transcending the less perfect order of being. Taken in this way, the conception of the holy does not presuppose the existence of a supernatural order, but focuses on human beliefs in an encounter between different levels of being. The holy is linked to the sacred, as the abstract realm has features in common with the holy, but sacredness is foremost a quality of the human elevation to that level, the process of abstraction, taking away certain qualities from human actions and things, in this way rendering them conceptual.[7]

Another feature of the abstraction of human action to the intersubjective world of ideals is that it, as indicated above, comes to share place not only with ritual norms, but with moral templates, ideal figures and exemplary narratives. The ritual thus becomes an arena in which the person comes into contact with these models of action and thought, also enabling him or her to fuse with them and in that way acquire a new character or nature. This coming together of the individual and the ideal underscores the basic social nature of ritual, as the intersubjective world of abstract actions and narratives is by definition upheld by social processes: language, teaching, discussion, reward and punishment. The world of ideals, into which the individual enters, is in a sense the collective memory of the social group, being in need of constant reactivation and transmission to new generations.[8] Ritualization is a means for individuals to enter into that world, in order to handle it, serve it and to benefit from it.

Once again the similarity with theatrical performance is close as also there the same processes are at play, actors holding up their persona to let the public engage with, for example, the template of moral and immoral love, of honour and shame. The abstract realm is acted out, perceived and felt, but in religious rituals a higher degree of seriousness is involved, a commitment entailing the notion of real transformation and not only catharsis. The theatrical performance can evolve into pure entertainment (catharsis as merely emotional activation) and would still be a performance, though of a superficial sort, while ritual as entertainment would have lost a significant part of its ritual character.

The borders are of course fleeting; rituals can be more or less performance oriented and theatre more or less ritualistic.[9] Nevertheless, theatrical performance builds on the distinction between actor and persona and characteristically the audience for the most part consists of passive perceivers being less committed than in living rituals, while it is the connection with the world of intersubjective ideal entities that unite theatre and ritual.[10] If theatrical action moves towards extreme realism, it cannot, nevertheless, escape the exemplary, letting one case represent a larger set, otherwise the problem of relevance will become acute: as in the case of Andy Warhol's 8 hour long film of a man sleeping.

Ritualization in its idealization of action, promoting it to the world of abstract entities, not merely facilitates the relation between the world of ideals and that of concrete life, but due to this it is also of central importance for religion. Or the other way around, religion as founded on the belief in the personification of the ideal order is vital for ritual action and the maintenance of a collective world of abstract principles. Because the realm of the supernatural is precisely this abstract ideal world: it encompasses moral norms, ideal persons and basic patterns of conduct – it is a supra-individual world of beings, entities and principles more or less abstracted from human finitude. Through ritualization the human person is able to become sacred, to ascend to the perfect world, and enter into relations with the ideal. But at this point, it is important to emphasize that though the road of abstraction can lead to total transcendence, along a consequent *via negativa*, such is mostly not the case when we come into contact with lived religion, and thus not merely focus on texts of speculative theology and metaphysics. It is this intermediate level where the ideal meets us in the form of persons and narratives which constitutes the arena of myth. A religion can, however, encompass both levels, for example, as a set of narratives of exemplary conduct and a more abstract system of ethical norms.

In order to understand the mentality behind religious ritualism it is necessary to abstain from the nominalist impulse inherent in modernity and instead *pace* Plato emphasize that the ideal, the abstract realm, in a religious context is not seen as the pale reflection of sensual real life, forcing us to breathe the thin air of metaphysical speculation, but, on the contrary, it is embraced as the result of an ascension on the ladder of being: the higher the more perfect realizations of being await us. The intersubjective cultural world is, hence, considered more objective than the changing earth, the norm more real than concrete action. Through ritualization, the human social group ascends to the level of the ideal, and this being typical of the religious impulse, tries to benefit from the richness of being found there. The holiness of a god or a goddess corresponds to its level of abstraction, and to reach the respective levels demands a similar effort of sacralization on the part of the human, or one has to take refuge in the idea of divine grace. The absolute being, the most abstract entity, is of course the most powerful, according to this way of reasoning, but confronted with heights of abstraction like that, the human intellect runs out of steam and the being thus conceived transcends the power of imagination – personification and the formulation of a narrative becomes problematic. To be intimate with such an abstract godhead entails leaving cognition and imagination behind and is the province of the mystic, who enters the path on which everything is abstracted, finally entering into nothingness, which at the same time is the fountainhead of being and power as such.

The raising of the individual by ritualization into the abstract world makes the question of individuation topical as the ritual person has become de-individuated, lost its specific personality by assuming an abstract persona, a ritual mask.[11] The question is then how the transformation back to the individual person takes place. In one sense, the problem of individuation is a question of relevance, of connecting the abstract actions to the lifeworld of the individual and to that of the social group. In rituals, there is, thus, not merely a movement towards the abstract, but reality in its earthly contingent form is very much present with all its pressing demands. Not only is ritual necessary for interaction with the notional and normative elements of a culture, but it presents itself also as a remedy due to the reality of *inter alia* death, diseases, misfortune, hatred, betrayal of trust, war, scarcity of food, defamation, persecution, anxiety, depression and injustice. These sources of pain motivate the ritual ascension of the human person, the search for contact with the holy, in order to overcome, or at least to be able to handle, evils such as death.

In a second sense, besides relevance, individuation in a more literal sense is a question of becoming an individual once more, because if a person cannot leave its abstract character achieved by ritualization, he or she has, in principle, to continue to live like a personification of a norm. Something which, on the other hand, can be a goal through a strategy of hyper-ritualization, a process in which increasingly more details of life are ritualized, not only governed by moral norms indicating the goodness or badness of actions, but ritual norms actually controlling the precise performance of the actions. Individuality is then deferred to the margins of life, to those areas where there is still room of manoeuvre for instrumental reasoning and action. In order to make profane life possible, the individual has to return to the level of the concrete going through a process of individuation thereby shedding the extraordinary abstract state into which he or she had entered. However, the person leaves the ritual transformed, the semiosis has left traces: if abstraction is the ascendance to the level of form partially leaving matter behind, a modified form re-enters into matter, a different person exits the ritual. The ritual functions as the fire of the goldsmith; it makes the material pliable to adopt a new form which when cooled preserves this new identity. The final ritual of the Vedic soma sacrifice was, for example, a bath, and in Hinduism water has *inter alia* this cooling effect, besides that of cleansing and removing the sacral state.

The contact with the ideal order of a culture is a way of tapping resources of being and power, at the same time as the world of ideals is upheld: the gods both give boons and are in need of the sacrificial food. And it is precisely on the ritual ground that the social and personal identity of the individual is made, and consequently moral-legal personhood conferred, weaving the web of interpersonal relations; and in all this the semiotic processes taking place on the surface of the person are of central importance.[12] The ritual person in its abstract state is placed in the ideal world which is enacted in the ritual setting and the abstraction of individuality makes it possible for the individual to enter into contact with the ideal entities: gods, norms (e.g. the divine law), social roles (the king) and notions (wisdom). As ritualization entails some degree of disembodiment, the person becomes in a sense conceptual and liable to manipulation in the manner of concepts, the person taking on signification in a radical way. Analogy, hence, works in the manner of identification: water cleanses in this state in a much more profound and radical way than ordinary water. However, in order for the water to be able to do this, it must also have been rendered abstract through sacralization; sacred water is not ordinary water; it is conceptual water on the level of the ideal. In the light of this, we can understand the viewpoint of pious Hindus bathing in the Ganges desiring purification though from a concrete perspective the river is intensely polluted.[13]

Ritual action semiotics

Ritualization opens up an avenue for internalization which differs from teaching in that it does not in principle depend on understanding, but on the efficacy of action. It is a form of semiotic action as indicated by speech act theory which focuses on discourse as actions, for example, the formula "Hereby I pronounce you man and wife." Ritual action, though bearing testimony to the same union of language and action, approaches this from the opposite direction: It is action functioning in the manner of language. The speech-act is an utterance which truly functions as an action, in that it brings about change, while the "act-speech" is an act which functions as language without distancing itself from the aspect of causality as discourse has done. For example, if hitting a person in the face first has as its object to render the opponent unconscious, but later evolve into a sign of enmity; it can in a third step, in analogy to a speech act ("I declare you my enemy") actually make a person your enemy; the formalized act functioning as a means of communication. As a ritual act, however, the ritual slapping can retain the primary aspect of efficient causality, namely the effect of rendering the opponent senseless, but this is now being achieved on a semiotic level. The slapping of the abstract notion of the enemy as represented in, for example, a statue is then not merely a way of openly declaring another group as the enemy, but can involve the idea of actually hurting the enemy. This is what has been labelled as magical thinking and its origin and nature, especially its rationality or lack of it, has puzzled scholars. According to the theoretical perspective elaborated here, this form of action done according to a special logic of meaning and often characterized as magical, is also natural to religious ritual, when the ideal world is taken as having a reality of its own. It is more a question of ritual thinking than a special magical mindset. For when matter is abstracted, analogy is the same as partial identity, and in the ideal world, identical twins are in fact only one person, making them on a conceptual level into a real nuisance: being two and one at the same time. A perfect copy cannot exist on this level, because a perfect copy cannot by any criteria be distinguished from the original. Two notions having the same characteristics are as the twins actually one notion and can only be individuated by being thought by different embodied minds. Disembodied minds would by thinking the same thought acquire partial identity. Naturally, the implications of this become evident first in a more intellectual religious tradition, as found in the Vedic *brāhmaṇas*, but also on lower levels of abstraction the same tendency can be witnessed.

A feature of the special action semiotics of ritualized action, however, points to a dilemma at the heart of ritual practice, namely that actions do not directly refer to any symbolical value, for example, concepts such as purity or salvation; they instead refer to the norms regulating the action. When an action is ritualized, it is made to conform to the ritual norm in such a way as to abstract away idiosyncrasies as much as possible; the person tries to become like the norm and not merely to follow it. In this way, the person is subjected to a semiotic process, but the person does not acquire what is usually called symbolical meaning, as the norm is a statement on how to act, not the "meaning" of the act. To ritualize an action is, on the one hand, to render it meaningless – it is divorced from the intention of the individual – but, on the other hand, this is a process of signification and thus also of meaning, but the meaning acquired is that of a norm. The foundational semantic double nature of ritualization is provided by the tension between, on the one hand, the disconnecting of action from individual intentionality, connecting it instead to the meaning of the ritual norm in this way achieving a focus on correct performance. And, on the other hand, ritualization allowing action to become semiotic, being able to act upon other abstract entities and in its turn being acted upon by them, everything according to the special logic of ritual semiotics. Action becoming ritualized thus loses its meaning and at the same time becomes meaning.

Notes

1. Cavallin 2003.
2. Humphrey and Laidlaw 1994: 236–237.
3. Ricoeur 1973: 95; cf. Bell 1992: 51.
4. The textual genre trying to formulate these norms in a systematic fashion is of course the śrauta sūtras.
5. Bell 1997: 139.
6. Humphrey and Laidlaw 1994: 211.
7. For a similar differentiation between the numinous and the sacred, both species of the The Holy, see Rappaport 1997: 277–405, though for him the bifurcation is based on that the sacred is discursive while the numinous is ineffable 1997: 371.
8. Hervieu-Léger 2000; Assmann 2006.
9. Cf. Turner 1988.
10. Rozik (2002: 75–6), however, remarks that the opposition between participation-spectatorhood is not valid as a criterion in distinguishing between ritual and theatre, as spectatorhood is a form of participation. He localizes the decisive difference instead in the opposition between efficacy and description, or action and thinking. However, the participation characterised by action and efficacy is mostly more intense than that taking place according to description and thinking.
11. When the aim of the ritual is a transformation of the person, its de-individualization can take the form of undressing. That is, the signs which

connect the personal identity with the social identity are removed, and the person is invested with new signs which establishes a new social identity and at the same time facilitates its internalization, establishing also a new interior personal identity.

12. The different levels of individuality, social identity, personality and universal concept comes together in the fascinating theme of personal names. These hover ambiguously between pure reference "Andrew" as a label affixed to this man and Andrew Smith as indicating inclusion in a family (or social group), however, vague; and Andrew as a concept signaling manliness (the etymological sense). The name can then have as one its "meanings" the unique essence of the person, but as language operates by concepts which are general, this unique constitution can only be comprehended as the participation in certain general qualities, or as devoid of meaning in being a sign with only reference, a mere arrow pointing toward the interior "hidden" kernel of the personality. Such a pure reference can then be seen as participating in that essence instead of describing it through general concepts and it hence takes on a partial identity with what it signifies, which cannot be linguistically expressed in any other way. The disclosure of one's true "name" is, therefore, an act of externalization which renders the person vulnerable: he or she is in one sense turned inside out. For the exploration of naming in an anthropological context see vom Bruck 2006. One problem which can arise in a religious context is to do with all the Andrews, are they one person, or do they share basic characteristics participating in Andrewness, or are names only nomina? In philosophy, these problems are discussed under the heading of "proper names" which have given modern philosophers much headache, see e.g. Zink 1963 and Stroll 1998; the decisive point being precisely the tension between reference and meaning (e.g. Makin 2000 on the theories of Russell and Frege).
13. Alley 2002.

References

Alley, Kelly. 2002. *On the Banks of Ganga: When Wastewater Meets a Sacred River*. Ann Arbor: University of Michigan Press.

Assmann, Jan. 2006. *Religion and Cultural Memory: Ten Studies*. Stanford, CA: Stanford University Press.

Bell, Catherine. 1992. *Ritual Theory, Ritual Practice*.Oxford: Oxford University Press.

Bell, Catherine. 1997. *Ritual Perspectives and Dimensions*. Oxford: Oxford University Press.

vom Bruck, Gabriele, and Barbara Bodenhorn, eds. 2006. *The Anthropology of Names and Naming*. Cambridge: Cambridge University Press.

Cavallin, Clemens. 2013. *Ritualization and Human Interiority*. Copenhagen: Museum Tusculanum Press.

Cavallin, Clemens. 2003. "The Efficacy of Sacrifice: Correspondences in the Ṛgvedic Brāhmaṇas." Göteborg University, Department of Religious Studies. (Skrifter utgivna vid Institutionen för religionsvetenskap Göteborgs Universitet, 29.)

Hervieu-Léger, Danièle. 2000. *[1993] Religion as a Chain of Memory*. Oxford: Blackwell.

Humphrey, Caroline, and James Laidlaw. 1994. *The Archetypal Actions of Ritual: A Theory of Ritual Illustrated by the Jain Rite of Worship*. Oxford: Clarendon Press.

Makin, Gideon. 2000. *Metaphysicians of Meaning: Russell and Frege on Sense and Denotation*. London: Routledge.

Rappaport, Roy. 1997. *Ritual and Religion in the Making of Humanity*. Cambridge: Cambridge University Press.

Ricoeur, Paul. 1973. "The Model of the Text: Meaningful Action Considered as a Text." *New Literary History* 5(1): 91–117. http://dx.doi.org/10.2307/468410.

Rozik, Eli. 2002. *The Roots of Theatre: Rethinking Ritual and other Theories of Origin*. Iowa City: University of Iowa Press.

Stroll, Avrum. 1998. "Proper Names, Names, and Fictive Objects." *Journal of Philosophy* 95(10): 522–534. http://dx.doi.org/10.2307/2564720.

Turner, Victor. 1988. *The Anthropology of Performance*. PAJ publications.

Zink, Sidney. 1963. "The Meaning of Proper Names." *Mind* 72(288): 481–499. http://dx.doi.org/10.1093/mind/LXXII.288.481.

About the author

Clemens Cavallin is Senior Lecturer at the Department of Literature, History of Ideas, and Religion at the University of Gothenburg, Sweden. Cavallin's research interests include Hinduism, Ritual theory and Catholic Studies. His dissertation "The Efficacy of Sacrifice" (2002) focused on Vedic sacrifices, while his second book, *Ritualization and Human Interiority* (2013) concerns ritual theory. He is presently working on a biography of the Canadian artist and author Michael O'Brien and on the project "Religion on Campus: A Study of Views on Religion at Two Indian Universities" which analyses the present situation of religious studies in India.

3

Lord Over this Whole World: Agency and Philosophy in Bṛhadāraṇyaka Upaniṣad

Anna-Pya Sjödin

> "Yajñavalkya," Ārtabhāga said again, "tell me -when a man [*puruṣa*] has died, and his speech disappears into fire, his breath into the wind, his sight into the sun, his mind into the moon, his hearing into the quarters, his physical body [*śarīra*] into the earth, his self (*ātman*) into space, the hairs of his body into plants, the hairs of his head into trees, and his blood and semen into water -what then happens to that person [*puruṣa*]?"
>
> Yajñavalkya replied: "My friend, we cannot talk about this in public. Take my hand Ārtabhāga, let's go and discuss this in private."
>
> So they left and talked about it. And what did they talk about? -they talked about nothing but action [*karman*]. And what did they praise? -they praised nothing but action. Yajñavalkya told him: "A man turns into something good by good action and into something bad by bad action" Thereupon Ārtabhaga fell silent.[1]

This article concerns in what way thinking the sacrifice could be understood as ordering thinking the human being as agent and in turn thinking the human being as knower. That is, how it could be possible to conceive of a relationship or connection between sacrifice and philosophy within Upaniṣadic thought. The analysis below will mainly take place within a close-reading of some of the ways that agency is conceptualized in the *Bṛhadāraṇyakopaniṣad* (BĀU). Towards the end I will turn to later philosophical thinking on agency and knowledge, here represented by Praśastapāda's commentary on the *Vaiśeṣikasūtra.*

Keywords: Bṛhad Āraṇyaka Upaniṣad, Praśastapāda, agency, knowledge

The discussion of agency in BĀU is centred around the question of an embodied self/person and the limiting or liberating circumstances that he/she is subject to or master over. In that way it touches upon the construction of an idea of a person or individual and in a wider sense an idea of what a human being essentially is. In a more technical vein I understand agency (ie. *kartṛtva*) here as an agents (*kartṛ*)[2] capacity to act and by that acting coming to results, in a causal way that is, as determined by the acting. Within the context of BĀU agency could be understood in terms of specified kinds of agency, for example sacrificial agency or soteriological agency and so on. But, at the same time also as a somewhat "general agency," that is, as said above, a capacity to act and thereby creating consequences, but also, and perhaps most important, an agency intimately connected to a knowledge of what these consequences might be.

The early Upaniṣadic texts, of which BĀU is one, are orally transmitted and remembered texts that were compiled approximately from 600 BC and onwards for up to several hundreds of years. These texts are concerned with the ideas of *ātman, brahman,* and *puruṣa*. *Brahman* is variously understood as an absolute reality, a cosmic force or a first cause but also as an object of worship and a personal entity depending on which *Upaniṣad* is read. *Ātman* is sometimes used in the meaning of body and/or human being but more frequently it is used in the sense of "self," here it should be remembered that *ātman* also functions as a reflexive pronoun within the Sanskrit language. The self in turn is understood sometimes as a vital force connected to breathing (*prāṇa*), sometimes as a deity, sometimes as a creator and sometimes as an individual self depending on which passage in the different Upaniṣads one reads. The relationship between *ātman* and *brahman* is of central concern in many of these texts. In the BĀU, *brahman* and *ātman* are often identified with each other, they are for example displayed parallel to each other, in identical text-passages, and in other passages they appear to be interchangeable.[3]

Puruṣa then is used in the meaning of "person" or "man" but it is important to remember that this term has cosmological connotations, the first man or cosmic man is also called *puruṣa*. The cosmic man was used as material for sacrifice and out of his body and bodily/mental functions the world came to be. His eyes became the sun and his mind the moon, his breath the wind and so on.[4] I want you to pay attention to the repetition of these connections in the citation that introduced this article. In that text-passage, *puruṣa* has been translated in two ways, first as "man" and then as "person," illustrating well the kind of hermeneutical difficulties that are frequent in the early Upaniṣads.

The relation between *puruṣa* and *ātman* is diversly described and elaborated in the texts. Sometimes they are equated with each other and sometimes they are put in hierarchical relation to each other and sometimes just separated in two categories. In the initial citation here for example, *ātman* and *puruṣa* are spoken of as two kinds of aspects of the human being. This all is to make clear that there is no apparent descernible unity in thought among the early Upaniṣads, and each *Upaniṣad* can, in turn, contain different strands or trends of thought. There is furthermore no apparent layering or classifying of for example epistemological, ontological or metaphysical issues, with the consequence that the different foci of the text come forth as somewhat blurred in a systematic reading.

What is apparent in all the early Upaniṣads, however, is that we encounter a thinking turned towards the human being, with the self in the centre of the discussion. The knowing of oneself as self, how this knowing can be reached and what consequences this knowing can have are themes that run through all these texts.

> This self is the trail to this entire world, for by following it one comes to know this entire world, just as by following their tracks one finds cattle.[5]
>
> This innermost thing, this self –it is dearer than a son, it is dearer than wealth, it is dearer than everything else.[6]

Framing the text

My choice of BĀU for the analysis here is not randomly made but rather has to do with which *śākhā*- which school or tradition of vedic recitation- that the text belongs to. The BĀU is attached to the white *Yajurveda* and to the *Śatapatabrāhmaṇa* texts. These texts are related to the ritual specialists called the *adhvaryu*, who handled the material actions of the ritual, for example preparing the sacrificial grounds and the oblations.[7] The grand vedic sacrificial rituals, in contrast to the vedic domestic rituals, were elaborate, time-consuming and very expensive. They furthermore required a host of different ritual specialists, whereas the domestic sacrifice was and still is individually performed. The horse sacrifice (*aśvamedha*) for example, lasted a whole year.[8] The theorizing of ritual and sacrifice within the *Brāhmaṇa* text-corpus exploded not long before the appearance of the first Upaniṣadic texts, that is, possibly around 700 BC. The structure of the theorizing of the ritual and sacrifice that takes place in these texts is mainly by way of equivalence or connection. Parts of the ritual are identified with or connected to parts of the agent of the ritual, and with parts of the world at large. Examples of this way of connecting is found in the BĀU passage on the sacrificial horse.[9] The phenomenon of such connections is amply illustrated in Stephanie Jamison's text above.[10]

Ritual action in the *brāhmaṇa* context is called *karma(n)* and this is a meaning that is partly retained in the BĀU, which is also said to be the first of the Upaniṣads to speak clearly of *karman* in terms of retributive activity. With this in mind I want the reader to be aware of the fact that there are connotations to the term *karman* that includes ritual/sacrificial action as well as action in a more general sense. So that sometimes in the BĀU, *karman* translates as sacrifice and sometimes as action (in general) and sometimes perhaps including both meanings simultaneously.[11] In relation to this it might be important to note that there are a number of researchers that have discussed the conceptualization of action/sacrifice within both the *brāhmaṇa* and *Upaniṣad* texts. Cavallin, for example, has pointed out that thinking sacrificial efficacy and activity in the *brāhmaṇa* texts seems to lead to a thinking concerning acting and agency in general.[12] Signe Cohen has claimed that there are connections between the reflection on the ritual activity of the *adhvaryu* (ritual specialists) to the ideas of *karman* as spelled out in the BĀU.[13] Both Cohen and the translator of the older Upaniṣads, Patrick Olivelle, emphasizes *karman* in the senses of both "ritual" and "ethic" action. But Olivelle also notes a shift towards an "ethicization" of action in the Upaniṣads.[14] The distinction between "ritual" and "ethic" action is not necessarily a clear cut one. Tull has, for example, pointed out that the passages in the BĀU where good and bad action (*su-/duṣ-kṛta*) have been understood in relation to an idea of *karman* in an ethical sense may very well refer to good and bad sacrificial action.[15]

In my opinion it is philosophically important here to clarify that "ethical" action could simply imply action that is retributive, that has consequences according to what is understood as "good" and "bad," irrespective of the particularities of that good and bad. So it is not the action in itself that is ethical but an idea that everything I do as a human being has consequences also outside of the sphere of what could be seen as an apparent material causality, that is, a so called karmic process, a process of cause and consequence. Given that we define ethical action as actions that have bearing upon other conscious beings then the very distinction between ethical action and sacrificial action might become incompatible with an idea of *karman* where *every action* that is conducted generates consequences. Hence, almost as if a particular sphere of an "ethical" or "a morality-based" action is not even discernible. That is, discernible in contrast to some other action, because every action performed has consequences. In the much later text of the Vaiśeṣika philosopher Praśastapāda, on actions producing merit and demerit, there appears no distinction between sacrificial acts and such acts that would be named ethical in the context of the above definition. In Praśastapāda's listing of actions producing merit and demerit are mentioned such diverse things as ritual bathing, being angry, performing or not performing sacrifices according to ones' station, stealing, fasting, and devotion to the god/goddess one prefers.[16] When using his text as a hermeneutical device, reading backwards so to speak, the problematic idea of a clear cut separation between ethical and sacrificial actions could be abandoned. On the other hand; however analysed, the ambiguity in how it is possible to understand the notion of *karman* within the BĀU underscores the present reading of the text.

It is in relation to the above discussions that I have written this paper along the lines of a certain presupposition. This idea entails a connection between the theories of sacrificial agency, that is, the *brāhmaṇa* thinking on sacrifice, and later theories of human nature and agency. This means that I believe that the consequences of thinking the sacrificial act appears as consequences in thinking the human being as agent, both in the Upaniṣads but also later on in the philosophical discourse of India. In that way I would like to call attention to a possible ideational connection between *brāhmaṇa* sacrificial theory and Upaniṣadic anthropology which leaves traces in the later systematic philosophical thinking, visible, for example, in Praśastapāda's commentary on the *Vaiśeṣikasūtras* on the self. Towards the end of this paper I have included a brief example of this assumed continuum of thinking the human being.

Upaniṣads as philosophy

Before continuing to further discuss the above connection I will turn to an important issue within the context of how "philosophy" is understood and could be understood. That is, in what way the Upaniṣadic writing of the human being as agent can be termed philosophy. The answer to this question obviously depends on what one takes the term "philosophy" to mean. The discussion of the import of the term "philosophy" is possible to relate to Larson's definition given in this volume. He makes a distinction between systematic philosophy and unsystematic thinking. Given that definition the Upaniṣadic texts are not to be considered as philosophy. And I will, towards the end, give an example of the difference between such systematic philosophy and Upaniṣadic thinking. I do not, in this respect, call into question the fact that there are huge differences between the systematic Indian philosophical discourse and the somewhat unsystematic thinking in the present texts. I do, however, contend with that this kind of systematic philosophy that we see emerge in later texts is the only kind of philosophy formulated in ancient India, that there is but one single understanding of philosophy available to us. An understanding that furthermore often mirrors a static notion of philosophy within western academia. An understanding that, in turn, is hard to find in any consensual form whatsoever within this same academia and throughout the history of a so called "Western philosophy."

I have argued, elsewhere, for a more reflexive and fluid understanding of what I call the "activity of philosophizing," so that it might expand and deviate from the idea of a static definition. A definition that defies the fact of both a heterogeneous history, and a present discourse, of "Western philosophy."[17] By this I do not mean to say that I see philosophical activity as a primarily national or ethnic endeavour (ie. "Western/Indian"), but rather that this is exactly how philosophy from outside the European and American discourse has been, and still is, viewed within academia. In order to get out of this kind of vicious circle of arguing against an already determined notion of philosophical activity in an ethnicized form, I turn instead to the idea of reflexivity. A reflexivity that exists along the very lines of the heterogeneity of conceptualizations of "philosophy" both from a synchronic and diachronic perspective. Accordingly, this reasoning does not imply that there is a self-evident list of elements that would, if present in the Upaniṣads, point to its being philosophy, or its being "worthy" of the term philosophy. Rather, it implies a reading of the texts in the same self-evident vein as when one considers the Herakleit fragments to be philosophy. In the present context this reflexive reading means that a certain reading of an *Upaniṣad* would produce a further understanding of what philosophy could be, a widening of the term so to speak. Thus, the understanding of the conceptualization of agency within the text, is thought of, in extension, as a way or means to understand how the text writes philosophy, or rather how philosophizing is done in the *Upaniṣad.* Furthermore, I assume the idea that a certain understanding of agency stands prior to a certain understanding of knowing or knowledge. To put it in another way: in order to understand the epistemological concerns of the text we have also to understand the "anthropological" concerns of the text. That is, the way in which a human being is conceptualized as acting and knowing.

The reader should note that my discussion of the understanding of "philosophy" here remains somewhat circular and in this sense also problematic. I do believe that the systematic discussions of epistemology in later Indian philosophical texts *are* more akin to what could be seen as a normative presupposition of what philosophy is understood to be at present.[18] At the same time I also believe that we have the ability to reformulate "philosophy" both in relation, and opposition, to that normative idea.

Agency in Bṛhadāraṇyaka Upaniṣad

The agentivity or agency (*kartṛtva*) of which the BĀU speaks could be understood as a central theme within the thinking of the human in general, thus overarching a number of other aspects of the human, such as the Upaniṣadic tropes of enjoyer *(bhoktṛ)*, knower *(jñātṛ)*, and perceiver/

seer *(draṣṭṛ)*.[19] These are all linked to what I would call an absolute subject, that is, the self (*ātman*). What appears important in the BĀU is the connection between self and cognition, as if cognition would be the central indicator of self. At least it portrays self in terms of, and in relation to, epistemological agency.[20]

> "The self within all is this self of yours"
>
> "Which one is the self within all, Yajñavalkya?"
>
> "You can't see the seer who does the seeing; you can't hear the hearer who does the hearing; you can't think the thinker who does the thinking; and you can't perceive the perciever who does the perceiving. The self within all is this self of yours, All else is besides this grief."[21]
>
> This *ātman* is -not -not. It is ungraspable, for it cannot be grasped. It is immortal, for it does not die.[22]

An absolute subject is something that is never a thing, that is, something that can never be made an object, insofar as always being subject in relation to all other objects. In one sense the self could here ontologically be understood as already given, hence being before knowing and acting takes place. I read this text as an expression of the centrality of the subject. The human being is thought in relation to this subjectivity as enjoyer, knower, perceiver and, of course, as agent. I am fully aware of how the citation above, and other similar passages often are read as expressing an idea that the knowledge of *ātman* and/or *brahman* surpasses any sensual or intellectual knowledge, that is, that *ātman*/*brahman* as such lies beyond language. Of course these readings do not negate the possibility of my understanding of an absolute subject that is, by its nature, beyond any objectively expressible or thinkable entity. On the other hand I think it important to continue to scrutinize the various expressions of knowledge and cognition that are present in the early Upaniṣads. Knowledge is thought with different terms and in different contexts. For even though one cannot make *ātman* an object of knowing one can indeed seek, and come to, knowledge of *ātman*. As Brereton notes; "For Yajñavalkya, the self that is the unknowable subject of all knowing is also the self of the whole world"[23]

> You see, Maitreyi –it is one's self (*ātman*) which one should see and hear, and on which one should reflect and concentrate. For when one has seen and heard one's self, one knows this whole world.[24]

In reading this it becomes, of course, important, to differentiate between the ontological status of *ātman* and the epistemological. The self exists as absolute subject and in that capacity *ātman* can never be the object of knowledge, but this status, on the other hand, can be known and understood.

The specific images of the self's agency that are present in the BĀU are the inner controller (*antaryāmin*), the lord (*adhipati*), the king (*rājā*), the master (*īśa*), the ruler (*vaśin*) and the overseer (*praśāstṛ*)[25]. The trope "lord over this whole world" can sound as follows:

> This person [*puruṣa*] here is made of mind and consists of light. Lodged here deep within the heart, he is like a grain of rice or barley; he is the lord of all, the ruler of all! Over this whole world, over all there is, he rules.[26]

The peculiar juxtaposition here of the very small and the very large is a common feature of the sayings in many of the early Upaniṣads. The being very small could be read as indicating an incapacitated state, unempowered as it were, whereas the very large of course produces the opposite. That the self is so very small but at the same time so very powerful gives us an acute sense of the extent of the agency expressed.

The inner controller then is expressed as follows:

> This self of yours who is present within but is different from all beings, whom all beings do not know, whose body is all beings, and who controls all beings from within –he is the inner controller, the immortal.[27]

I think it possible, as a hypothesis, to understand these tropes of controller and ruler as attempts to delineate a certain kind of agency that, even though it extends beyond, and in some cases functions as the opposite of, the sacrificial ground, has gathered momentum within the reflection upon sacrificial agency. Indeed, this could be understood in terms of a diffusion or extension of the agency of the sacrificial agent within the sacrificial universe to the soteriological, ethical and epistemological agency of the human being within the world at large. Here it is necessary to call to mind the power of manipulation that the Vedic sacrificial acts gained within the Brāhmaṇic world. Stephanie Jamison comments thus:

> Participants and objects in the ritual stand for, embody, and indeed actually *become* participants and objects in the larger sphere of human life and in the cosmos...In other words, the performance of the ritual is a way of exerting control on the unruly human and natural forces in the universe by controlling their representatives within the restricted compass of the ritual ground.[28]

In the BĀU the sacrificial acts or ritual acts are also repeatedly linked to the constituents of the human and the human in turn is tied to, or equated with the rest of the world.

> ..and his body (*ātman*) is the rites [*karma*], for one performs rites [*karma*] with one's body [*ātman*]. This is the fivefold sacrifice – the sacrificial animal is fivefold, the human being [*puruṣa*] is fivefold, and this whole world, whatever there is, is fivefold. Anyone who knows this obtains this whole world.[29]

The linking of the sacrifice, the performer of the sacrifice, and the "outside" world enables the thought of agency to spread outside the limits of the sacrifice. Outside of the sacrificial ground this entails, among other things, to become lord over all that there is, or in other words to become the central point of reality.

> This very self is the lord and king of all beings. As all the spokes are fastened to the hub and the rim of a wheel, so to one's self are fastened all beings, all the gods, all the worlds, all the breaths and all these bodies.[30]

We could think this in terms of a sacrificial agent, so to speak, who stands within the sacrificial ground and acts within this ground, everything that he does in there is linked to, or connected to, or identified with, an outside of the ground so that the actions within has consequences on the outside. If he does everything right, in proper order, the sponsor of the sacrifice (*yajamāna*), and the sacrificial agent, receives the proper consequences.[31]

One way of understanding the connection between the ritual specialist within the sacrificial grounds and the outside of this is to construe it in terms of the ideal and real converging. That is to say that the agency expressed here is not, in one sense, metaphorically understood at all, but rather as a quite concrete exchange. On the other hand, this thinking agency allows for a metaphorically expressed understanding of the human being. I am not saying here that it is possible to know how the performers of sacrifice actually thought about the capacity to determine a sequence of events as the distinction between the real and ideal could imply. What I am saying is that the very idea of ritual agency allows for a certain thinking about agency in general and consequently about knowledge. That is, the one who knows the precise connections "*obtains this whole world.*"

The thought that a person, being the hub of the world as *ātman*, can achieve consequences when acting in general or all the time, and not only within the frame of sacrifice, is not, in my opinion, so foreign here. The "outside," that is "the whole world" comes within grasp and control of the self.[32] In such a thought it would be possible to talk about an "absolute agency" of an "absolute subject," an agency that could mean the capability not only to uphold and behold the world but also to make or create the world.

> This is how he dreams. He takes materials from the entire world and, taking them apart on his own and then on his own putting them back together, he dreams with his own radiance, with his own light. In that place this person becomes his own light. In that place there are no carriages, there are no tandems, and there are no roads; but he creates for himself carriages, tandems and roads. In that place there are no joys, pleasures, or delights; but he creates for himself joys, pleasures, and

> delights. In that place there are no pools, ponds or rivers; but he creates for himself pools, ponds and rivers – for he is a creator (*kartā*).[33]

This very interesting, and arresting, imagery appears in the dream-analogy in the fourth *adhyāya* of BĀU. The text itself instructs us in a paragraph further down that this could be understood as an analogy, at least to the extent that there is a pronounced correspondence between the dream-world and the awake-world.[34] In a more speculative vein the above text-passage calls to mind a child at play, building landscapes, taking things apart and putting them together again, apparently emphasizing the creative aspect of agency. The phrase "to be one's own light" is in the context of this article also an important marker of the close connection between acting (*karman*) and knowing (*jñāna/veda*). The light which lives in the sun is connected to the eye, the visual sense-organ. Although there is no clear formulation of what is called projective perception in the BĀU, this has been read, for example by David Gordon White, as pointing to a capability of sight.[35] The notion of projective perception entails the idea that the sense-organs are actively reaching out for the objects they need to be in contact with in order for perceptual cognition to take place. This actively pursued perception is more clearly emphasized in later texts on cognition and I will come back to this further down.

Expressions of self and subject

There is an obvious tension in the BĀU between the acting transformable subject and the still static self. Good acting creates good and bad acting creates bad but *ātman* remains the same, nothing good or bad attaches itself to it. So on one side there is an active agent and on the other a passive unchangeable, constant existent subject that is moved by nothing and no one.

> What a man turns out to be depends on how he acts and on how he conducts himself. If his actions are good he will turn into something good. If his actions are bad he will turn into something bad.[36]

> He does not become more by good actions or in any way less by bad actions! He is the lord of all, the ruler of creatures! He is the guardian of creatures![37]

> He sees the self in just himself and all things as the self. Evil does not pass across him, he passes across all evil, he is not burnt up by evil he burns up all evil.[38]

This static/dynamic tension is something that stays in later philosophical thinking and sometimes it becomes an important theme for debates and discussions concerning what the human being is, that is, whether she really could transform herself or if she already is perfect. Transformation or activity in order to reach perfection/liberation in the case of the later becomes futile; she just has to realize that she already is everything that is possible. This tension is visible in the way that BĀU writes its human being. Although one essentially is oneself there are passages that suggest a kind of rift between the self and the rest of the human so that one can, in principle, remain unaware of oneself or even hide from oneself. It is in these passages the self is described as something that has come into the body, or lives within the body.

> The self has entered this body, this dense jumble;
> if a man finds him,
> recognizes him,
> He's the maker of everything – the author of all!
> The world is his – he's the world itself![39]
> When a man clearly sees this self as god,
> the lord of what was
> and what will be,
> He will not seek to hide from him.[40]

In a cursory reading this and other similar passages obviously express that the human being is thought of in terms of body and self (*ātman*). But this kind of image is not the only one found in the text, nor is the meaning and implication of the term *ātman* fixed. This is indicated by how the self (*ātman*) or sometimes the person (*puruṣa*) appears to be used as including the body.[41] Apart from that, the body is, of course, also an important aspect of agency, the body is used in order to execute actions, such as sacrifice, and this is something that the text appears to be aware of. For example when dreaming one can, in some fashion, bring the body along:

> Wherever he may travel in his dream, those regions become his world... just as a great king, taking his people with him, may move around in his domain at will, so he, taking the vital functions here with him, moves around his body at will.[42]

The human being is often expressed as constituted by the so called vital powers or functions; breath, thought, speech, sight and hearing. The centrality of these in the text is an indication that one should be wary of expressing a common sense division or distinction between body/self. The vital powers are sometimes identified with *ātman*, sometimes they stand alongside *ātman* and sometimes they are separated from *ātman*.[43] That there are distinctions and categorizations of the human being at work in the BĀU is clear but how these categorizations work is not so readily understandable.

What the above mentioned tension also might indicate is that the text is caught in a negotiation of its categories for thinking the human being.

These negotiations could be understood by a simplified structure in terms of ranging, from a sacrificial agency where bodily/physical activity is at the centre, to the agency of the unmoved self which is one of inner activity, that is, one of cognitive, or perhaps one could say mental, activity. In another vein we may also understand the expressions of this tension as expressions of an absolute agent much in the same way as the expressions of the absolute subject. That is, as a subject who can know, feel and touch but cannot be known, felt or touched. The agent then can act, good or bad but cannot really be changed as a result of good or bad action, which is, nothing at all could really influence or transform the self in any way. One way of phrasing this is the distinction between being a mover and being moved.

> About this self, one can only say -not -not. He is ungraspable, for he cannot be grasped. He is undecaying, for he is not subject to decay. He has nothing sticking to him, for he does not stick to anything. He is not bound; yet he neither trembles in fear nor suffers injury.[44]

Continuity of thought

I will conclude here with a brief note on the continuum of thinking the agency of the self and point to some important issues that need to be analyzed further. When the philosopher Praśastapāda writes about the self around 600 AD, he writes with images of the agent-self that echoes those in the BĀU. The self is according to Praśasta situated within the heart (*hṛdaya*), and when we are asleep it shares this space with the inner sense (*manas*) or, as it is also termed, the inner cause (*antaḥkaraṇa*).[45] This obviously echoes Upaniṣadic descriptions of *ātman* (self), *puruṣa* (person), or sometimes *manas* as being situated in the heart.[46] But it is foremost visible in the analogies or inferences that Praśasta utilizes to point to *ātman*, the so called indicators. Here a trope like *adhiṣṭhātṛ* (ruler, governor) is used for *ātman* and the images of the agent ranges from a charioteer, a string puller, a blower of bellows, a master of the house to a little boy throwing a ball. The extent to which the agency of *ātman* is thought is visible in the image of healing as indicating that the body has an owner looking after it and making repairs or in the image of breathing as indicating that there is someone who blows. And in the image of the blinking indicating someone pulling strings:

> Just as a charioteer is inferred by means of the motion of the chariot so also is a controlling agent[47] of the body inferred from the inherence in the body[48] of activity-towards and activity-against[49] in order to reach for the pleasant and avoid the unpleasant; and from breathing. How so? From seeing the motion of change[50] when wind is contained within the body, just like a blower of bellows[51]; from the regulated/controlled

> motion of closing and opening the eyes, just like a puller of strings; from effecting the growth [of the body] and from healing of the torn and broken body and so on, just like that which is done (i.e. caused) by the master of the house [when it is broken].[52] From the motion of the inner sense being a prerequisite for (*nimitta*) the connection between instrument, grasper (subject) and intended (*abhimata*) object just like a boy setting a ball in motion in the corners of a house.[53]

For Praśasta the self is thought through the terms governor (*adhiṣṭātṛ*) and acquirer (*prasādhaka*), that is as agent (*kartṛ*) and subject/knower (*jñātṛ*). Here below exemplified by the process of causality, the cutting down a tree, analogous to the process of sense perception; hearing, seeing, touching and so on.

> As it is imperceptible, because of its subtleness, it is obtained by means of there being instruments of hearing and such [sense-capacities] that are inferred from the grasping of sounds and such [objects of perception]. An acquirer (*prasādhaka*) is [thus] inferred from the acquirement of sounds because it is seen that instruments, as an axe or some such, are employed by an agent (*kartṛ*) and an acquirer from the attainment of sounds etc.[54]

The inferences that he draws on the phenomena of perceptual grasping and purposeful animation of the body are indicative of how knowledge of the self is reached. What is important to remember here is also that ordinary sensual perception (seeing, hearing, tasting, smelling and touching) is, for Praśasta, a completely active preoccupation for the human being. Our sense-organs, most pregnantly the eye, reach out for their corresponding objects. Perception, in this sense, is not automatic or given but require an agent for whom the object is an intended (*abhimata*) target as it were.

The terminology of agency that Praśasta uses in these passages indicates three main aspects of action, first the intention (*abhimata*), the willing or wishing for something to take place and second the control or regulation (*niyata*) of the body being steered towards the desired or away from the undesired and third the impetus to move/act which is called effort (*prayatna*). The controlling is seen in the image of pulling strings, that is, to control the blinking of the eyes.[55] The steering of the chariot in Praśasta's text is guided by someone wishing to go in a certain direction as it were. The body, "the chariot," is moved according to the effort (*prayatna*) of the self, the moving directed then by either desire or aversion. The idea of intention (*abhimata*) comes forth in the image of a boy throwing a ball. Through Vyomaśiva's commentary on the passage we get a clearer picture of how this is possible to understand. The game the boy is playing involves three balls, the first one for the boy to throw and a second one that he aims at and a third one for the second ball to connect with. The boy is the self, the ball in his hand is the inner sense (*manas*)[56], the ball he aims at is the sense-organ, the third ball is the intended object. The aiming is, in the example, correlated with the act of turning towards an object in sensory perception, emphasized by the word *abhimata* (intended or desired). This "turning towards the desired" presupposes what is called effort (*prayatna*).[57]

The connection between Praśasta's text and the BĀU is not obvious in the sense that they have the same way of articulating thought. Praśasta follows certain parameters in his writing that are not shared by the BĀU, the systematic use of inferential reasoning is, among other things, expressive of this. What is interesting, however, is that there seems to be, in both texts, a certain structure to how the human being is thought, and that this thinking in turn has consequences for how knowledge is conceptualized. That the possibility of knowledge or knowing in a way presupposes agency, without which it would be meaningless, or even, as a category, unattainable. And, if it would be feasible to define a kind of minimal idea about how philosophy is done in the BĀU I would say that we find it in the very activity of structuring thought through agency and knowledge.

In conclusion then, we might say that one way of understanding how agency is formulated in the BĀU is that the text does not so much express a literal or ontological agency but rather visualizes a specific image of the human being; forming an idea that can function as a prerequisite for the very possibility of systematic philosophizing. That is to say, the enabled human being of the BĀU has everything within her grasp, every possibility of knowing the world, through knowing herself. In a way then the agency as lord or controller could be understood as that which makes knowledge possible to know. And, of course, in extension; knowledge possible to control.

Notes

1. BĀU 3.2.13 [my italics within brackets]. I have used the Olivelle 1998 translation of BĀU for all citations in this paper. The passages from the BĀU cited in this paper are reprinted by permission of Oxford University Press, USA. This concerns extracts from the following pages; 73, 81, 83, 89, 113, 121, 123, 125, 129, 135.
2. *Kartṛ* and *kartṛva* (ie. agentivity) are derived from the verb √*kṛ* (to do). By adding the suffix -*tṛ* to verb-roots a so called agent-noun is formed, signifying then the performer of the verb in question.
3. Cf. BĀU 1.4.1–8 and 1.4.10–11, see also Olivelle 1998: 22–23.
4. Cf. Smith 1989: 203–204, Tull 1989: 54–55., for the *Puruṣasūkta* see RV. 10. 90, in German translation by Geldner 1951: 286–288.

5. BĀU 1.4.7
6. BĀU 1.4.8
7. Cf. Minkowski 1991: 21, Jamison 1991: 20–23.
8. Cf. Minkowski 1991: 18–19, Jamison 1991: 22–25.
9. BĀU 1.1.1
10. See Jamison, present vol. p. 15–16.
11. Cf. Cohen 2008: 49, Olivelle 1998: 21 and Tull 1989: 28–30.
12. Cavallin 2002: 220–223, 231.
13. Cohen 2008: 48–49, 78.
14. Olivelle 1998: 11.
15. Tull 1989: 30–32. For the different terms of good and bad ritual action see also Gonda 1966: 115–117.
16. Praśastapāda 1991: 622–623.
17. Sjödin 2011: 539, 544.
18. Cf. Larson, in the present vol. p.xxx
19. See for example; SU 1.12, KaU 2.7, 3.4, CU 7.8.1, 7.9.1, 8.5.1, BĀU 3.7.23, 4.3.23, 4.3.32
20. Cf. Black 2012: 13, 15.
21. BĀU 3.4.2
22. BĀU 4.4.22
23. Brereton 1990: 129.
24. BĀU 4.5.13
25. Cf. BĀU 2.1.2; 2.5.15; 3.7.2–23; 4.4.15, 22; 5.6.1; 6.3.4–5. Note that the *praśāstṛ* is also the name of a sacrificial expert; *maitrāvaruṇa*. Minkowski 1991: 40.
26. BĀU 5.6.1, my italics within brackets.
27. BĀU 3.7.14
28. Jamison 1991: 25–26.
29. BĀU 1.4.17. My italics within square brackets. The fivefoldedness of the human being appears to be; speech, breath, sight, hearing and self/body.
30. BĀU 2.5.15
31. Cf. for example Minkowski, 1991: 19, on the role of the *yajamāna*.
32. This is an ideational elaboration on thoughts expressed by Cohen 2008: 78–79.
33. BĀU 4.3.9–10. (my italics) The last words could very well be translated "–for he is an agent" whereas the verb for creating that is used in the other lines, √*sṛj*, connotes creating, procreating and emitting rather than a mere "doing."

34. BĀU 4.3.14
35. White 2009: 127–129.
36. BĀU 4.4.5
37. BĀU 4.4.22
38. BĀU 4.5.23
39. BĀU 4.4.13
40. BĀU 4.4.15
41. BĀU 3.9.10
42. BĀU 2.1.17
43. BĀU 3.9.4, BĀU 2.1.20, BĀU 4.3.7, 4.4.8, 4.4.38,
44. BĀU 4.4.22
45. *uparatendriyagrāmasya pralīnamanaskasyendriyadvāreṇaiva yad anubhavanaṃ mānasaṃ tat svapnajñānam... vādṛṣṭakāritaprayatnāpekṣād ātmāntaḥkaraṇasaṃśayogāt manasi kriyā prabandhād antarhṛdaye nirindriye ātmapradeśe yadā niścalaṃ manastiṣṭhati, tadā pralīnamanaska ity ākhyāyate.* Praśastapāda 1991: 429–430.
46. "*Manas*" does not, of course, have the same technical and mechanical function in the early Upaniṣads as it receives by Praśastapāda. The term is, however, in both cases identified with inner (mental/cognitive) processes.
47. That is, a controller possessed with effort (*prayatnavān adhiṣṭhātā*).
48. Vyomaśiva 1929: 402, *vigrahasya śarīrasyādhiṣṭhātā.*
49. Here Praśastapāda outlines two kinds of activities, one avoiding (*nivṛtti*) and one reaching (*pravṛtti*). There is no reason to translate *nivṛtti* with inactivity, since avoidance or turning back from something would count for an activity of sorts as it requires effort/incentive (*prayatna*).
50. *vāyvāśrayatvam anyeṣām apy astīti vkṛtagrahaṇam. vikāras tu tiryaggatiśīlasya vāyor yad etad ūrdhvam adho gamanam*, Vyomaśiva 1929:403.
51. Jhā 1982: 153, 185 translates *bhastrā* with wind-pipe and bagpipe.
52. Cf. Vyomaśiva 1929: 404.
53. *śarīrasamavāyinībhyāṃ ca hitāhitaprāptiparihārayogyābhyā ṃ pravṛttinivṛttibhyāṃ rathakarmaṇā sārathivat prayatnavān* vigrahasyādhiṣṭhātānumiyate *prāṇādibhiś ceti. katham śarīraparigṛhīte vāyau vikṛtakarmadarśanād bhastrādhmāpayiteva. nimeṣonmeṣakarmaṇā niyatena dāruyantraprayokteva. dehasya vṛddhikṣatabhagnasaṃrohaṇādinimittatv āt gṛhapatir iva. abhimataviṣayagrāhakakaraṇasambandhanimittena manaḥ karmaṇā gṛhakoṇeṣu pelakapreraka iva dārakaḥ*, Praśastapāda 1991: 210
54. *tasya saukṣmyād apratyakṣatve sati karaṇaiḥ śabdādyupalabdhyanumitaiḥ śrotrādibhiḥ samadhigamaḥ kriyate, vāsyādīnāṃ karaṇānāṃ*

kartṛprayojyatvadarśanāt, śabdādiṣu prasiddhyā ca prasādhako 'numīyate. Praśastapāda 1991: 277

55. Cf. KaU 3.11–9, SU 2.9.

56. The inner sense (*manas*) functions as a mediator between the outer sense-organ and the self. The self, the inner sense, the sense-organ and the object need to be in contact with each other in order for perception to take place.

57. *yathā hi gṛhe dārakaḥ pelakaiḥ saṃkrīḍamāno hastasthitapelakena madhyasthapelakam abhihatya pelakāntareṇa sambandhayati tadvad ātmāpi śarīre manasā cakṣurādikamabhihatya viṣayaiḥ saṃyojayatīti. tathā cābhimataś cāsau viṣayaś ca rūpādistadgṛhṇātīti tadgrāhakam. tacca grahaṇaṃ cakṣurādi tena saha sambandhaḥ tannimittena manaḥkarmaṇā jñāyate. prayogastu jīvaccharīram, prayatnavadadhiṣṭhitam abhimataviṣayagrahakakaraṇādhāratvāt gṛhavat. mano vā, prayatnapreryam, abhimataviṣayagrāhakakaraṇasambandhitvāt, hastasthitapelakavat* Vyomaśiva 1929: 404–405.

Abbreviations

BĀU:	Bṛhadāraṇyaka Upaniṣad
CU:	Chāndogya Upaniṣad
KaU:	Kaṭha Upaniṣad
RV:	Ṛg Veda
SU:	Śvetāśvatara Upaniṣad

References

Black, Brian. 2012. "Senses of self and Not-self in the Upaniṣads and Nikāyas." In *Hindu and Buddhist Ideas in Dialogue: Self and no-self*, edited by I. Kuznetsova, J. Ganeri, and C. Ram-Prasad, 11–24. Aldershot: Ashgate.

Brereton, J. 1990. "The Upanishads." In *Eastern canons: Approaches to the Asian Classics*, edited by W. Theodore and I. Bloom, 115–135. New York: Columbia University Press.

Cavallin, Clemens. 2002. "The Efficacy of Sacrifice, Correspondences in the Ṛgvedic Brāhmaṇas." Dissertation, Department of Religious Studies, University of Gothenburg.

Cohen, Signe. 2008. *Text and Authority in the Older Upaniṣad.* Brill's Indological Library 30. Leiden: Brill. http://dx.doi.org/10.1163/ej.9789004167773.i-320.

Geldner, E. trans. 1951. *Der Rig-Veda.* Harvard Oriental Series vol. 35. Cambridge, MA: Harvard University Press.

Gonda, Jan. 1966. *Loka, World and Heaven in the Veda.* Amsterdam: N. V. Noord-Hollandsche Uitgevers Maatschappij.

Jamison, Stephanie. 1991. *The Ravenous Hyenas and the Wounded Sun, Myth and Ritual in Ancient India.* Ithaca, NY: Cornell University Press.

Jhā, Ganganātha. 1982. trans. *Padārthasangraha of Praśastapāda with the Nyāyakandalī of Śrīdhara*. Chaukhambha Oriental Studies no. 4. Varanasi: Chaukhambha Orientalia.

Minkowski, Cristopher. 1991. *Priesthood in Ancient India, A Study of the Maitravāruṇa Priest*. Vienna: De Nobili Research Library.

Olivelle, Patrick, trans. 1998. *The Early Upaniṣads: Annotated Text and Translation*. Oxford: Oxford University Press.

Praśastapāda. 1991. *Praśastapādabhāṣya. In Nyāyakandalī being a commentary on Praśastapādabhāṣya, with three sub-commentaries*, edited by J. S. Jetly and V. G. Parikh. Gaekwad's Oriental Series no. 174. Baroda: University of Baroda Oriental Institute.

Sjödin, Anna-Pya. 2011. "Conceptualizing Philosophical Tradition: A Reading of Wilhelm Halbfass, Daya Krishna, and Jitendranath Mohanty." *Philosophy East & West* 61(3): 534–546. http://dx.doi.org/10.1353/pew.2011.0034.

Smith, Brian K. 1989. *Reflections on Resemblance, Ritual, and Religion*. Oxford: Oxford University Press.

Tull, Herman W. 1989. *The Vedic Origins of Karma, Cosmos as Man in Ancient Indian Myth and Ritual*. Albany: State University of New York Press.

Vyomaśiva. 1929. *Vyomavatī*. Edited by G. Kaviraj. Chowkhamba Sanskrit Series no. 375 (fsc 5). Varanasi: Chowkhamba Sanskrit Series Office.

White, David Gordon. 2009. *Sinister Yogis*. Chicago, IL: University of Chicago Press. http://dx.doi.org/10.7208/chicago/9780226895154.001.0001.

About the author

Anna-Pya Sjödin is Senior lecturer in the study of religions at Mid Sweden University, department of Humanities, affiliated researcher at Uppsala University, department of Linguistics and Philology. Sjödin received her PhD in Indology at Uppsala University 2007. Her research interests include Indian epistemology, ontology and the relationship between action (*karma*) and knowledge (*veda/jñāna*) in early and later Indian philosophical texts. Her dissertation "The happening of Tradition: Vallabha on Anumāna in Nyāyalīlavati" (2007) concerns medieval Hindu epistemology. More recently she has published on yogic cognition in Vaiśeṣika.

4

"The End of Sacrifice" and the Absence of "Religion": The Peculiar Case of India

Gerald James Larson

Guy Stroumsa's provocative monograph, *The End of Sacrifice: Religious Transformations in Late Antiquity*, called to mind an earlier article of mine, entitled, "An Old Problem Revisited: The Relation between Sāṃkhya, Yoga and Buddhism." It also called to mind an article by Frits Staal, entitled, "The Himalayas and the Fall of Religion."[1] What led me to associate the two latter articles with Stroumsa's monograph is the relationship in all three to the role of the notions of "Christian" and "religion" in Late Antiquity, the term "late antiquity" broadly understood by Stroumsa as stretching "from Jesus to Muhammad."[2]

In the case of Stroumsa's work, the notion of "religion" seems to correlate with the "end of sacrifice," traceable to a significant extent to the destruction of the Second Temple of Jerusalem by Titus in 70 CE and the resulting impossibility of performing blood sacrifice thereafter. In the case of my article, I was examining the intellectual history of ancient India, arguing that the traditions of Sāṃkhya, Yoga and Buddhism are indeed related but not in their most important aspects in the fifth and fourth centuries BCE, as was thought by many older Indologists, but, rather, in the first centuries of the Common Era, the period roughly coterminous with Late Antiquity in the Mediterranean world. In the case of Staal's work, he poses the interesting thesis that the very term "religion" itself is not a common noun but, rather, a naming or proper noun. In other words, Staal suggests that the term "religion" is a proper name, another name in an abbreviated form for the term "Christian." Stroumsa comments towards the end of his monograph:

Keywords: concept of religion, Axial Age, Indian philosophy, Indian soteriology

> The world of Late Antiquity was therefore a new axial time, or *Achsenzeit*, no less crucial for the future than the one identified by Karl Jaspers around the middle of the first millennium before our era. It was a world of transformations....[3]
>
> Here I have sought to address a...series of transformations, religious in essence. In dealing respectively with what I have called a "new care of the self," the rise of religions of the Book, the end of sacrifices, and the shift from civic religion to communitarian religion, I have tried to show that some of the major anthropological, cultural and political transformations of Late Antiquity can only be understood as directly linked to certain far-reaching changes in the very concept of religion.[4]

"Christian" "religion" appears to have been the basic model, both for the Jewish people as well as the later Arab peoples. Daniel Boyarin refers to what he calls "heresiological terms of art" that were determinative for the formulation of the "religions" of "Judaism" and "Islam," that is, names, terms or concepts generated largely by Christian heresiologists by way of determining the uniqueness of an incipient "Christian" "religion."[5] Boyarin quotes the following argument of Steve Mason in this regard.

> By about 200 C.E. the Church was making headway as a popular movement, or a constellation of loosely related movements. In that atmosphere, in which internal and external self-definition remained a paramount concern, Tertullian and others felt strong enough to jettison earlier attempts to portray themselves as Judaeans, and to see commitment to Christ as *sui generis*. Rather than admitting the definitive status of the established forms and responding defensively, they began to project the hybrid form of *Christianismus* on the other groups to facilitate polemical contrast... The most important group for Christian self-definition had always been the *Ioudaioi*, and so they were the groups most conspicuously reduced to such a treatment, which generated a static and systemic abstraction called *Ioudaismos/Iudaismus*.[6]

Boyarin concludes:

> The clear and critical conclusion to be drawn from this argument...is that "Judaism" as the name of a "religion" is a product of Christianity in its attempts to establish a separate identity from something else which they call "Judaism," a project that begins no earlier than the mid-second century..., gathers strength in the third century, and comes to fruition in the processes before and following the Council of Nicaea.[7]

Mutatis mutandis, similar processes are operating later in the designation of "Islam" as a "religion."[8] In any case, the notions of an abstract belief system centering on one God (Yahweh, the Triune God, Allah), a master text (Torah, New Testament, Qur'an), a master historical narrative (*Heilsgeschichte* as Passover, Crucifixion/Resurrection, Hijra), a master community (Synagogue, Church, Mosque), and a specific sacred space (Jerusalem, Rome, Mecca) all largely emerged from Christian intellectual reflection in Late Antiquity and was thereafter superimposed as a category upon other traditions. "Christian" "religion" then becomes the touchstone for testing the qualities of all other sacral traditions. Even "Hellenism" becomes a "religion" in this sense of the Christian model in the fourth century in the writing of Julian "the Apostate."[9]

Let me now turn to the title of my presentation, "'The End of Sacrifice' and the Absence of 'Religion': The Peculiar Case of India." If Stroumsa's and Staal's arguments are worth pursuing [and perhaps obviously, I think that they are to a significant extent], there would appear to be some interesting questions to ask about the manner in which we identify and construct (or de-construct) our studies in South Asian "religion," "philosophy," and "theology."

(1) First and most striking in this regard, if Stroumsa and Staal are correct, there is nothing remotely like "religion" in India in the sense that the notion came to be formulated in the Mediterranean of Late Antiquity. To be sure, the notion of "religion" (in the sense of Christian/Jewish/Islamic "religion") is introduced in South Asia in the later centuries of the Common Era, but in many ways such a notion has little if anything to do with what had been going on culturally in the South Asian region. If such is the case, then how does one characterize cultural traditions that do arise after the "end of sacrifice" in India? In other words, when the Vedic sacrificial system begins to lose its prominence and other kinds of cultural performance begin to emerge in South Asia, if the notion of "religion" is seriously misleading, what alternative conceptions might be formulated?

(2) Second, if the term "religion" is problematic in a South Asian environment, prior or apart from "religion" in the sense of Christian/Jewish/Islamic "religion," what about terms such as "philosophy" and "theology" in the South Asian cultural environment? Could there be merit in likewise considering these terms also as "naming" terms or proper nouns rather than as common nouns or generic categories? Is it plausible to argue, therefore, that there is an "absence" of "philosophy" and "theology" in South Asia on analogy with the absence of "religion"? If such is a plausible suggestion, then, how does one characterize the theoretical and/or speculative traditions that do arise in the South Asian region in the early centuries of the Common Era?

(3) Third, if Stroumsa is correct that the cultural transformations in the Mediterranean region in Late Antiquity represent what he calls a second *Achsenzeit* (Axial Age), is there a comparable second "Axial" period in the South Asian region? If so, how does it differ from the

changes taking place in the Mediterranean region and how does it differ from the transformations that occur in the first *Achsenzeit*?

(4) Fourth, if the terms "religion," "philosophy," and "theology" must be re-configured or rectified in the light of evidence in a so-called second *Achsenzeit* in the South Asian region that run parallel with the transformations occurring in the Mediterranean region in Late Antiquity, is it necessary to re-think the meaning of "religion," "philosophy," and "theology" in Late Antiquity as well, no longer now as generic, universal concepts but, rather, as historically derived "naming" terms or proper names? In other words, is there a dialectic operating here, or some sort of "blowback" effect, that can shed some new light on our own western intellectual history?[10]

(5) Finally, fifth, *pace* the neo-colonialist, post-modernist, post-structuralist, and deconstructionist *aficianados* among us, is it possibly the case that our most difficult conceptual misunderstandings and conundrums arise not only long before the Enlightenment and the rise of modernity but as well before the medieval periods in Europe, the Mediterranean, the Near and Middle East, South Asia, and elsewhere, namely, in a second *Achsenzeit*, that is to say, the Mediterranean of Late Antiquity and comparable developments in roughly the same period of the Common Era in South Asia?

In the sequel, I shall address each of these five questions, not by way of suggesting definitive answers to the questions, but, rather, by way of posing possible future research trajectories for our comparative studies. My intention, in other words, is to compare and contrast what is going on in the Mediterranean of Late Antiquity with what is happening in roughly the same period in the South Asian region. Put somewhat differently, what I am trying to do in this paper is something along the lines of what the ancient sage, Confucius, called "the rectification of names" *(cheng ming)*.[11] Or perhaps, somewhat more bluntly: what in the world have we been talking about when we use the terms "religion," "philosophy" and theology" in our studies?

The term "religion" in the South Asian region

Half a century ago, Louis Renou commented, "*Le dharma ou 'loi' hindoue - le Sanskrit n'a pas d'autre pour désigner approximativement la religion.*" ["*dharma*" or "law" – Sanskrit has no other term in order to designate approximately the notion of religion.][12] Daniel H. H. Ingalls put it even more bluntly: "Ancient India...has no word for 'religion'."[13] The distinguished Indian historian, Romila Thapar, extends the issue to cover the term "Hindu" as well. Says Thapar:

> The term Hindu was first used to mean all those who lived in al-Hind but were not Muslim. In terms of religious definition, reference is made

> in Persian sources to various Hindu religions....[as many as 42 in all] "'Hindu" became a term of administrative convenience when the rulers of Arab, Turkish, Afghan and Mughal origin – all Muslims – had to differentiate between "believers" and the rest. The first step towards the crystalisation of what we today call Hinduism was born in the consciousness of being the amorphous, undefined, subordinate other.[14]

The modern historian of India, R. E. Frykenberg offers the following comment:

> The terms "Hindu" and "Hinduism" have always been used – and are still being used – to cover a wide-ranging multitude of meanings.... during the late 18th century when the concept first began to be used, the term "Hindu" was applied to anything which was of India, anything "Native" or "Indian." "Hindu" was also a negative term. It was the term used, in negative ways, to characterize *all things in India* which were *not* Muslim, *not* Christian, *not* Jewish, or hence, *not* Western. ... In a still narrower sense...Hindu and "Hinduism" were the terms which were later applied to all high culture and religion in India, but especially that which was of Aryan, Brahmanical or Vedic origin. ....The result has been a jumbling and scrambling of signals. Vagueness of usage has led this concept into trackless deserts of nonsense. ... One can find no single, all-embracing religion which can be traced all the way back to the Vedas.[15]

Most recently, of course, is Wendy Doniger's massive volume, *The Hindus: An Alternative History*, in which she largely avoids any attempt at definition and focuses instead on what she calls the "pluralism," "tolerance," "hybridity," and "multiplicity" of the "Hindus."[16]

Clearly there is a problem with the term "religion" as well as the terms "Hindu" and "Hinduism." Neither in what Jaspers calls the first Axial age (ca. 800 BCE to 200 BCE) nor in what Stroumsa is suggesting as a second Axial age (ca. 100 to 700 CE) is there anything like "religion" as formulated in the Mediterranean of Late Antiquity. Instead, as Renou notes, there is only the polymorphic, or, if you prefer, the polyvalent term, *dharma*, inclusive of such meanings as "law," "duty," "custom," "obligation," "virtue," "righteousness," and so forth. Moreover, the polymorphic or polyvalent term *dharma* is broadly used in Vedic-cum-Brahmanical contexts as well as in Śramanical contexts, that is to say, Buddhist, Jain and other (ascetic) traditions.

In the case of the Vedic-cum-Brahmanical context, *dharma*-traditions begin to become prominent as social reality expands from a largely rural, agricultural base in the northwest regions of the Indus Valley, the Punjab, and so forth, into the more complex Gangetic plain regions with the emergence of towns (sometimes referred to as the period of "second urbanization"), trade, a money economy, and the greater use of iron technology (ca., the sixth or fifth centuries BCE) [roughly contemporary with what Karl Jaspers identified as the Axial Age, a period between ca. 800 BCE and 200 BCE, with important comparable transformations in Greece, the Middle East and China]. The transformations that are occurring are reflected in some of the oldest Upaniṣads, for example, the *Aitareya, Taittirīya, Bṛhadāraṇyaka, Chāndogya*, and so forth. There are gods (*deva*) of one kind or another, of course, but speculations for the most part focus on cosmic abstractions and neuter absolutes. The older Vedic sacrificial system is clearly still operative, and speculative reflections are emerging that go beyond simply textual exegesis and explanations of the sacrificial process. The external fire sacrifice is analogized symbolically with the interior heat of the breath and body that supports life, and correlations are drawn between the cosmic ultimate that supports the sun and fire (the *Brahman*) with the inner, subjective-cum-cosmic Self (the *Ātman*) that supports the life of the body, using what has been called a peculiar 'magical' "logic of identity." Early speculative traditions relating to "*Sāṃkhya*" (or what Franklin Edgerton has called "reason-method") and "*yoga*" ("disciplined meditation" or "action-method") are also first appearing.[17] Comparable speculations carry over into the narrative texts of the epics (*Mahābhārata* and *Rāmāyaṇa*), as, for example, the *Bhagavad Gītā* the *Mokṣadharma*, and so forth, the middle verse-Upaniṣads, as well as in the law books (e.g., the *Manusmṛti*) and the other Śāstras. These traditions eventually come to be referred to overall simply as *varṇāśrama-dharma*.

These Vedic-Brahmanical *dharma*-traditions are strikingly different from the notion of "religion" in the Mediterranean of Late Antiquity. Instead of one transcendent deity, there is a polymorphic set of disparate deities. Instead of a single *Heilsgeschichte* or master narrative, there is a wide-ranging multi-narrativity. Instead of a single authoritative text, there is a pervasive multi-textuality. Instead of an abstract set of beliefs or credo (orthodoxy), there is the absence of any sort of cognitive regulation but various traditions, instead, of ortho-praxis that differ from one *varṇa/jāti* to another and from one stage of life to another. And in place of a cohesive believing community, there are pluralistic sets of mini-communities, to some degree normatively hierarchical in an official idiom of *varṇa* or "caste," but in reality a splintered texture of birth-groups (*jāti*-s) that vary from region to region on the subcontinent. To cite Frykenberg again, there is in such environments, "no single, all-embracing religion which can be traced all the way back to the Vedas."

Even more puzzling are the *dharma*-traditions among the Non-Vedic *śramaṇa* and *yati* groups in the Gangetic plain regions. According to Buddhist textual evidence (to be found primarily in the Pali *Sāmañña-phala Sutta, Dīghanikāya* I, 47–86) there were many such groups of "wandering ascetics" (from which the terms *śramaṇa* and *yati* derive), two of which become especially prominent in the subsequent intellectual history of South Asia, namely the Buddhists and the Jains. Both use the term *dharma*, the Buddhists as a proper name for their tradition (in the sense of "teaching," "righteousness," "truth"), and the Jainas as a unique technical term for motion or movement.[18] These *dharma*-traditions are non-theistic, reject the authority of the Vedic-Brahmanical sacrificial system, reject therefore as well the system of *varṇa/jāti*, consider personal awareness or even the notion of the "individual/person" as deeply flawed and afflicted with ignorance; accept a notion of beginningless sorrowful (*duḥkha*) and recurrent re-birth (*karman* and *saṃsāra*); reject embodiment as a painful bondage from which they seek radical release (*nirvāṇa, kaivalya, kevala, mokṣa,* and so forth) through the pursuit of strategies of meditation (*yoga*), either in monastic environments or in total isolation – almost what would have to be called "irreligion" when measured against the touchstone of what is emerging as "religion" in the Mediterranean of Late Antiquity. Put simply, there is very little even roughly comparable to Mediterranean-region notions of "religion" that develop following the "end of sacrifice" or among groups that reject the authority of the Brahmanical sacrificial system in the South Asian region.

The terms "philosophy" and "theology" in the South Asian region

It has been frequently claimed that 'philosophy' as a discipline has been uniquely present only in western intellectual history, a point of view among many philosophers who argue that philosophy begins with the pre-Socratics and classical Greek traditions of reflection, and continues exclusively down to the present in European and American intellectual history, a point of view that is still often accepted among many continental philosophers (e.g., Heidegger) as well as analytic philosophers (e.g., A. J. Ayer, and more recently, Richard Rorty). Such a point of view comes close to suggesting that "philosophy" is also a proper noun or a naming term on analogy with "religion." In this regard I recall the amusing story that my former colleague Ninian Smart tells about the great A. J. Ayer. In a lecture course Ayer was vigorously asserting that there is nothing like "philosophy" in India's intellectual history at which point Ninian raised his hand and asked, "Professor Ayer, you must have read extensively in Indian literature to have reached that conclusion." Ayer then sheepishly admitted that he had not read a single Indian text but that he had read about the claim in a number of western philosophical texts.

Be that as it may, it is the case that the terms "philosophy" and "theology" have tended to be used in discussions of South Asian intellectual contexts that are, at best, highly confusing and, at worst, seriously misleading. It is important to be clear about what we mean when we use the western term "philosophy" in the South Asian context.[19] Many Indologists and Buddhologists become involved in both an anachronism and an equivocation with respect to the word "philosophy." One reads, for example, about the "philosophy" of the Vedas and Upaniṣads, or the "philosophy" of the Bhagavadgītā, or the "philosophy" of the epics even in as sophisticated a work as Erich Frauwallner's *Geschichte der indischen Philosophy*.[20] There is hardly any "philosophy" in any of these texts in the western classical sense or European sense, or even in the later Indic sense, beyond the most elementary speculative intuitions that hardly rise above a "magical" logic of identity. Most serious researchers are fully aware, of course, of the fundamental difference between speculative intuitions in environments of received authority, on the one hand, and systematic reflection that seeks overall coherence and persuasive presentation, including the identification of the means of knowledge (*pramāṇas*), precise definitions of terms, and vigorous polemic with other traditions, on the other. The former, that is, speculative intuitions in environments of received authority are as old or older than the Vedic tradition itself, almost all of which are themes and variations on the notion of *dharma*. The latter, namely, systematic reflection [called in Sanskrit, *ānvīkṣikī*, from *anu + īkṣ*, meaning "to follow with one's look," or "reflection," and eventually coming to mean something like "logic" or "logical investigation"] that seeks overall coherence is much more recent, hardly to be dated earlier than the first centuries of the Common Era, or, in other words, roughly contemporary with developments in the Mediterranean world of Late Antiquity.[21]

Much the same can be said about the term "theology" as it is used in Late Antiquity in the Meditrranean region. There is no "theology" at all in India in this sense, primarily because systematic discussion about the existence and nature of God (*īśvara*) is almost completely absent in precisely the same manner as the notion of "religion" is absent. Devotional piety (*bhakti*), whether of the constrained type as found in *Bhāgavata* or early *Vaiṣṇava* piety (e.g., as exhibited in the *Bhagavadgītā*), or the exuberant devotionalism of the later vernacular traditions, fail to develop "theologies" until many centuries later, and then for the most part probably due, in my view, to Christian and Islamic influence.

It seems to be the case that the earliest embryonic or exploratory attempt to do something like a coherent discourse about God that is appropriate to the Indic intellectual environment is to be found, oddly enough, in the *Yogasūtra* of Patañjali (see Yogasūtra, Pāda I, *sūtras* 23–29, Pāda II, *sūtras* 1 and 32, and Pāda III, *sūtra* 26) together with the *Bhāṣya* attributed to Vyāsa, from about the fourth century of the Common Era.[22] Pātañjala Yogic discourse about God (*īśvara*) appears to grow out of the confluence of two older non-theistic Indic worldviews (*bhuvana-jñāna* and/or *bhuvana-darśana*), namely, the old *Sāṃkhya* cosmology/cosmogony and the old Buddhist meditation traditions. Notice that I use the expression "worldview" (from German *Weltanschauung*), since a general term such as "worldview" comes closer, in my view, to identifying older *Sāṃkhya* traditions and older Buddhist traditions than do the terms "religion," "philosophy" or "theology," at least prior to about the fourth century of the Common Era. Even in the fourth and fifth centuries of the Common Era when they become coherent theoretical systems and become incorporated into *Pātañjala* Yoga [and later into the various *Vedāntas*], they are perhaps still better thought of in terms of worldviews rather than the conventional designations of "religions," "philosophies" or "theologies."

When I use the expression "appropriate to the Indic intellectual environment" and when I suggest that I prefer to use the general term "worldview" (*Weltanschauung*) instead of the conventional terms "religion," "philosophy" and "theology," I have in mind the common cosmology/cosmogony of karma (*karman*) and rebirth (*punarjanman*) that is presupposed among the various *dharma*-traditions (Hindu, Buddhist and Jaina) in South Asia, or what Gananath Obeyesekere has characterized as the "...karmic eschatologies...found only in Indic religions."[23] Obeyesekere in his massive study entitled, *Imagining Karma*, documents a fundamental distinction between "rebirth eschatologies" and "karmic eschatologies." The former, rebirth eschatologies, are found throughout the world, often in small-scale tribal contexts, or in more complex social contexts (e.g., the Pythagoreans in Hellenic and Hellenistic traditions, and so forth), frequently linked with ancestor-rituals, and with or without "ethicization." The latter, karmic eschatologies, are unique to Indic traditions and have highly ramified accounts of "ethicization" in terms of good and evil deeds, appropriate moral behaviour, moral retribution, and so forth.[24]

Many texts can be cited by way of documenting the overall "karmic eschatologies" of the Indic worldview. Two, however, are typical but also diagnostically interesting in terms of exhibiting the common framework of world-periods (*Yugas*) and world geography (*loka, dvīpa*), namely, (a) the Vi*ṣṇu-purāṇa*, Book I, Chapter III and Book II, Chapter II; and (b) "knowledge about the world" (*bhuvana-jñāna*) as set forth in the commentary attributed to a certain Vyāsa on *Yogasūtra* III.26.[25] The account in the *Viṣṇu-purāṇa* is a simple mythological characterization, but the account in the *Yogasūtra* represents a more theoretical interpretation.[26] As I say, both accounts are typical of the sorts of discussions one finds in most of the other *Purāṇas*, the great epics, the Hindu law books, and in most Buddhist and Jaina accounts as well.[27]

Descriptions in detail of cosmological time in terms of *Yugas* and the descriptions of cosmological geography in terms of the "world egg"

(*Brahmāṇḍa*) or "knowledge of cosmological space" (*bhuvana-jñāna*) are not necessary in terms of what I want to focus on in this article. Suffice it to say, that the former has to do with the well-known theory of declining *Yugas* or "world periods" from the perfect *Kṛta* (abiding for 1,728,000 human years), through the *Tretā* (1,296,000 years), to the *Dvāpara* (864,000 years) and, finally, to the *Kali* (432,000 years), together with the various permutations of these numbers in a declining progression through 72 Manvantaras that are without beginning (*an-ādi*). The latter, namely, the "world-egg" has to do with the tripartite division of the cosmos in terms of the seven heavenly *sattva*-worlds (*lokas*), the terrestrial *rajas*-worlds of our earth with its seven continents, and the seven "nether" (*pātālas*) *tamas*-worlds together with the seven "hells" (*narakas*) (also *tamas*-worlds, ending with the lowest "hell," Avīci).

Throughout the worlds are all sorts of beings working out their karmic trajectories through ongoing cycles of manifestation or coming forth and withdrawal (*pralaya* and *mahā-pralaya*). Such is true for *Brahmā* and the world-egg or universe itself. Brahmā, sometimes identified with *Hiraṇyagarbha*, the "golden germ or womb," and the world-egg itself both under-go periodic manifestation and withdrawal. The worlds, whether in manifestation or in withdrawal, are subject to a beginningless process (*pariṇāma*) of time or becoming (*bhava*). How the cycles unfold is determined by the trajectories of the various species of beings that have been self-constructed by the afflictions (*kleśas*), actions (*karman*), ripenings (*vipāka*) and resulting residues (*vāsanās, āśayas, saṃskāras*) of their own behaviour or functioning.

What is unusual about God in the Yoga "theological" account of the Indic worldview is that God is construed in an unusual manner. God is neither any of the conventional "gods," for example, *Brahmā, Viṣṇu, Śiva, et al.*, nor is God involved in the spatio-temporal content or functioning of the manifest universe. God is described, rather, as a particular pure, that is, non-thetic, consciousness, an "eternal excellence" (*śāśvatika utkarṣa*) untouched by afflictions, actions, the consequences of actions, or long-term karmic predispositions of any kind. God, therefore, cannot be a "creator" in any meaningful sense in a beginningless world, nor can God be "personal" in any intelligible sense, since the notion of "person," whether analogical or literal, presupposes precisely what is being denied of God. God as consciousness cannot be a thing or entity, and because consciousness is non-thetic or object-less, it can only appear or be described in terms of what it is not, an apophatic or negative theology, or, if you will, a negative theology that borders on an "a-theistic" "theism."

Apart from the traditional idiom in which these unusual notions of time, space and deity unfold, what is of greater interest are three interrelated presuppositions that appear to provide a basis for this common

Indic worldview that is taking shape in the first centuries of the Common Era in many areas of South Asian cultural life, namely, what I would identify as a presupposition of synchronic phylogeny (*varṇāśrama-dharma*), a presupposition of diachronic ontogeny (*punarjanman*), and a presupposition of precessional transformation (*saṃsāra*). By the term "phylogeny" I mean the Indic account of the development of the material world and its sentient species, derived primarily from the old Sāṃkhya philosophy. By the term "ontogeny" I mean the Indic account of the development of the individual sentient being (whether human, animal, divine, and so forth). By the term "precessional" I mean the manner in which Indic transformation unfolds in keeping with the notion that the universe is overall running down or declining. I am using the term "presupposition" in the general sense of an established cultural presupposition accepted commonly in a social environment.[28]

The presupposition of synchronic phylogeny

Our modern notions of history and conventional historical thinking are for the most part absent in Indic thought. There is, of course, a notion of history that is operating. It is just not our western notion. What is striking about the Indic worldview is that everything is perfect, properly formed and excellent at the outset of the world process with the accompanying claim that the process is beginningless. In other words, nothing new can emerge that is not already presupposed and fully formed at the outset, but that which is fully formed was or is, as it were, without beginning! Madhav Deshpande (1979: 9–10) points out that there is a deep "preservationism" in classical Indic thought. He comments:[29]

> Thus there was no history in a real sense. All forms existed, and it is a matter of pure accident that certain forms are or are not found in a particular text, a particular time or a particular region. Thus, the problem of "existence" was separated from the problem of "attestation." Non-attestation did not imply non-existence. While eternal existence was the fact, the attestation and non-attestation of forms was a matter of historical accident.

Whatever changes occur either in language or in society are treated as "options," hence, the system of *varṇāśrama-dharma*. Language, society and cosmos are dealt with largely in a deductive fashion. The human community is not to be viewed as developing over time diachronically. It is to be viewed, rather, in terms of "synchronic phylogeny."

Western science and civilization are based on a continuously self-improving process of experimentation and induction of new general principles, but classical Indian tradition "claims" to be authoritative by being a purely deductive tradition whose first principles have been unalterably established....

> History as viewed from this deductive perspective is not a matter of new creation of events or new inventions, but simply an unfolding of implicit aspects and values of the eternally self-existing reality.[30]

The main task for the Indic worldview is to look back and remember the eternal first principles that are truly authoritative and make possible the options with which we must live.

The presupposition of diachronic ontogeny

The synchronic phylogeny wherein everything is fully formed at the outset carries with it a second presupposition, which in a puzzling way appears to undercut the first presupposition. The second presupposition can be expressed in the following manner. Everything is fully formed at the outset, beginninglessly, then so likewise are all sentient creatures throughout the extended universe. There never was a time, in other words, when I or any other sentient being was not, since all were there at the outset. Hence, through all the unfolding periods of becoming, I, along with all other sentient creatures, must also have been becoming, or, in other words, the notion of karma and rebirth (*punarjanman*). My identity in this particular rebirth is shaped by a linear series of preceding rebirths stretching back to a beginning-less beginning! In any particular rebirth of a sentient being, the sentient being is part of an unfolding synchronic whole, but the particular identity of a given rebirth has been shaped by an incredibly complex series of linear actions (*karman*) which have determined my synchronic place in this particular rebirth. Moreover, since the process is beginningless and, hence, infinitely so, then my actions as a sentient being have undoubtedly brought me into every possible life-form that has been formed from the outset, beginninglessly!

There are, therefore, two continually intersecting processes. On the one hand, there is the synchronic phylogeny of everything having been fully and perfectly formed at the outset. On the other hand, there is a continuously operating linear ontogeny of individual rebirths whose trajectories in rebirth after rebirth are determined both by the synchronic presuppositions coming from the past being projected into the future. From one point of view, the system appears to be completely determined (synchronically) along the lines of *varṇāśrama-dharma*. From another point of view, however, the system is completely open and free, in the sense that at any given point-instant, I, along with all sentient beings, must engage in action (*karman*) that will shape my future becoming (ontogenetically). There is a simultaneous synchronic-cum-diachronic inter-subjectivity in all forms of sentient life whereby sentient beings are regressively and progressively "creating" a common life-world.

The presupposition of precessional transformation

There is still another presupposition in Indic thinking that always accompanies the intersecting processes of synchronic phylogeny and diachronic ontogeny. Not only is everything present in its perfect and well-formed nature at the outset beginninglessly (synchronic phylogeny), and not only are all sentient beings nevertheless undergoing recurring diachronic identities based upon their karma in rebirth after rebirth, the entire cosmic drama is declining. The world is continually running down, falling backwards or regressing from an original excellence. The Indic worldview, of course, is not unique in this regard. The notion of the world running down is frequently accepted in the ancient world. What makes the notion of decline especially poignant in the Indic worldview is the strong linkage of decline with karma and rebirth. The reasons for decline are not always clear. In this regard, Madhav Deshpande's comment is typical.

> It is not very clear why such a doctrine of decline developed in ancient India. It is conceivable that the invasion of the Greeks and the emergence and dominant political and social position of the non-Vedic religions like Buddhism and Jainism were viewed to be "darker times" in comparison with previous ages, and this might have led to the theory of four ages.[31]

Such speculation probably is not necessary, however. In my view, there is considerable empirical evidence in the texts that the notion of declining ages has a great deal to do with ancient traditions of "astronomy"/ astrology that were widespread throughout the ancient world. The plane of the earth's equator is at a slight angle (23 and one-half degrees) to the ecliptic, and the vernal equinox of the beginning of spring "precesses" or moves backward through the ecliptic or the zodiac one degree of arc about every 72 years. It takes approximately 26,000 years (or more precisely just under 26,000 years) for this precession or falling backwards to make a full circle so that the vernal equinox can occur again at its starting-point. According to one calculation, the oldest zodiacs were constructed by using the fixed star Aldebaran in the exact middle of Taurus, thereby making the vernal equinox at one degree of Aries around 4139 BCE.[32] Other calculations have also been used. Quite apart from the precision of such "Ages," the basic notion of "precession" or falling backwards along the ecliptic or zodiac in a time frame of roughly 26,000 years was widely recognized in the ancient world. It is known as the "Great Year," and I would suggest that it has its analogue in the *Yuga* theory. All of the numbers mentioned in the *Yuga*-theory discussed earlier, namely, 1,728,000, 1,296,000, 864,000 and 432,000 years together with some 72 "human-intervals" (*manvantaras*), appear to reflect a comparable understanding of the "Great Year." The basic number 432,000 is a multiple of both 60 (= 72) or 360 (= 12), the latter providing a characterization of the year and the former (viz., 72 × 360 "days" in the life of Brahma, or 25,920 "years") the "Great Year" or "Cosmic Year."

The large numbers used are probably due to the desire to express mathematical ratios and relations in terms of whole numbers. Since so much ancient knowledge relating to astronomy/astrology is traceable to the ancient Near Eastern cultures of Babylonia and Sumeria, it could well be the case that the Indic numbers also reflect that influence. Clearly ancient India learned a great deal from the ancient Near Eastern cultures and the Greeks. A. L. Basham comments,

> Western [that is, Greek, Near Eastern and Mediterranean] astronomy brought to India the signs of the zodiac, the seven-day week, the hour, and several other ideas.... Like all ancient astronomy, that of India was restricted owing to ignorance of the telescope.... For purposes of calculation the planetary system was taken as geocentric, though Aryabhata in the 5th century suggested that the earth revolved round the sun and rotated on its axis.... The precession of the equinoxes was known...as were the lengths of the year, the lunar month, and other astronomical constants.[33]

In using the expression "precessional transformation," however, it is not my intention to enter into the problem of origin or diffusion or scientific explanation, but, rather, to point to a unique mind-set regarding the unfolding of time. The mind-set is one of falling backwards, of "precessing," and, hence, at least in the classic Indic formulation, of the present and future always becoming the past (or, in other words, karma and rebirth). What is and what will be has already been, and my "historical" task is to understand what I was, to lift the amnesia or remove the cobwebs so that I can re-member and be mindful about the construct of what I am. The Indic traditions recognize that when one acts in the present for the future, one is re-living and re-enacting much of what has already been. Our emotions, our basic drives, and our physical bodies come to us from the past. To be sure, we are free to act in what appears to be the "present" moment, but we are not changing only the present. We are also re-membering and re-arranging the past, thereby projecting what will be our future.

Given such a mind-set of "precessional transformation," there are only two possible options: either acquiescing or adjusting or harmonizing with what is (was), that is to say, the option of *varṇāśrama-dharma* (synchronic phylogeny), or somehow renouncing in terms of the quest for *mokṣa* or *nirvāṇa* or some other renunciatory technique (linear ontogeny in an environment of precessional transformation).

These presuppositions appear to be present, *mutatis mutandis*, throughout the *dharma*-traditions (Hindu, Buddhist and Jaina) of the Indic worldview of karmic eschatologies. To be sure, these presuppositions are clearly "cyclical" so long as it is remembered that the critical intuition is a cycling neither into the present nor the future but, rather, a cycling into the past, a "falling backwards" or "precessing" or "re-membering" for which my own "linear" karma is fully accountable.

A possible second "axial" age (*Achsenzeit*) in the South Asian region

Having addressed the problematic notions of "religion," "philosophy," and "theology," and what I am suggesting might be a more appropriate set of notions for South Asia, let me turn now to some brief comparative reflections. Max Weber in an essay entitled, "The Social Psychology of the World Religions," argues that there are only three consistent "theodices" [= cogent explanations for the suffering and injustice that one finds in the world]. Says Weber,

> The metaphysical conception of God and of the world, which the ineradicable demand for a theodicy called forth, could produce only a few systems of ideas on the whole – as we shall see, only three. These three gave rationally satisfactory answers to the questioning for the basis of the incongruity between destiny and merit: the Indian doctrine of Karma, Zoroastrian dualism, and the predestination decree of the *deus absconditus*. These solutions are rationally closed; in pure form, they are found only as exceptions.[34]

As I have suggested in this presentation, the notions of "religion," "philosophy" and "theology," deriving from the Mediterranean of Late Antiquity, appear to have no counterpart in the South Asian region until quite late, namely, in the first centuries CE from roughly the fourth through the eighth centuries. In South Asia there is nothing comparable to "religion" beyond the notion of *dharma* as "law," "duty," "righteousness," and so forth, whether one is referring to the various *varṇāśrama-dharmas* that emerge out of the old Vedic-cum-Brahmanical traditions, or one is referring to the *dharma*-traditions of the Buddhists and Jainas, that is, the *śramaṇa* traditions of the so-called "second urbanization" in South Asia.

I have suggested further that in South Asia the term "worldview" is perhaps more appropriate for what is developing in the first centuries CE, involving the confluence of the two streams of what I have characterized as the two older non-theistic Indic worldviews, namely, the old *Sāṃkhya* cosmology/cosmogony and the old Buddhist meditation traditions. Polemical interaction between these traditions gives rise to what comes to be known as *"ānvīkṣikī"* (systematic logical investigation) or what is conventionally often referred to as the beginning of Indian "philosophy" proper. The *Yogasūtra* (called a "*Sāṃkhya-pravacana*" or "an explanation of *Sāṃkhya*") and its earliest commentaries (ca., 350 to 450) reflects the interactions between the old *Sāṃkhya* and the first systematic Buddhist technical schools (*Sarvāstivāda, Sautrāntika, Mādhyamika* and *Yogācāra*). The various other schools of Indian thought are also developing, including the schools of logic and epistemology, grammar, and, of course, eventually the later *Vedāntas*. Dating is difficult to determine for this earliest period in Indic systematic reflection, but a reasonable approximation would be anywhere between ca. 100 BCE and 100–200 CE and continuing up to the time of the great Śaṃkara (ca. 700).[35] This period of systematic Indian thought, including *Sāṃkhya*, Yoga, Buddhist, Jaina, hermeneutics, logic, grammar, as well as the later *Vedāntic* traditions, all without exception operate within a worldview that presupposes the karmic eschatologies described earlier with the presuppositions of synchronic phylogeny, diachronic ontogeny and precessional transformation.

This period, of course, is also roughly contemporary with the Mediterranean of Late Antiquity and its worldview of quite a different set of axioms, namely, as a "new care of the self," the notion of a religion of the book, the end of sacrifice, and the shift from civic to communitarian religion, as set forth in Stroumsa's *The End of Sacrifice*. It is also the case (and possibly not an accident) that this period is also the period in which the first documented encounters take place between the Mediterranean of Late Antiquity and the South Asian region via the trade routes of the Near East, Middle East and Persia.

Clearly, I am inclined to argue that this is, indeed, a second Axial Age in which dramatic transformations are occurring on almost all levels of cultural development. Moreover, the changes occurring are reflective of the three great Weberian theodices: the *deus absconditus* (the "hidden God") or, if you will, the inscrutable will of God (as revealed in a single holy Book), on the one side, and the ethicized karmic eschatology of *varṇāśrama-dharma, punarjanman* and *saṃsāra* (as revealed in the *samādhis* and *anubhava* of Yogic meditation), on the other side, both extremes being mediated, conceptually and possibly historically as well (via the Near East and Persia) by the Zoroastrian dualism, the various Gnostic dualistic systems and the mystery cults of one kind or another.

The possibility of a "blowback" effect

Here I can be brief, since I only want to call attention to a possible revisionist perspective in our own western historical understanding. If Stroumsa is correct that the very notion of "religion" is dramatically transformed in the Mediterranean region of Late Antiquity, and if what I have been arguing about the cultural development of the *dharma*-traditions in the South Asian region are in any sense correct, or at least plausible, could it be the case that Jaspers's notion of a first "Axial" Age has been wrongly framed and is seriously anachronistic? Stroumsa describes Jaspers's "axial age" in the following manner:

> The German philosopher Karl Jaspers characterized the first half millennium before our common era as an *Achsenzeit* (axial age), when across different (often imperial) civilizations there developed a hierarchical differentiation between the visible and invisible, the material and spiritual, worlds. Confucius, Buddha, Zarathustra, the prophets of Israel, and the first Greek philosophers represented for Jaspers the types of this intellectual and religious transformation. It seems to me that the era and domain we are studying also has a claim to this title of "axial age," an epoch in which the very frameworks of a civilization are transformed in a radical way.[36]

A. L. Basham has commented,

> "Jaspers's theory is not universally accepted by scholars of religion. His identification of charismatic religious leaders who characterized a transformation in the way human beings perceived the world simply does not fit in every case. Where the identification does fit, no concrete causal connections can be found."[37]

The key phrase in Basham's comment is, "...no concrete causal connections can be found." What if, however, there are clear causal connections, not from an imagined "axial age" in the fifth and fourth centuries BCE, but, rather, from an historically documented "axial age" in the Mediterranean region of Late Antiquity and the cultural developments in classical Indian thought in the first centuries of the Common Era of roughly the same period? In other words, what if, just as there has been a tendency to project the notion of "religion" in Late Antiquity on to other cultural contexts in terms of the future, so there has been a comparable projection on to the past? Put somewhat differently, could it be the case that a so-called second "axial age" is, in fact, the first "axial age" that has been anachronistically projected on to the past? The Indic evidence is important in this regard, it seems to me. Almost all of our evidence for the Buddhist and Jain traditions derives from texts hardly earlier than the first centuries of the Common Era. Moreover, the thought-world of the oldest Upaniṣads and the middle verse *Upaniṣads* together with the thought-worlds of the *Bhagavad Gītā*, the *Mokṣadharma*, and the epics and law books generally, are hardly intellectually systematic apart from later ramified commentarial elaborations.

Even the Greek evidence strikes me as being problematic, at least in some instances. For example, I have been interested in looking at notions of karma and rebirth in Pythagorean traditions, but most of the evidence about early Pythagoreanism, other than inconclusive references in Plato and Aristotle, comes from sources that are clearly Neo-Pythagorean and closely linked to Neo-Platonism. In a similar fashion, most of what can be said about Pre-Socratic philosophy comes from highly ramified later accounts that are clearly reconstructions of what might have been the systematic significance of early Greek philosophizing.

Contemporary conundrums and misunderstandings

Finally, and again only briefly, I find myself thinking that some of our most important conceptual challenges in contemporary scholarship have hardly been satisfactorily addressed by the discourses of Enlightenment or Colonialism or Neo-Colonialism or Post-modernism or Post-structuralism or Deconstruction. As important and productive as these discourses have been, they are all themes and variations on the notions of "religion," "philosophy," and "theology" that were formed in the Mediterranean region of Late Antiquity (the period "from Jesus to Muhammad," to use Stroumsa's idiom) and thereafter projected forward and backward to encompass the entire range of world intellectual history from the time of the Pre-Socratics to the most recent theorization of globalization or world-systems analysis.[38]

Peter Gordon in a fascinating recent book, *Continental Divide: Heidegger, Cassirer, Davos,* offers the following summary comment about Heidegger's philosophical program.

> The history of philosophy was therefore nothing less than a history of the forgetting of Being, or *Seinsvergessenheit.* To retrieve what had been forgotten, Heidegger promised a "destruction" of the history of ontology: a vigorous and even violent reinterpretation of the philosophical tradition that would demonstrate, in stepwise fashion through key moments in the canon, just how humankind had fallen into error.[39]

It is generally recognized that Heidegger failed to accomplish his program. Let me conclude, then, by suggesting that that task remains to be accomplished, not only for "philosophy," however, but for "religion" and "theology" as well!

Notes

1. Stroumsa 2009, passim; Larson 1989:129–146; and Staal 1982:38–51. Staal, 1989: 387–389, develops the argument further in his book, *Rules without Meaning.*
2. Stroumsa 2009: 34.
3. Stroumsa 2009: 108.
4. Stroumsa 2009: 108–109.
5. Boyarin 2009: 7–36. Boyarin argues that in Late Antiquity, Jewish literature nowhere refers to the Jewish people in terms of Jewish "religion" or "Juda-

ism." It is only with the Christian writer Tertullian in the mid-third century (see p. 10) that one first finds the word "Judaism" as a "religion" in reference to the sacral traditions of the Jewish people.

6. Mason 2007: 457–512, 476. Cited in Boyarin 2009: 10–11.
7. Boyarin 2009: 11.
8. See Smith 1978. This is the classical discussion of the history of the term "religion" [from Latin, religio, derived either from relegere, 'to be scrupulous,' or from religare, "to bind," 204] in the West in which Smith argues that by the time of Lactantius (ca. 325), early Western civilization was at the threshold of "... taking a decisive step in the formulation of an elaborate, comprehensive, philosophic concept of religio. However, it did not take it. The matter was virtually dropped, to lie dormant for a thousand years." (28). Boyarin 2009:12 challenges this view of W. C. Smith and persuasively shows that the modern notion of "religion" was invented already in the fourth century and helped to make possible a "transethnic Christendom." See the subsequent discussion pages 12–27.
9. Boyarin 2009: 13.
10. Johnson 2004: 3–33.
11. Confucius, *The Analects*, 13.3, in de Bary *et al.* 1999: 56. "The Master said: 'What is necessary is the rectification of names (cheng ming).' ...If names are not rectified, then language will not be appropriate, and if language is not appropriate, affairs will not be successfully carried out.... In regard to language, the noble person allows no carelessness, that is all."
12. Renou 1947:480, cited in Smith 1978: 248.
13. Ingalls 1954: 34, also cited in W.C. Smith 1978:248–249.
14. Thapar 1985: 17.
15. Frykenberg 1991:31–33.
16. Doniger 2009 especially Chapter 1 pages17–49.
17. Edgerton 1965: 26–27 for the 'magical' logic of identity, pages 35 and following for the terms *sāṃkhya* and "yoga.". See also Larson and Bhattacharya 1987: 4–9. See also Larson and Bhattacharya 2008: 30–52.
18. For a useful discussion of *brāhmaṇas* and *śramaṇas* see Hirakawa 1990:13–19. See also Jaini 1979: 1–41, 99–101.
19. Larson, 1979: 75–153. Larson and Bhattacharya 1987: 3–41; and Larson and Bhattacharya 2008: 30–52. See Gerald J. Larson 1995: 75–101.
20. Frauwallner 1953 and 1956. See chapter, "Die Philosophie des Veda," and "Die Philosophie des Epos."
21. This is the thrust of my article mentioned at the outset of this presentation, namely Larson 1989.

22. See section entitled, "Theism of Yoga" in Larson and Bhattacharya 2008: 91–100.
23. Obeyesekere 2006: 17.
24. Obeyesekere 2006: 17–18.
25. Wilson 1972:19–24, 134–141, see also Larson and Bhattacharya 2008:91–99.
26. I have written about both texts in some detail in Larson 2012: 113–123.
27. Jacobi 1961a vol. 1: 200–202 and 1961b 4:129–138. See also La Vallée Poussin 1961a vol. 1: 187–190 and 1961b 4:129–138.
28. I have written about these matters in several other publications. See, for example Larson 1980: 303–316; also, Larson 1983:161–167; also, Larson 1993: 373–378; and most recently, Larson and Bhattacharya 2008: 91–100.
29. Deshpande 1979: 9–10.
30. Deshpande 1979: 18–19.
31. Deshpande 1979: 6.
32. Gleadow 1969: 55–58
33. Basham 1981: 492–493.
34. Gerth and Mills 1946: 275–279, 358–359.
35. I have discussed this early history of Indian systematic reflection in detail in the following: Larson 1989 and Larson and Bhattacharya 1987 and Larson and Bhattacharya 2008, see also Doniger 2009, esp. chap. 1: 17–49.
36. Stroumsa 2009: 6. See also, of course, Karl Jaspers 1949, *Vom Ursprung und Ziel der Geschichte.*
37. Basham 1989: 126.
38. The most recent documentation of what I am suggesting is the collection of articles given over to current theorizing on the nature of "religion" in the Journal of the American Academy of Religion, Volume 78, No. 4, December 2010. Among the ten articles in the collection, not a single one deviates from the notions of "religion," "philosophy" and "theology" as fashioned in the Mediterranean region of Late Antiquity. The same is true of the hundreds of scholarly notes that document the articles. Not a single theoretical reference can be found from non-western sources. The provincialism of the scholarly discourse is remarkable.
39. Gordon 2010: 32.

References

Basham, A.L. 1981. *The Wonder That Was India*. Calcutta: Rupa and Co., Repr.

Basham, A.L. 1989. *The Origins and Development of Classical Hinduism*. Edited and completed by Kenneth G. Zysk. Boston, MA: Beacon Press.

Boyarin, D. 2009. "Rethinking Jewish Christianity." *Jewish Quarterly Review* 99(1): 7–36.

de Bary, W. T., *et al.*, eds. 1999. *Sources of Chinese Tradition*. 2nd ed. vol. I. New York: Columbia University Press.

Deshpande, M. 1979. "History, Chance and Permanence: A Classical Indian Perspective." In *Contributions to Asian Studies*, vol. I. edited by G. Krishna, 1–28. Oxford: Oxford University Press.

Doniger, W. 2009. *The Hindus: An Alternative History*. London: The Penguin Press.

Edgerton, Franklin. 1965. *The Beginnings of Indian Philosophy*. Cambridge, MA: Harvard University Press.

Frauwallner, E. 1953. and. 1956. "Geshcichte der indischen." Otto Muller Verlag. *Philosophie* 1–2:.

Frykenberg, Robert E. 1991. "The Emergence of Modern Hinduism as a Concept and as an Institution: A Reappraisal with Special Reference to South India." In *Hinduism Reconsidered*, edited by G. D. Sontheimer and H. Kulke, 31–33. Delhi: Manohar.

Gerth, H. H. and C. W. Mills, eds. 1946. *From Max Weber: Essays in Sociology*. Oxford: Oxford University Press.

Gleadow, Rupert. 1969. *The Origins of the Zodiac*. New York: Atheneum.

Gordon, Peter. 2010. *Continental Divide: Heidegger, Cassirer*. Davos: Harvard University Press.

Hirakawa, A. 1990. *A History of Indian Buddhism*. Translated and edited by Paul Groner. Honolulu, HI: The University of Hawaii Press.

Ingalls, D. H. H. 1954. "Authority and Law in Ancient India." *Journal of the American Oriental Society*. Supplement No. 17.

Jacobi, H. 1961a. "Ages of the World (Indian)." In *Encyclopedia of Religion and Ethics*, vol. 1. Edited by J. Hasting, 155–161. New York: Charles Scribners Sons.

Jacobi, H. 1961b. "Cosmogony and Cosmology (Indian)." In *Encyclopedia of Religion and Ethics*, vol. 4. Edited by J. Hastings, 200–202. New York: Charles Scribner's Sons.

Jaini, P.S. 1979. *The Jaina Path of Purification*. Berkeley: University of California Press.

Jaspers, K. 1949. *Vom Ursprung und Ziel der Geschichte*. Munich: Piper Verlag.

Johnson, C. 2004. *Blowback: The Costs and Consequences of American Empire*. New York: Henry Holt and Co.

Larson, G. J. 1979. *Classical Sāṃkhya: An Interpretation of Its History And Meaning*. 2nd ed. Delhi: Motilal Banarsidass.

Larson, G. J. (1980) "Karma as a 'Sociology of Knowledge' and a 'Social Psychology'of Process/Praxis," In *Karma and Rebirth in Classical Indian Traditions*, edited by W. Doniger, 303–316. Berkeley: University of California Press.

Larson, G. J. 1983. "McClain's mathematical acoustics and classical *Sāṃkhya* philosophy." *Journal of Social and Biological Structures* 6(2): 161–167. http://dx.doi.org/10.1016/S0140-1750(83)80015-3.

Larson, G. J. 1993. "The Trimūrti of Smṛti in Classical Indian Thought." *Philosophy East & West* 43(3): 373–388. http://dx.doi.org/10.2307/1399575.

Larson, G. J. 1995. *India's Agony over Religion.* Albany: State University of New York Press.

Larson, G. J. 2012. "Hindu Cosmogony/Cosmology." In *The Routledge Companion to Religion and Science*, ewdited by J.W. Haag *et al.*, eds. 113–123, London and New York: Routledge.

Larson, G. J., and R.S. Bhattacharya, eds. 1987. *Sāṃkhya: A Dualist Tradition in Indian Philosophy*, Encyclopedia of Indian Philosophies vol. IV,edited by Karl H. Potter. Princeton, NJ: Princeton University Press and Motilal Banarsidass.

Larson, G. J., and R. S. Bhattacharya, eds. 2008. *Encyclopedia of Indian Philosophies, gen*, vol. XII. Yoga: India's Philosophy of Meditation. Delhi: Motilal Banarsidass.

La Vallée Poussin, L. de. 1961a. "Ages of the World (Buddhist)." *Encyclopedia of Religion and Ethics*, vol. 1, edited by J. Hastings. New York: Charles Scribner's Sons.

La Vallée Poussin, L. de. 1961b. "Cosmogony and Cosmology (Buddhist)." *Encyclopedia of Religion and Ethics*, vol. 4, edited by J. Hastings. New York: Charles Scribner's Sons.

Mason, S. (2007) "Jews, Judaeans, Judaizing, Judaism: Problems of Categorization in Ancient History." *Journal of the Study of Judaism* 38: 457-512.

Obeyesekere, G. 2002. *Imagining Karma: Ethical Transformations in Amerindian, Buddhist and Greek Rebirth.* Berkeley: University of California Press.

Renou, Louis. 1947. *L'Inde classique*, vol. 1. Paris: Payot.

Smith, W.C. 1978. *The Meaning and End of Religion.* New York: Harper and Row.

Staal, Frits. 1982. "The Himalayas and the Fall of Religion." In *The Silk Route and the Diamond Path*, edited by D. E. Klimburg-Salter, 38–51. Berkeley: University of California Press.

Staal, Frits. 1989. *Rules without Meaning.* Toronto Studies in Religion, vol. 4. Bern: Peter Lang.

Stroumsa, Guy J. 2009. *The End of Sacrifice: Religious Transformations in Late Antiquity*, Translated by S. Emanuel. Chicago, IL: University of Chicago Press.

Thapar, Romila. 1985. "Syndicated Moksha." *Seminar* 313: 60–88.

Wilson, H.H. 1972. *The Viṣṇu Purāṇa.* Calcutta: Punthi Pustak.

About the author

Gerald James Larson is Rabindranath Tagore Professor Emeritus of Indian Cultures and Civilization, Indiana University, Bloomington, and Professor Emeritus, Religious Studies, University of California, Santa Barbara. Larson is the author or editor of some 12 books and well over 100 scholarly articles on cross-cultural philosophy of religion, history of religions, classical Sanskrit and South Asian history and culture. Among the most recent books are *Religion and Personal Law in Secular India: A Call to Judgment* 2002, and Volume XII of the *Encyclopedia of Indian Philosophies*, co-edited with the late Dr. Ram Shankar Bhattacharya, entitled *Yoga: India's Philosophy of Meditation* (2008)

5

The Crisis of Sacrifice

Peter Jackson

I

Before delving into the intricacies of sacrificial ideology in early Greek and Indian thought, let me begin by making a few general propositions concerning the cross-cultural relevance of what may be termed the "two religiosities." This bifurcation of religious actions and orientations is suggestive of what Jan Assmann has recently discussed under the heading – borrowed from the 17th century Cambridge theologian and philosopher Ralph Cudworth – of *religio duplex*. When this concept first began to circulate in early modern Europe it implied a division between the contingent aspects of public worship and theology (*positive religion*), and a universal religiosity of the pure intellect (*natural religion*).[1] It would make little sense to maintain such an idealizing mindset in this connection, especially as regards the putative universality of "primeval" thought. Nevertheless, I do believe that we need to assign some typological value to the distinction between a civic religiosity that celebrates and seeks to consolidate an existing community, and a sectarian religiosity that rather seeks emancipation from the civic community through voluntary ordeals of initiation and ascetism in a quest for truth, immortality, salvation, and so forth. I am not suggesting that this distinction is universally valid, nor that the two religiosities are necessarily incompatible, yet it does seem narrow-minded to imagine that the familiar pattern emerging in Archaic and Classical Greek society – soteriological and cosmopolitan teachings introduced by wandering sages

Keywords: apotheosis, care of the self, *Homeric Hymn to Hermes*, Orphism, Ṛbhus, Pythagoreanism opposing the traditional ways of civic religion – did not result from some generalizable social dynamic. If we accept this premise it would seem likewise narrow-minded to take the unfamiliarity of certain speculative doctrines (such as metempsychosis) and ascetic conducts of life (such as sexual abstinence and vegetarianism) as a pretext for their exotic origin.[2] In so far as change and innovation are not solely attributed to foreign influence, we should also acknowledge the in-group tensions and potentially shifiting perspectives that constantly thrive within an existing social order. The institution of sacrifice is precicely such a seat of shift and tension.

I wish to explore how the notion of a synergetic ritual interaction between ritual specialists, patrons, and imaginary divine recipients – linked as it was to the promise of fame and immortality – is likely to have stimulated a parallell development of new and sometimes analogous modalities of philosophy and secteristic religiosity in early Greek and Indian society. While the reality of Greek religion was certainly more complex and ambiguous than such a dyadic model might intimate, the opposing poles of "civic" and "unlicensed" religion still constitute a necessary prerequistie for identifying the figures and phenomena moving between them.[3]

II

The surviving descriptions of Orphic and Pythagorean religiosity may aptly illustrate how these new modalities of thought and conduct derived benefit from a traditional economy of sacrifice. This was done in two seemingly opposed fashions. Although these groups performed sacrifices on certain occasions, the traditional sacrifice of the established polis was clearly rejected. When dietary taboos prevented Orphics and Pythagoreans to participate in the communal meals, the attention of their contemporaries was not merely directed at the doctrine of metempsychosis. From the perspective of the polis such taboos invalidated the very token of civic allegiance (*eusebeia*), because they exposed the disloyalty of a self-chosen association based on a common disposition of mind.

On the other hand, such oblique customs and dispositions of mind were also indicative of a virtual introjection (or internalization) of sacrifice. A new life in purity and strict observance implied a radicalization of civic piety, through which everyday life was transformed into a constant state of ritual liminality. The sense in which Pythagorean and Orphic groups simultaneously rejected and introjected traditional doctrines and customs through their radicalization was surely not a tendency restricted to secteristic religiosity, which was often (as we shall see) depicted in rather derogatory terms. The impact of so-called "Orphic" ideas on 5th century poetry and philosophy is widely acknowledged among contemporary scholars, despite a lingering disagreement as regards the precise meaning of the labels "Orphic" and "Orphism." A familiar example is Pindar's doctrine of the soul, which clearly grows out of a Homeric (and aristocratic) notion of immortality through fame.[4] Another case is the adjacent radicalization of civic "care" (*epimeleia*) as exemplified by the Socratic "care of the self," to which I shall return below.[5] Yet we may find support for similar ideas in much earlier sources.

If we consider how the social importance of sacrifice was asserted and negotiated through the medium of myth, most likely in narratives predating the "Orphic" currents of the 5th century, the theme of immortality seems intrinsically linked to the raison d'être of sacrifice. The mythical treatment of Hermes' "invention" of sacrifice is a case in point. As the myth unfolds in the *Homeric Hymn to Hermes*, the protagonist is seeking recognition as a member of the Olympic family, and eventually achieves fame among the immortals (*kleos estai en athanatoisi* [458]) in reward for his inventiveness and performative skills (the newly invented lyre and his singing). Another crucial detail in the plot is the fact that Hermes avoids the edible parts of the slaughtered animals, thus affirming his divine status by rejecting the communal meal in which a human sacrificer would usually take part. The peaceful settlement between Hermes and Apollo (signalled by the verb *diakrinō* [438]) marks the resolution of an original crisis (signalled by the verb *krinō*). According to another well-known etiology of sacrifice, gods and mortals first "parted" or "had a dispute" (*ekrinonto*) at the ancient city of Mekone (Hesiod's *Theogony*, 535–544). The reason for the dispute was a trick played by Prometheus against Zeus during the preparation of a communal meal. By placing the edible parts of a great ox inside the animal's stomach and smearing its bones in fat, he violates a fundamental principle of hospitality and fair distribution. Although the trick sets the standard for future sacrifices, it also causes the community of men to be forever alienated from the community of gods.

If the two etiologies are analyzed contiguously, sacrifice not only appears as something serving the interests of a community, but also as something that can be manipulated and restored so as to induce a change of status and community. The crisis of unfair distribution and divine discontent can be resolved. More than literary fancies, these myths reflect a social reality in which patrons and ritual specialists are constantly negotiating.

III

The ancient institution of sacrifice was, both in Greek and Vedic society, grounded in a treaty between ritual specialists and chieftains, who spent wealth and effort in order to achieve everlasting fame (**k̂leu̯os*) and immortality. The Vedic poets ceaslessly employed their own clever idiom to project the excellence of their own guild into the mythical past. The divine recipient of ritual services could thus assume the role of a generous patron, who accepted the gift of ritual and confirmed approval through the redistribution of wealth. Furthermore, along a similar line of analysis, immortal fame was not only incumbent on the patron through his wealth and generosity, it was also conceived as a divine reward for the ritual service.

In a small group of Rigvedic hymns, a mythical episode about the R̥bhus, a group of three travelling singers and artisans led by a certain R̥bhu (from which the group collectively derrives its name), is allusively touched upon. The myth is obscure – Karl Friedrich Geldner (1951) called it a "Dunkler Sagenzug" – and cannot be grasped in its detail, yet there are a few recurrent traits in the episode that appear decisive enough for our current analytical purposes. The R̥bhus are said to arrive at the house of the sun-god Savitar/Agohya (1,110,3; 1,161,11), where they seem to spend a period in somnambulistic transition before being rewarded by the gods with immortality and fame (110,3 and 5) for their artistic wonders, many of which are associated with the fixtures of ritual.[6] They multiply the Soma-vessels, (1,161,10), generate the cow, "fashion sacrifice" by straightening up the stones (for pressing out Soma) (3,54,12) – actions which seem to lend them a place in a new sacrificial community.[7]

The appellation (from the stem *r̥bhú-*) of these wandering singers provides a clue to their role in this curious drama. Craig Melchert has recently re-examined the philological evidence for a PIE etymon *$*h_3erb^h$-*, which, in so far as it is said of a voluntary action, had the etymological sense "change sides, change allegiance."[8] Behind its homely use to refer to a straying animal (e.g. Hittite *ḫarp[p]*) lies, Melchert argues, "a complex notion of change of group membership with rich associations in the vocabulary of social institutions."[9]

Among the possible derivatives of the root, Sanskrit *r̥bhú-* is given passing attention in one of Melchert's footnotes. He considers the possibility, first raised by Hisashi Miyakawa, that the Sanskrit name reflects the etymon *$*h_3erb^h$-* in the specific sense *"one who has left humankind and joined the gods." Unable to pursue the issue further, Melchert calls it an "intriguing suggestion."[10] This is also said of the possible connection between R̥bhu and Orpheus, which was most recently defended by Michael Estell in a paper from 1999. I should not be reharsing all the details pertaining to the much-debated comparison between R̥bhú- and Orpheus here, suffice it to say that the etymological sense "change sides, change allegiance" adds a certain depth and complexity to the common background of the figures. Let me give a few examples.

Apart from being losely associated with the theme of apotheosis, Orpheus and the Ṛbhus are depicted as skillful performers with an uncertain commitment. Their ritual skills arouse amazement and alacrity among the gods. Much like Hermes, Orpheus is associated with the perfection and handling of the lyre as a particularly potent means of persuation. If the mythical appearance of Orpheus and the Ṛbhus had some bearing on the social factuality of ritual, it seems plausible that the characteristic features of these figures were in fact modelled after (or at least informed by) the ritual specialist's innate propensity to surrender his current patron and seek a more beneficial commitment.

IV

The importance of patronage is still clearly reflected in Plato's derogatory remarks on the wandering followers of Orpheus and Musaios in the *Republic*, from which we learn that these "beggar priests and seers" [*agurtai de ke kai manteis*] were not only seeking individual converts among the rich, but also tried to purusade whole cities.

> [They] come to the doors of the rich and convince them that in their hands, given by the gods, there lies the power to heal with sacrifices and incantations [...] and they offer a bundle of books of Musaios and Orpheus [...] according to which they perform their sacrifices; they pursuade not only individuals but whole cities that there is release and purification from misdeeds through sacrifices and playful pastimes, and indeed for both the living and the dead; they call these *teletai*, which deliver us from evil in the afterlife; anyone who declines to sacrifice, however, is told that terrible things are waiting for him.[11]

It is worth noticing that the etymological sense "change sides, change allegiance" was a characteristic feature of the mythological person Orpheus as well, who appparently sets an example of any proselyte through his fatal shift of devotion. In one of the few surviving testimonnies of Aeschylus' lost tragedy *Bassarides*, a possible source of inspiration for Euripides' *Bakkhai*, the following story is told about Orpheus:

> [Orpheus,] after going down to Hades in quest of his wife and seeing what things were like there, ceased to honour Dionysos, by whom he had been glorified, and regarded the Sun (whom he also called Apollo) as the greatest of gods (*ton de Helion megiston ton theōn enomizen einai, hōn kai Apollōna prosēgoreusen*); he would rise before daybreak and await the sunrise of the [Thracian] mountain Pangaeum, so as to be the first to see the Sun. Dionysos was angry at this and sent against him the Bassarides (as the tragic poet Aeschylus says), who tore him to pieces and scattered his limbs far and wide; but the Muses collected them together and burried him at a place called Leibethra (in Macedonia).[12]

The introjection of sacrifice here reaches its climax and most radical expression of devotion. More than just submitting to a ritual life in purity and abstinence, Orpheus is torn apart in the manner of a Dionysian *sparagmos.* He is transformed into a sacrificial victim.

Philosophical discourse invites us to construe the practice of prayer and animal sacrifice in public space as a mischievous satisfaction of appetite and desire perverting the virtues of philosophy. It was this interpretation of sacrifice that led Aristotles' successor Theophrastus to feel such admiration for the Jewish practice of *holokaustos* ("burnt whole," "burnt-offering"). The Jews, conceived as a people of philosophers, are said not to feast on the sacrifices, but to burn them whole and to fast for the intervening days. During this time they converse with each other about the deity and observe the stars at night. While they were the first to institute sacrifices, they did it by compulsion and not from eagerness.[13] We need not scrutinize the historical accuracy of this description in order to appreciate the ideals that inform it. Regardless of their arbitrary means of projection, they remain the ideals of a Greek writer and peripatetic philosopher.

The account contains a detail that curiosly reflects the trial against Socrates. The Jews are described as theologians-cum-astrologers. When they fast, i.e., while renouncing the communal meals, they converse about the deity and observe the stars at night. Since their noble devotions are somehow perceived to counterbalance the atypical nature of their worship, the typical nature of civic worship in the Greek polis is bound to turn the philosopher into an "unwanted" (*atopos*) and ridiculous figure. The distracted astrologer, turning his eyes beyond the immediate concerns of the local community, was in fact the familiar subject of an Aesopian fable about an astrologer who falls into a well while studying the stars. Plato's revised version of the fable takes the form of a philosophical foundation-myth. It is also ingenously designed to have Socrates predicting his own tragic destiny, which is forshadowed at the immediate end of the same dialogue.

> Thales was studying the stars (*astronomoūnta*) and looking up ... he fell into a well. A Thracian servant girl with a sense of humor, according to the story, made fun of him for being so eager to find out what was in the sky that he was not aware of what was in front of him right at his feet.[14]

The same joke, Socrates adds, can be applied to anyone who devotes himself to philosophy.

Although I hesitate to speak of any direct "Orphic" echoes here (despite the Thracian origins of the servant girl), the structural similarities between Thales' humiliating downfall and Orpheus' tragic destiny on the mountain Pangaeum will not have escaped the readers' attention.

Both figures have surrendered a former ally – Dionysos in the case of Orpheus, the city of Miletus in the case of Thales – and both are paying dearly for chosing a more distant and elevated ally.

Hans Blumenberg, who devoted a whole book to the philosophical fable and its repercussions in Western thought, was eager to emphasize the importance of conflicting perspectives in the plot: the exploratory gaze of the philosopher and the condescending gaze of the Thracian maid.[15] These conflicting perspectives, both easilly recognizable to anyone involved in the less pragmatic endeavours of scholarship and science, imply a reversal of the expected power relations. She, the low-cast woman from a foreign country, now speaks with the authority of the polis, whereas he, the nobleman from the ancient city, has abandonded his civil duties and turned his attention to a foreign cause. In the direction of his gaze she recognizes no domestic divinities. They exist only at the place where he falls into the well. For this reason, her malicious joy is fully justified and attuned to the interests of the city.[16]

V

When Socrates stood accused of having corrupted the youth, and of *asebeia* ("impiety") for dishonoring the gods of Athens by introducing new deities into the city, his philosophical activities were consequently deemed to invert the most prominent token of allegiance to the community. These putatively pious gestures of *eusebeia* are referred to in the *Apology* as foil for the groundbreaking notion of "care of the self" (*epimeleia heautoū*).

> Most excellent man, are you who are a citizen of Athens, the greatest of cities and the most famous for wisdom and power, not ashamed to care for the acquisition of wealth (*epimeloumenos*), and for reputation and honor (*doxēs kai timēs*), when you neither care (*ouk epimelē*) nor take thought for wisdom and truth and the perfection of your soul?[17]

In order to appreciate the semantic subtleties of the Socratic precept (an elaboration of the famous Delphic maxim *gnōthi seauton*), we must take into account that the term *epimeleia* was already intrinsically associated with the exigencies of public worship. It could evoke a sense of "care" (if not even "zealusness") bestowed upon sacred things, a sense likewise testified by the early usage of Latin *religio, religiosus.*[18] We also need to recall that the cultic apparatus of the Greek polis was largely a matter of wealth and reputation. This means that Socrates is placing the civic sacrificial economy under scrutiny, but, more importantly, he is also propagating its replacement by a new economy of the self – it is only when you start occuping yourself with yourself, and not with the tokens of wealth and reputation, that you will learn how to occupy yourself with the city.

The notion of the philosopher as an asocial and apolitical drop-out should not be exaggerated, for there were certainly philosophers who merely served the interests of the established political order. Nevertheless, the stereotype is prominent enough in some of the early biographies of philosophy and soteriological religiosity to deserve serious attention – just think of what Heraclitus is claimed to have told the men of Ephesus while playing knuckle-bones with the children inside the temple of Artemis. When expected to write a constitution for the city, he allegedly told them: "What are you staring at, you bastards? Isn't doing this better than playing politics with you?"[19]

The renunciation of home and family, the abandonment of the old gods (the old customs, the old bonds of loyalty), the irresponsible attitude towards political obligations, all these breachs of etiquette mark a quest for spiritual refinement and transformation. When a traditional economy of sacrifice is internalized, inner life is economized through ascetism and self-care. The expected gain is no longer the increasing quantities of wealth and honour, but rather spiritual qualities that may seem redundant, possibly even threatening and corrosive, to a loyal member of the pre-existing in-group.

I began this short survey by touching upon the generalizable social dynamic from which such a development might ensue in discrete historical contexts. Still, I have also pointed to certain hereditary elements in early Greek and Indian society that may provide a window on a possible prelude to this development.

Notes

1. Assmann 2010: 16–17.
2. Regarding the Indian origins of Orphic and Pythagorean metempsychosis, cf. Burkert (1972: 133) with references to earlier research.
3. Kindt 2012: 98. Max Weber once came close to formulating a sociological law in order to capture this tension: "A religiosity of salvation is elaborated in its most durable form by privileged classes of a people when they are demilitarized and excluded from the interest of political activity" (Weber quoted in Kippenberg 1991: 88)
4. Burkert 1987: 301.
5. For a seminal treatment of the topic, cf. Foucault (1988 and 2001).
6. Cf. the recent interpretation by Witzel and Gotō (2007).
7. Cf. Witzel and Gotō (2007: 722).
8. Melchert (2010: 181–183).
9. Melchert (2010: 180).

10. Melchert (2010: 186).
11. 364b-365a.
12. The paraphrase occurs in pseudo-Eratostenes i *Catasterismi* (24).
13. Theophrastus quoted in Porphyry's *On Abstinence* (2,26). Cf. also the discussion in Stroumsa 2009.
14. *Theaitetos*, 174a4–8.
15. Blumenberg 1987: 12. Jonathan Z. Smith touches upon similar themes of *policing* and *counterpolis* in his readings of Euripides' *Bacchai* and the Jonestown incident (see especially Smith 1982: 114).
16. Blumenberg 1987: 12.
17. 29d-e.
18. E.g. Aristotle, *Pol.* (1322b19) (*e. pròs toùs theoús, pròs tên pólin* [D.22.78]?
19. *Diogenes Laertius* 9.1–6.

References

Assmann, Jan. 2010. *Religio duplex. Ägyptische und europäische Aufklärung*. Frankfurt am Main: Verlag der Weltreligionen.

Blumenberg, Hans. 1987. *Das Lachen der Thrakerin. Eine Urgeschichte der Theorie*. Frankfurt am Main: Suhrkamp.

Burkert, Walter. 1972. *Lore and Science in Ancient Pythagoreanism*. Cambridge, MA: Harvard University Press.

Burkert, Walter. 1987. *Greek Religion*. Cambridge, MA: Harvard University Press.

Foucault, Michel. (1988) "Technologies of the Self." *Technologies of the Self: A Seminar with Michel Foucault*, edited by Luther H. Martin, Huck Gutman and Patrick H. Hutton, 16-49. Tavistock: University of Massachusetts Press.

Foucault, Michel. 2001. *L'Herméneutique du sujet. Cours au Collège de France: 1981–1982*. Paris: Seuil.

Geldner, Karl Friedridrich. 1951. *Der Rig-Veda. Aus dem Sanskrit ins Deutsche übersetzt*. Harvard Oriental Series, 33–36, vol. 1–3. Cambridge, MA: Harvard University Press.

Kindt, Julia. 2012. *Rethinking Greek Religion*. Cambridge: Cambridge University Press. http://dx.doi.org/10.1017/CBO9780511978500.

Kippenberg, Hans G. 1991. *Die vorderasiatischen Erlösungsreligionen*. Frankfurt am Main: Suhrkamp.

Melchert, Craig. 2010. "Hittite ḫarp(p)- and Derivatives." In *Studien zu den Boğazköy-Texten*, edited by J. Klinger, Elisabeth Rieken and Christal Rüster, 179-188. Investigationes Anatolicae 52. Wiesbaden: Harrassowitz Verlag.

Smith, Jonathan Z. 1982. "The Devil in Mr. Jones." In *Imagining Religion. From Babylon to Jonestown.*, 102-120. Chicago, IL: University of Chicago Press.

Stroumsa, Guy. 2009. *The End of Sacrifice: Religious Transformations in Late Antiquity*.Chicago, IL: University of Chicago Press.

Witzel, Michael, and Toshifumi Gotō. 2007. *Rig-Veda. Das heilige Wissen. Erster und zweiter Liederkreis.* Frankfurt am Main: Suhrkamp.

About the author

Peter Jackson is Professor at the department of History of Religions at Stockholm University, Sweden. Jackson received his PhD in the History of Religions from Uppsala University in 1999. He specializes in the study of Indo-European religions, with a particular emphasis on ancient Indian and Iranian religions, the religions of ancient Greece and Rome, and Old Norse religion. He also works on more general theoretical and conceptual concerns in the study of religion. His most recent book is *The Transformations of Helen: Indo-European Myth and the Roots of the Trojan Cycle* (2007).

RITUAL TRANSFORMATIONS IN LATE ANTIQUITY

6

The End of Sacrifice Revisited

Guy G. Stroumsa

Some years ago, I published a short monograph on the religious transformations of late antiquity, which I entitled *The End of Sacrifice*, in order to highlight the most dramatic change in religious life in the Christianized Roman Empire, namely, the end to public animal sacrifices.[1] For the historian of religions, the end of animal sacrifices as the centerpiece of public religion is certainly one of the most important problems at the end of the ancient world. Indeed, the early Christian attitudes to animal sacrifices have attracted considerable scholarly attention of late. The main problem with most of these books, however, is their almost exclusive focus upon Christianity, while ignoring Rabbinic Judaism, a religion born concomitantly with Christianity, and from the very same roots, the Second Temple version of the religion of Biblical Israel. From a methodological perspective, such an approach is seriously mistaken, as what obtains in Judaism may give us some important clue as to the more general trend in late antique religion.

Among the many interesting papers presented at the Stockholm Colloquium on Philosophy and the End of Sacrifice, Gerald Larson's essay, "'The End of Sacrifice' and the Absence of 'Religion': the Peculiar Case of India" sought to take my own thesis as its starting point. Larson, in particular, pointed out some puzzling similarities between the way religion and theology, as we traditionally understand these terms, seem to appear in India in the first centuries of the Christian era. Referring to the idea of an "Axial Age" (more or less around the middle of the first millennium B.C. E.), Larson expresses doubts about its significance for India.

Keywords: Axial age, sacrifice, Late Antiquity, transformation of ritual, individualization, Religions of the book

Larson, then, suggests that one might look at Late Antiquity as a second "Axial Age," perhaps even one endowed of more significance than the 'first' Axial Age, the one heralded by the German philosopher Karl Jaspers. The Axial Age has been most recently discussed anew by the leading American sociologist Robert Bellah. I propose to devote some paragraphs to the idea of the axial age as understood by Bellah in his recently published *magnum opus, Religion in Human Evolution: From the Paleolithic to the Axial Age.*[2] In the book, Bellah deals successively, with the civilizations of Israel, Greece, China and India around the middle of the first millennium B.C.E. This discussion represents to my mind the core of his book, and is a renewed attempt to highlight and understand the nature of what has been dubbed since Karl Jaspers (1949) "the axial age." At the onset of *The Origin and Goal of History* (*Vom Ursprung und Ziel der Geschichte*), the German philosopher Jaspers highlighted the fact, already noticed in the eighteenth century, that approximately around the mid-first millennium BCE, a series of exceptional figures appeared in a number of civilizations, which had a dramatic impact on thought and religion. Confucius and Mencius in China, the Buddha in India, Zarathustra in Iran, the Prophets of Israel and the Ionian Pre-Socratic philosophers all transformed the cultures in which they were born in radical ways (Zarathustra's dates are anything but certain. He may well have preceded the axial age by a few hundred years). Jaspers was fascinated by this seeming synchrony, which he could not really explain. For Jaspers, the axial age constituted the great divide in human history. Civilizations before and after it were different in some fundamental ways. In Jaspers' perception, civilizations that had no obvious contacts between them underwent, at more or less the same time, which he called *Achsenzeit* (axial age), a spiritual "quantum leap" which introduced self-consciousness and gave an ethical dimension to myths and to the perception of the universe. Through the spiritualization that this transformation involved, the axial age established the grounds on which the great historical religious and intellectual traditions emerged. In 1975, Jaspers' insight was picked up, as it were, by the participants of a special issue of *Deadalus*, the journal of the American Academy of Sciences, edited by the American Sinologist Benjamin Schwartz. The interest in the axial age recently gathered momentum with *The Origins and Diversity of Axial Age Civilizations* (Eisenstadt 1986), a book edited by the leading Israeli sociologist Shmuel Noah Eisenstadt. The current trendiness of the axial age is perhaps best highlighted by the publication, in 2006, of Karen Armstrong's *The Great Transformation: The Beginnings of Our Religious Traditions* (Armstrong 2007).

The idea of the axial age, with its undertones of a scholarly approach emphasizing the spiritual unity of humankind and deep similarity between the "great civilizations" and their intellectual and spiritual heroes is easily seductive. This reviewer retains fond memories of exhilarating interdisciplinary seminars on "axial civilizations" jointly taught with Eisenstadt and other colleagues in the early 1980s at the Hebrew University of Jerusalem: Eisenstadt (who died in 2010) was urging us to dare dreaming, to speculate on the essence of the dramatic changes in patterns of thought and behaviour as a consequence of the axial age. Play, indeed, is as essential an ingredient of intellectual creativity as it is of ritual. For him, the main axial transformation was the birth of cultural "reflexivity"' and of "second order thought." Thanks to the chasm that had opened between the heavenly world and the human realm, axial age cultures learned to express discursively their own cosmology and anthropology. This chasm also had another impact on religion, which now entailed a demand for salvation.

If I have insisted upon Eisenstadt's contribution, it is not only because of my personal recollections. It is, mainly, because Bellah himself had co-taught a course at Harvard, in 1963, together with Eisenstadt (and with Talcott Parsons), from which was born Bellah's seminal article on "Religious Evolution" (*The American Sociological Review* 29 [1964], 358–374). In this article, Bellah mentions neither Jaspers nor the Axial Age, but Weber's name figures prominently. Indeed, sociologists like Eisenstadt and Bellah saw themselves as walking in Weber's footsteps when they sought to compare ancient civilizations. Weber's Sisyphean attempt at highlighting the main articulations of societies, economics and religious views, from a comparative perspective, an attempt that was cut short by his death in 1920, remains to this day the most impressive and sustained effort to analyze religions in the context of the different societies in which they were born and grew, and the dialectical relationship between religion, economy and society.

In a sense, *Religion in Human Evolution* is the sequel to "Religious Evolution," a sequel which remained in gestation for almost half a century. This long gestation may partly explain why the book will more likely than not leave the reader with a sense that Bellah has overplayed his hand. Less, here, would probably have meant more. In "Religious Evolution," Bellah had identified five stages of religious evolution in human history: religion moved for him from "primitive" to "archaic" to "historical" to "early modern" to "modern." *Religion in Human Evolution*, however, does not deal with religion beyond the ancient world, although Bellah speaks of tribal, archaic, axial, post-axial, modern and post-modern stages. It remains unclear to me where exactly the axial age fits in Bellah's early taxonomy. I guess that the "axial" and "post-axial" stages correspond to the previous "historic" stage. A certain lack of terminological clarity here prevents a clear-cut perception. But Bellah is not concerned by such "details," as crucial as they may be to the historian. What does concern him is the essential idea of "evolution." It is on purpose that Bellah borrows this term from Darwin's historical physiology. Just as the species evolve and eventually transform themselves, so do societies, and so do religions.

Like Durkheim, Bellah conceives the stages of religious development as following the evolution of societies moving from the less to the more complex. This Durkheimian trope is compounded by a Darwinian one: human evolution also belongs to the evolution of a species. Societies move from the simplest structures (the tribe) in the early stages of human history to more and more complex ones: the city, the early state, the empire. The transformations of society are accompanied by transformations of ritual and myth, of religion. "As societies became more complex, religions followed suit," writes Bellah, indicating that such transformations are not linear. They are mainly accomplished through mutations, radical structural changes which appear to be the answer to crises and challenges. The axial age, he argues, witnessed a major crisis in the ritual system, as people stopped believing in the system's efficacy. Bellah can thus speak about a burst of 'anti-ritualism,' and of 'demythologization (Bellah uses here, in a new fashion, a concept coined by the theologian Rudolph Bultmann, referring to the mental activity necessary for a modern apprehension of the New Testament). To be sure, antiritualism does not entail the end of ritual, any more than de-mythologization means the end of myth. It does point, however, to a new, critical attitude to traditional ritual, as well as to the new central importance of ethics in religion – hence, the new universal dimension of religion. It is only with the break of former ritual systems that major breakthroughs could open new vistas in religious attitudes and beliefs.

The fascination with the axial age reflects the similarity of intellectual and spiritual trends and culture heroes, across civilizations seemingly unrelated. This concept is a perfect antidote to accusations of Eurocentrism in an age of globalization. The problem is that the axial age seems to be a *fata morgana*. The riddle of synchrony, as Jan Assmann has argued, evaporates at the mention of Akhenaton, Jesus or Muhammad, who should obviously belong to the club of "axial" figures together with Socrates, Isaiah or Zarathustra. While it sometimes happens that different cultures reach a similar turning point at approximately the same point in time, what really counts, in each case, is the cause (or causes) of this turning point. Moreover, the obvious possibility of diffusionism should be entertained: if chariots and goods could move so easily, ideas could too. But religious change can also be brought about by new technologies. The clearest case is probably that of the emergence and diffusion of script systems. The development of writing, which is directly related to the establishment of empires and huge, centralized societies, entailed the need, for the literate elites, to educate and train new generations of scribes, and eventually the redaction of books, and hence of holy texts, often remaining esoteric, not to be divulged to all and sundry. Religion inscribed in a book has become a portable religion, one that can and will travel. On various occasions in his book, Bellah points to the crucial importance of writing in the evolution of cultures, but fails to grant the topic all the focused attention it requires.

The concept of axial age, then, is misleading. Rather than focusing on one epoch when everything, everywhere, tipped over, it is probably wiser to identify major cultural changes, whenever they happen. New configurations of culture and their social consequences are just as interesting as new configurations of society and their cultural consequences. Bellah's interest in early religion is no simple intellectual curiosity. For him, the axial age mutations are so significant because they would eventually shape our own world. More precisely, we are the inheritors, he says, of the legacy of both Greece and Israel. This may very well be the case, but it is only through the major intellectual re-modelling effected by the Church Fathers (and before them by Philo of Alexandria) and of the Medieval Scholastic theologians (who could read Aristotle mostly thanks to the Arabs!) that these two legacies were integrated.

Scholarly attempts to deal with the foundations of the different disciplines are usually not crowned by success: since they cannot prove, they usually do not convince, and other scholars are prone to present detailed arguments refuting the main theses of the new theories. This is, to my mind, rather unfair. Failure, in such cases, is the price of aiming high. An intellectually ambitious work may not win approval in its discipline, but it often sets the tone for a whole generation of researchers, or more. There is such a thing as a respectable, even a noble failure.

If aiming high often entails missing the target, it also clearly points in the right direction. Bellah's book teaches us, once more, that religions should be studied in their different societal and cultural contexts. If there is no single *homo religiosus*, from all times and all cultures, as the phenomenology of Mircea Eliade wanted us to believe, that does not mean that there is no common ground between the rituals and myths of all nations. And if the axial age proves to be an illusion, that does not mean that religions, like societies, do not undergo at some turning points in history some major transformations, or even mutations. Analyzing such mutations in comparative perspective, dismantling their inner mechanisms, is not merely possible. It is the key to a better understanding of the very nature of religious revolutions, past and present.

The challenge is how to dissolve false categories without giving up on the grand ambition to find laws, i.e., to retain the principle of unity beyond diversity – and what else is science, what else is scholarship? If the idea of the axial age fails to convince, it is not because there is "nothing in it," but because it is less unique and less universal than it claims to be. Rather than one single axial age, one might then prefer to speak of a number of axial periods, in each cultural eco-system, while it is possible, of course, to identify also some synchronic similarities between different cultural eco-systems. The longer late antiquity, for example, is such a period for the cultures of the Near East and of the Mediterranean. From Jesus to Muhammad, a series of religious movements (together with the Christians, one should mention, at least, the Rabbinic Jews, Gnostics, Manichaeans and Mandaeans) insist on the redaction and preservation of holy, revealed books. These books, which are often learned by heart, at least in part, are commented upon, sometimes translated, often sung during ritual. One can speak of a "Scriptural movement" in the late antique Near East and Eastern Mediterranean. It is essential to understand how this new role played by books will soon transform the religious systems of the area, ushering in new configurations from the old building blocks. These new religious configurations, namely Eastern and Western Christendom, as well as Caliphate Islam, will soon form what I called above an "eco-system," which will endure throughout the Middle-Ages. And since in late antiquity the religion of Biblical Israel underwent a series of dramatic transformations with the Rabbis, it is what we have recently learned to call the Abrahamic religions that the "Axial Age" ignores. In this "eco-system," religious and cultural trends will constantly circulate and evolve, creating the basis of our world. These reflections on the idea of an axial age, evoked by Bellah's new massive book, are meant to cool unleashed enthusiasm, as tempting as it may be, for seeing in late antiquity, or in any other given period, a time of dramatic cultural, intellectual and religious transformation in many highly different societies. Hence, the following pages, which seek to summarize some of the salient arguments of *The End of Sacrifice*, do not claim a global heuristic value, beyond the Mediterranean and Near East. While it may be far-fetched to speak about an axial age, the search for similarities and parallel developments in distinct civilizations, which do not have much interface, can certainly lead to interesting, or even important conclusions about the mechanisms through which civilizations undergo deep transformations.

A series of major political, cultural and social changes affected all aspects of life in the Near East as well as around the Mediterranean under the Roman Empire. Religious beliefs and attitudes, in particular, underwent some dramatic transformations.[3] Indeed, those scholars who, rejecting the Gibbonian paradigm of decline and fall, have taught us to look at the Roman Empire in the *longue durée*, as to a time when new cultural frames were developed, have all insisted on the religious dimensions of late antique creativity. Each in his own way, Henri-Irénée Marrou, E. R. Dodds, Peter Brown, Robin Lane Fox, have been able to speak of the *religious revolution* of late antiquity.[4] One might argue that our period is no less capital for future developments than the *Achsenzeit* identified by Karl Jaspers with the middle of the first millenium BCE.[5] In order to do justice to the dramatic nature of the transformations in our period, from, say, Jesus to Muhammad, one can also speak of "religious mutations." By borrowing this metaphor from the field of biology, I intend to highlight the fact that we do not only witness the passage from paganism to Christianity (to follow the traditional perception), or that of polytheism to monotheism. Rather, I wish to claim that we can observe nothing less than a transformation of the very concept of religion. To encapsulate the nature of this transformation, one may perhaps speak of "the end of sacrifice," in reference to the fact that at the time of Jesus, religion meant, for Jews and Greeks alike, the offering of sacrifice, while the situation had changed in some radical ways in the sixth century. But the multifaceted nature of this revolution encompassed other areas than the ritual and its transformations. One can also observe a series of transformations: of psychological conceptions, of the place and role of books in religious life, and the passage from an essentially civic to a mainly communitarian nature of religion.

One question that has often been asked is that of the nature of these transformations: are they Christian by nature, or do they rather reflect the *Zeitgeist*? Such a question, it seems to me, is fundamentally flawed. The kind of Christianity (or Christianities) that emerge from our period is not quite identical to the Christian beliefs of the early Church Fathers, and reflect themselves the evolution of Christian beliefs and praxis during those centuries.

A new care of the self

In order to assess the mutations of religion in late antiquity (late antiquity being here understood in the very broad sense of the word), one should probably focus first on what happened to the self during our period. Following Pierre Hadot, who had offered subtle analyses of what he called "spiritual exercises" in the practice of philosophy under the Empire, Michel Foucault sought in his later years to analyse "the care of the self" (*epimeleia heautou*) among ancient intellectuals.[6] For him, the radical denigration of the body among early Christian thinkers and ascetics brought this care of the self to an end. It seems to me, however, that Foucault's analysis is flawed in various ways. In particular, the corpus from which he drew his evidence was particularly limited (Foucault used mainly texts from Cassian's interpretation of Egyptian monasticism). It is true, of course, that he did not have the time to broaden and fully develop his analysis. Even if more time had been granted to him, however, he probably would not have been able to offer a convincing analysis of the psychological transformations accompanying the passage from paganism to Christianity. This is so, I argue, because of his attempt (an attempt he shares with many) to understand this passage as an internal transformation of the Greco-Roman world, thus ignoring the Jewish dimensions of Christianity. Arnaldo Momigliano, would have been a better guide here, as he recognized the triple matrix of intellectual and religious life under the Empire: Jerusalem, together with Athens and Rome.[7] Indeed, the oriental nature of early Christianity seems to remain often undervalued.

A crucial psychological transformation occurred in our period, with the new recognition that what happened after death was so much more important than what happened to one in this life. This transformation, of course, was endowed with a religious nature, and would have far-reaching religious consequences. Think, for instance, of the profound differences between Marcus Aurelius's *Meditations* and Augustine's *Confessions*. Personal eschatology would soon change in some radical ways both attitudes to the self and the foundations of ethics. *Askēsis*, the constant exercising through which one sought to work upon oneself, was then endowed with a new meaning. *Askēsis* now meant an attempt at re-forming rather than discovering oneself. Christian anthropology was built on some conceptions, both explicit and implicit, which entailed attitudes quite different from those of both Stoic and Platonic philosophies (the two main schools of thought in our period). These conceptions were directly inherited from the Hebrew Bible (more precisely, from its Greek translation, the Septuagint). One such conception was the idea (Gen 1: 26) that man had been created in the image of God (*homo imago dei*). That usually entailed, in contradistinction with Platonic thought, a recognition of the intrinsic value of the human body, as the nature of man, for most Christian thinkers, encompassed both soul and body. Another one was the insistence on God's transcendence: the whole cosmos had been created by Him *ex nihilo*. This entailed a refusal to accept the Platonist idea of a real parenthood, or *sungeneia*, between the soul and the divine. Although Christian intellectuals accepted for a very long time many of the intellectual assumptions of the Platonists, without recognizing that this would lead them into some serious self-contradictions, they usually stopped short of thinking that the human soul could, thanks to its *sungeneia* with the divine, reach deification (*theōsis*) at the end of the ascetical praxis. This praxis, rather, was usually conceived in the terms of an *imitatio Christi*, leading to sanctification, sometimes through martyrdom. In contradistinction with the *askēsis* of the philosophers, Christian *askēsis* (as well as Jewish *askēsis*) sought more a *metanoia* (Heb. *teshuva*) than an *epistrophē*, a repentance of one's sins more than a turning over from matter to the divine.

In the religious world of late antiquity, one can distinguish different *Idealtypen* of religious virtuosi. While the priest and the prophet seem to have either disappeared or retreated into the background, the stage is mainly left to the sage, the gnostic and the saint. To be sure, all three characters appear at once in the major religious trends. It stands to reason, however, that the various traditions show different constellations between these *Idealtypen.* It seems to me that while the Jews hesitate mainly between the figure of the sage and that of the saint, the main figures for the Christians are that of the saint and that of the gnostic, while "pagans" value mainly the figure of the sage and that of the gnostic.

For Christians and Jews, the revealed Scriptures entailed a "dialogical" way of deciphering the self through a constant reading of the Scriptures (in particular of the Psalms). The growth of religious conceptions based on a revealed Book, in the centuries between Jesus and Muhammad, reflects indeed a major transformation of religion.

The rise of the religions of the book

The first centuries of the Roman Empire witnessed what is probably the most radical revolution in the history of the book until Gutenberg. This revolution has two sides. On the one hand, the passage from roll to codex – a passage at first slow and gradual, from the first to the fourth century, except among the Christians, who adopt the codex almost instantaneously – transforms the very appearance and circulation of the book. On the other hand, the development of silent reading permits a new attitude to the book and its contents, and introduces a new, reflexive dignity of the single reader. In a sense, both transformations point to a privatization of reading, to a more personal, and less public, relationship between the reader and the text. Such a privatization would in its turn permit an almost unbounded spectrum of hermeneutical possibilities. Now when such a new approach to books is linked to the emphasis on a single corpus of texts ennobled as revealed Scripture, it is easy to see the dramatic implications of this cultural revolution on religion itself.[8]

In order to identify and highlight the common denominator of a series of religious trends from early Christianity to early Islam, the comparative historian of religion Wilfred Cantwell Smith has referred to "the scriptural movement" of Late Antiquity.[9] Indeed, a series of religious movements appeared in late antiquity throughout the Near East and the Mediterranean which were all identified through their Scriptures. While this view of things has much to commend itself, it does not tell the whole story. Indians and Orphics, for instance, had had a long tradition of sacred books, while both Jewish and Zoroastrian scriptures had been redacted much earlier. The Gathas seem to have represented, for perhaps as long as a millennium, a very special case of book: a book preserved orally, in a quite fixed form. (Similarly, the Qur'an seems to have existed, at least for some decades, only in oral form). The Gathas would be put in writing only much later, after the Muslim conquest of Iran, when the Zoroastrian community was much weakened and fearing for its identity. For the Rabbinic movement, a strong propensity to move away from the written text of the Bible to oral traditions (the Oral Torah, *torah she-be-al-peh*) can easily be detected in the first centuries of the Christian era.[10] The writing phase among the Jews had taken place earlier, under the Second Commonwealth, when a plethora of works, eventually called Pseudepigraphical and Apocryphal books of the Hebrew Bible, had been written.

Indeed, the library at Qumran seems to have been very significant. One has calculated that only in the ninth century would the library in the Sankt Gallen monastery surpass Qumran in the number of the volumes it held. Their relationship to books represents a major difference between Jews and Christians in late antiquity. Rabbinic Judaism seems to have been satisfied with one, revealed book, remaining therefore ignorant of all other books, preferring oral commentaries (in Talmud and Midrash). The Christians read their books mainly in order to follow Jesus Christ, the supreme exemplar, whose life (and death) one sought to imitate. For the Jews, there was no single Biblical figure comparable to that of Jesus for the Christians. The Christians had offered a radical simplification of myth, while the Jews proposed a radical simplification of the notion of holy text. The Christian ideal of *imitatio Christi* permitted the development of a puzzling phenomenon: the saint, the holy man, would soon be described in terms of writing: the saint would himself be presented as a book to be deciphered, read, commented upon.[11]

A puzzling parallelism can be observed in the redaction and canonization process of the Mishna and the New Testament. Both seem to have been edited at more or less the same time: in the eighties of the second century. This synchronization has not been explained, and I suggest it reflects the result of the race, between the now distinct communities, throughout the second century, to identify themselves from their competitors. Both communities sought to offer the correct interpretation to the same text (a text that the Christians read in a [Jewish] translation): the Hebrew Bible. In a sense, one can claim that Mishna and New Testament represent two different hermeneutical keys to the Bible. The Mishna (in Greek *deuterōsis*, repetition) represents, just like the New Testament, the *kainē diathēkē*, the way through which the community can read and understand the true religious meaning of the Bible. The respective registers of Mishna and New Testament, of course, reflect the deeply different religious structures of the two religions.[12]

Among the new religious movements of late antiquity, Manichaeism is perhaps the most fascinating. One deals, here, with a strongly dualistic movement perceiving itself, from the start, as a world religion, based upon revealed Scriptures. In various ways, Manichaeism appears as a radicalization of some trends already delineated in early Christianity, and also as a preview of characters usually identified with early Islam. When he invented, in 1873, the locution "religions of the book," Max Mueller was seeking to modernize and generalize an early Islamic conception. While the concept of "people of the book" (*ahl al-kitāb*) does not seem to appear before the Qur'an, Mani himself, around the mid-third century, was well aware of the various scriptural traditions of different religious systems. The first of the Manichaean *Kephalaia* represents in this regard an understudied key text. Mani lists various prophets, Jesus, Zarathustra, Buddha, who each made the mistake of not carefully committing to writing his oral teaching. The distortion of their respective teachings by their followers would be the unavoidable consequence of such a mistake. Therefore Mani, in contradistinction to his predecessors in the long chain of prophecy, took great pains to retain a written version of his message. One can clearly see in this text a deep fear about falsifications of Scriptures, a fear also reflected in Jewish-Christian traditions and in the Qur'an about the Hebrew Scriptures. What is peculiar to Manichaeism, of course, is the total rejection of the Jewish claims, a rejection reflected in the absence of Moses from the list of prophets.

Manichaean rejectionism highlights the close connection, to be broken only by Marcionism, between Judaism and Christianity. Throughout their long polemics with the Jews in late antiquity, the Christian authors were not able to deny the advantage of the Jews upon them: only the latter could read their own writings in the original language. The Church Fathers perceived the Jews as *librarii nostri*,[13] *custodes librorum nostrorum* (Augustine),[14] and when the mob, encouraged by the local bishop, organized a pogrom, plundering Jewish houses and properties in Minorca, in 418, they took great care of salvaging from the fire the Torah scrolls in the synagogue.[15] But the evidence is here too scarce to permit important conclusions. Another instance of the deep ambivalence towards the Hebrew Scriptures is highlighted in Justinian's *Novella* 146, dating from 553. Forbidding the cultic reading of the Bible in Hebrew, the Novella reflects the Emperor's perception of the symbolic power that the Jews derived from their knowledge of the revealed Scriptures' original language.[16]

The Christians, who were not bound by cultural, religious or linguistic traditions, offered a new attitude to religious language. For them the *traduttore* was no *traditore*. On the contrary, the idea of translation, from an archaic to a common language, understood by all and sundry, was of the essence of their religion. The ease with which Christians accepted, encouraged, and used translations of their Scriptures has no parallel in the ancient world, before the Manichaeans, who would even offer a more radical version of this approach. Their disregard for archaic language and hieratic forms of expression is also reflected in Christian polemics with Hellenic intellectuals about sublime language versus *sermo humilis*. Christian intellectuals insisted, against their Hellenic counterparts, that their religion was the same for philosophers and fishermen, a fact that explained and justified the Gospels' low language. While Emperor Julian, in the second half of the fourth century, condemns and derides the Christians for the mediocre literary level of their Scriptures, his very polemics shows the extent to which even he was influenced by the Christian conception of Scriptures. To give another example, when Proclus, the leader of the Academy, states that he would seek to retain, on a desert island, only Plato's *Timeaus* and the *Chaldean Oracles*, he too shows the deep influence of the concept of Scriptures. Together with its marked lack of emphasis on the power inherent to original language, the Christians, more than any other religious movement, were willing to reject the idea of an oral, esoteric tradition existing side by side with Scriptures. This rejection, which fitted the ethos of Christianity as offering salvation equally to all, was certainly enhanced by the fight against such esoteric traditions embedded in the Gnostic trends.[17]

The Christianization of the Empire entailed the subtle transformation of the educational system. Before the end of the fourth century, the Christians learned to teach also those texts of Greek mythology to which they had been so vehemently opposed. Hellenic culture, then, would now be transmitted thanks to its former enemies, the Christians. In order to do so, Christian intellectuals were brought to apply also to the Hellenic tradition the set of hermeneutic rules they had developed in order to appropriate to themselves the Israelite Scriptures. To borrow a metaphor invented by Cricks and Watson to describe the structure of DNA, one could perhaps speak here of a "double helix." The Christian thinkers sought to find a series of similarities and parallels between the two cultural systems of Athens and Jerusalem. It is this double helix which stands at the root of Christian culture, which was first elaborated in late antiquity, and which informed European culture to the modern times. Christian culture, then, constituted itself, both in the East and in the West, through slipping from biblical to cultural hermeneutics.[18] The monasteries are the *locus classicus* where this work on books was achieved, a complex effort involving reading, writing and interpreting. The complex cultural system developed in the monasteries was based upon the central figure of Jesus Christ, through which all mythology revolved. Similarly, the libraries were built, as a whole, around the one book of Scripture, which contained, if properly understood, all secrets and all wisdom. Similarly to the Rabbinic Sages, who, borrowing the Greek concept of *paideia*, had transformed it into their central religious value, Christian intellectuals of late antiquity succeeded to a great extent in applying to the Greek intellectual tradition and to their own Scriptures the same hermeneutical rules. In both cases, such attitudes entailed quite a new place and role of books in religious life and thought.

Transformations of the ritual

We have seen so far how some deep psychological and cultural transformations in the Roman world both permitted and imposed a radical re-structuring of the very idea of ritual. The rise of Scriptures as the very backbone of religious movements transformed attitudes towards religious stories, or myths. It stands to reason that a similar transformation of the ritual should be discerned, as all religions hinge upon the two functions of myth making (or telling) and ritual action. To a new conception of *historia sacra* should correspond a new kind of religious praxis.

I suggested above that the traditional distinction of polytheistic versus monotheistic religions is not always particularly useful from a heuristic viewpoint. Indeed, in the ancient world, both polytheists and monotheists used to offer blood sacrifices to the divinity or divinities, and considered such sacrifices to represent the very acme of religious life. Thus Emperor Julian, in the second half of the fourth century, could write that "the Jews behave like the Gentiles, except the fact that they recognize only one god. On everything else, however, we share the same things: temples, sanctuaries, altars, purification rituals, various demands on which we do not diverge from one another, or else only in insignificant ways."[19]

"*Sacrificiorum aboleatur insania*. Let the madness of sacrifices end!" This law of Constantinus II, preserved in the Theodosian Codex, encapsulates the revolution started by Constantine and pursued by his successors.[20] This revolution was radical in its consequences: it brought an end to public sacrifices. To be sure, the idea of animal (or for that matter human) sacrifice never quite disappeared, and various traces of it are retained in later forms of Christianity, while Islam has a feast of sacrifice (*Id al-adha*).

Much before the fourth century CE, a major debate had been raging in Hellenic thought on the value of sacrifice. Lucian of Samosata, that second-century Voltaire, who knew how to poke fun at various ritual practices and religious attitudes, had sharply criticized sacrifices in his diatribe *peri thusiōn*. In the third century, Porphyry, following Theophrastus and his *peri eusebeias*, could claim that the philosopher was the true priest of the supreme god, and that his thought was the true temple. It is this identity that isolates the philosopher from the *polis* and its public rituals. In his treatise *de abstinentia*, Porphyry, drawing the logical consequence of his repulsion from animal killing, argues in favour of vegetarianism. In this context, one should call attention to his belief that the Jews are a race of philosophers, precisely because their sacrificial practices, in contradistinction with those of other peoples, are due to historical necessities rather than to low instincts. For Porphyry, then, true sacrifice is the union with god, accomplished by the wise man through *apatheia*.[21] Even a traditionalist like Iamblichus, who argues in favour of sacrifices, recognizes that they are not needed by the superior beings. Blood sacrifices, for him, are expected only by the lower gods, and represent only the material aspect of cult. For him, thus, spiritual sacrifices exist side by side with blood sacrifices.[22]

When their single Temple, in Jerusalem, was destroyed by Titus in 70 CE, the Jews had to reinvent their religion in some dramatic ways, while arguing that they were changing very little, and this only under duress. If Jews could be perceived by some as a race of philosophers (for instance by Numenius, who argued in the second century CE, that Plato was "an atticizing Moses"), it seems to me that it is to no small measure due to the fact that they could now be perceived as a religion without blood sacrifices. Some dramatic consequences followed from the destruction of the Temple. The first one was the birth of two new religions, rather than one. Side by side with the birth of Christianity, the appearance of Rabbinic Judaism after 70 CE and its growth in the following centuries represents a real mutation of the religion of Israel: indeed, a religion now with no sacrifices, a religion whose priests were out of business, in which religious specialists had been replaced by the intellectual elite. In a way, early Christianity, a religion centred upon a sacrificial ritual celebrated by priests, represents a more obvious continuity with the religion of Israel than that of the Rabbis. The Temple's fall, and the impossibility to offer sacrifices, entailed the transformation of the ritual: daily sacrifices were now replaced by prayers recalling the sacrifices of old. The absence of a Temple and the neutralization of priests, in turn, brought at once to a spatial explosion of Jewish ritual and its democratization. There was no *omphalos* anymore, no obvious place that God could call His own house.

According to a famous Rabbinic conception, the *shekhina*, or divine presence (from the root *shakhan*, to dwell), exiled from the destroyed Temple, was now staying within "the four cubits of *halakha*," within the small limits of personal religious duties.[23] In other words, religion had now moved from the public to the private sphere. *Askēsis*, prayer, almsgiving: the various duties of private religion (duties to be ideally accomplished in private, even in secret) were all considered as due replacements for sacrifice. A Rabbinic text compares, for instance, the fat burnt during a fast to the fat of a sacrificial animal.[24] When the Rabbis say that after the destruction of the Temple, an iron wall rose between God and Israel, they mean to insist on the fact that Judaism has become a religion of alienation, a religion of God's absence.[25] Man must behave as if he did not expect a clear and distinct voice to answer his prayers, as if the time-consecrated *do ut des* formula did not work anymore. In a way, this attitude is rather similar to that of the Church Fathers, about whom one could speak, in Weberian sense, of an *Entzauberung*. The religion of the Rabbis had replaced that of the prophets. The priests had disappeared for all practical purposes. They might have been a catalyst for the development of new mystical attitudes within the Jewish community. It stands to reason that some of the characters of mystical experience, as they are preserved for us in Late Antique Hebrew literature, and also in Gnostic and Judeo-Christian texts and traditions, are similar to those developed by the priests in the Temple, who must have been feeling powerful experiences.[26]

In strong opposition to post-Yavneh Rabbinic Judaism, early Christianity unabashedly presented itself as a sacrificial religion, although one of a new kind, in which the central ritual was called *anamnēsis*, a re-actualization, or even re-activation – rather than our weaker term "memory" – of Jesus' sacrifice. It was a religion without temples, in which the same sacrifice was offered perpetually, on a daily basis. It was offered by priests, organized in a hierarchy (in contradistinction to the basic equality of rank between the rabbis). The very metaphorizing of biblical traditions by Christian thinkers permitted the conservation of the terms of Israelite religion. In Christian literature of the first centuries, one can follow the clear development of sacrificial vocabulary. The language of martyrdom, strikingly, is replete with allusions to sacrifice. The clearest testimony of this perception of martyrdom as a sacrifice is probably the *Martyrdom of Perpetua and Felicity*. *Imitatio Christi*, when it goes up to the willingness to give one's life for one's faith, transforms the martyr, like Jesus, into a sacrifice, more precisely, a human sacrifice. This is very significant, as human sacrifices were considered by pagans and Christians alike in the Roman Empire as representing the very border between humanity and barbarism.[27] As the historian of art Jas Elsner has been able to show, the transformation of Roman art from Augustus to Justinian reflects a deep evolution of subjectivity in Roman culture. The martyrs do not offer sacrifice, they are the sacrifice, and no reciprocity, no immediate *quid pro quo* is expected from the divinity.[28] In that sense, Christian martyrdom reflects a radical change in the conception of sacrifice, a fundamental break in the very nature of religion. One also finds in early Christian literature, like in Rabbinic texts, a metaphorical use of sacrifice: Clement of Rome, already, refers to "a contrite heart" as the true sacrifice, whereas the fourth-century Euchites, or Messalians, will develop, like in Qumran, a theory and practice of continual prayer in order to keep Satan away in terms alluding to the "perpetual sacrifice" in the Jerusalem Temple.

More than the Rabbis, the Church Fathers were quite aware of the novelty of their religion and of the originality of their thought. This awareness is reflected, for instance, in their ability to offer what one can call "histories of religion," theses about the evolution of religious doctrines and practices, in particular sacrifice, from the earliest times. Similar conceptions are much rarer among Jewish thinkers, and only Maimonides, in the twelfth century, will develop a full-fledged historical and comparative theory of sacrifice, a theory which retains traces of a Christian influence.[29]

To conclude these brief reflections on the transformation of the ritual, one should perhaps point out once more the deep ambiguity of sacrifice. Transformed, reinterpreted, metaphorized, memorized, it seems never to die out quite completely. Late antiquity experienced the end of public sacrifices as the core of religious praxis, but that did not mean the end to the very idea of sacrifice.

From civic religion to communitarian religion

The end of sacrifices as a central, public religious practice, in late antiquity, led to a major crisis in the conception of ritual purity. Since the prophets of Israel, through Jesus and Mani, the value of the ancient ways of re-establishing ritual purity had been seriously questioned.[30] The abandonment of the temples, and often their destruction through fits of iconoclastic violence, raised other questions regarding religious identity, which had usually been centred around the shrines. Traditionally, the temples had been built on central, clearly visible places, either within or without the cities. Now the *oikoumenē* was being emptied from its temples, as it were, and in their place, churches were being built. In their place, but not always quite on the same places. Various studies of the transformation of the urban texture in late antiquity show that churches were much more dispersed, in the different neighbourhoods of the cities, and not necessarily at their centre. Moreover, in most religious cults of the ancient world, the ritual was usually performed in the open, in public (Mithraic cult represents here a striking exception), while synagogue and church ritual was almost only performed inside, for the community of the faithful. A central aspect of this ritual was the reading, singing, translating and commenting of Scriptural passages, a fact that imposed a closed building, usually of rather limited dimensions. The new forms of ritual entailed, then, new forms of cultic buildings. Such concrete transformations of religious life, and the new importance of religious communities, permit a better understanding of the nature of the changes than E. R. Dodds' talk about a new spirituality.

While Christian authors usually insisted with pride upon the novelty of their religion, this novelty was precisely what the traditionalists feared most. Thus, Emperor Julian expressed his wish to avoid novelty altogether, but in particular in the religious domain. But this very expression of his fear reflects the fact that such deep changes were precisely occurring at the time. While civic rituals, by definition open to all, were meant to reaffirm collective identity, the new forms of identity that were becoming prevalent were by nature religious, and open only to the members of the community – in contradistinction with the society at large.

As argued by John Scheid, a deep transformation of religious practice had occurred in Rome since the end of the civil wars, and was amplified with Roman expansionism, and then under the Empire. With the growth of the cities, the direct participation of all citizens in the cult was eventually made impossible, and the cult became the business of their representatives. Hence, a more abstract religion, which had not yet changed in nature, became more internalized: for many, religious participation was now intellectual, done through reading. Scheid, who sees here a *praeparatio evangelica* of sorts, suggests a parallel with the Jewish communities from the diaspora, which had learned to function without the Jerusalem Temple.[31] This is certainly true, although one should be careful not to overemphasize the differences between the Jewish communities in Palestine and in the diaspora. The term of "Scriptural communities," coined by Brian Stock to describe medieval phenomena, is applicable in the ancient world to philosophers and Jews alike. Such communities were found in Palestine as well as in the diaspora, around the *batei midrash*, the synagogues where the Scriptures were interpreted. Psycho-sociological analysis, then, can bring us to a better understanding of the nature of the new religiosity emerging in the Roman Empire: the forms of ritual, focusing around Scriptures to be read and interpreted, and offering the basis to calls for personal repentance from sin.

Already in the second and third centuries, the willingness of urban elites to retain the traditional values of the old civic model began to be questioned. In the fourth century, these elites too often showed no real interest in exercising their political duties. Together with the slow depopulation of the cities, this trend helps to explain the growth of religious communities. Such communities, to be sure, had existed for a long time. But under the Empire, in particular since the third century, what John North, using a metaphor borrowed from Peter Berger, has called "the supermarket of religions" offered multiple possibilities for a religious identity freely chosen. Garth Fowden, on his side, argues that the broad acceptance of such conceptions of communitarian identity became characteristic of late antiquity.[32]

In Rome, religion had meant, almost exclusively, the observance of the ritual. Questions of truth were quite absent from the religious sphere. In order to understand the transformation of such a conception into that of Augustine, for whom *vera religio* represents, first of all, an internalized phenomenon, we must recognize the inversion of the relation of two couples of notions: sacred versus profane, and public versus private. As both Cicero and Marcian tell us, religion, or the sacred, was in Rome essentially a public affair, while what remained private was profane. With the internalization and individualization of religion, the two couples would become inversed. Among both Jews and Christians, the field of the sacred was identified with the private domain, while the public domain remained essentially profane. This was certainly the case until the fourth century. With the progressive, but rapid, Christianization of the Empire, things changed, and religion (i.e., "orthodox" Christianity) sought to reclaim the public sphere. From Constantine to Theodosius II, religion eventually became an affair of state again, and received all the attributes of civic religion in ancient Rome, but with a twist. As the principle of religious authority was now rooted in personal conscience, and religion identified also with truth, the rejection of the right path (i.e., the interpretation of religion adopted by the Emperor) would have immediate and radical consequences.

Since Gibbon, various explanations have been offered to the rise of religious intolerance and violence (two different but connected phenomena) in the world of late antiquity. As such violence and intolerance was mainly the work of Christians, it is in either the nature of Christianity (i.e., its origins in Jewish exclusiveness) or in its history (i.e., in the collusion, not before the fourth century, between state and church) that the roots of Christian violence and intolerance have been sought. It seems to me that both approaches err in their static character: they are unable to account for the deep transformation of mental patterns within Christian communities from the first to the fourth century. Early Christian communities, which remained *entpolitisiert* in the strongest sense of this Weberian expression, could, like the Qumran community, develop freely, upon a radical interpretation of their Scriptures, some violent ideas about the *Endzeit* and the final eschatological war. The trouble began when they were suddenly put in a position of power. Most were unable to realize at once that the new political fortune demanded a new hermeneutics. As we know too well, similar phenomena are known elsewhere, also in contemporary history.[33]

In order to understand the growth in religious intolerance and violence in late antiquity, one must recognize the new fact of an identity defined, more than ever before, in religious terms. People now perceived themselves as belonging to a freely chosen community. While Jewish exclusiveness made space for non-Jews (for instance as "God fearers," fellow travellers of sorts, or as "pious among the nations"), Christian universalism could not easily tolerate outsiders. By definition, such outsiders were heretics, pagans or Jews. Only the latter could be, to a certain extent, tolerated on the fringes of society. With time, these fringes had a tendency to shrink. As we have seen, Justinian cannot tolerate their use of Hebrew anymore, and in the early seventh century, forced baptism is demanded in the Byzantine Empire.

Jews and Christians knew exactly the stakes of the conflict between them, and the rules of the game (true prophecy and the correct understanding of the common Scriptures). Between Christians and "pagans," on the other hand, a *dialogue de sourds* was soon established. On both sides, it seems, there was a total lack of understanding of the nature of the other side's religion. Both Christians and "pagans" sought to understand one another in their own terms. From one of the most impressive intellectual testimonies to this conflict, Origen's *Contra Celsum*, at least (a text written around the mid-third century), it would appear that the main argument between them focused around the idea of civic religion, or of the relationship between state and religion.[34]

To the extent that it claimed to be the sole representative of true prophecy, Islam was similar to Christianity. But its success in transforming the community of the faithful (the *umma*) into imperial society, (a transformation probably due mainly to the fast pace of the Arab conquests) permitted the Muslims to set a relationship between state and religion that ever evaded the Christian rulers, East and West.

Notes

1. See G. G. Stroumsa 2009 and the original, French version of this book, Stroumsa 2005a.
2. Bellah 2011.
3. The following pages (until p. 16) seek to summarize, at the request of the editors of this volume, some of the salient points of *The End of Sacrifice*. There is no need to emphasize the necessarily schematic character of these pages. In order to allow for easy reference, I follow the chapters of the book in the four sections of this article. For a slightly different version of this article, see Misset and van der Weg (eds.) 2008: 29–46.
4. See for instance Marrou 1977. For Marrou, the new religiosity constituted the main originality of Late Antiquity. Dodds 1965, Lane Fox 1986, Brown 1987: 27 (a review of R. Lane Fox's book).
5. For a new analysis of Jaspers' thesis, see Eisenstadt (ed.) 1986.

6. Hadot, 2002: 19–74 and 313–19. Foucault 2001.
7. See for instance Momigliano's "Religion in Athens, Rome and Jerusalem in the First Century B.C.," in Momigliano (ed.) 1987: 74–91. On Momigliano as a historian of religion, see Stroumsa 2007: 286–211.
8. I have dealt with aspects of this revolution in Stroumsa 2003 in Finkelberg and Stroumsa ed. 2003: 153–173.
9. Smith 1993. See further Stroumsa 2008: 61–76.
10. For the most thorough study, see Sussmann 2005: 209–384.
11. See for instance Magdalino 1999: 83–113.
12. Developments in Stroumsa, 2005b: 79–91.
13. Augustine, *Enarrationes in Psalmos*, 56.9, PL vol. 36, col. 666.
14. Augustine, *Sermo* 5.5, PL vol. 38, col. 57.
15. See Bradbury ed. And trans. 1996.
16. For the text of the Novella, see Linder 1987: 402–11; See further Rutgers 2003.
17. See Stroumsa 2005b.
18. See Stroumsa 1999: 27–43.
19. Julian, Against the Galileans, fragment 72.
20. *Theodosian Codex* XVI.10.2. See Belayche 2001: 455–86.
21. Porphyry, *On Abstinence*, II. 26–27.
22. Iamblichus, *The Mysteries of Egypt*, V.15.
23. Babylonian Talmud, *Berachot* 8a.
24. *Berachot*, 17a.
25. *Berachot*, 32b.
26. Elior, 2004.
27. See Rives 1995: 65–85.
28. Elsner 1995: esp. ch. II, 157 and following.
29. See G. G. Stroumsa, 2004, and G. G. Stroumsa, 2001: 268–81.
30. Missing reference
31. J. Scheid, 1989. See further J. Scheid, 2001 [1985]: 119 and the following.
32. J. North, 1992: 174–93. G. Fowden, 1999: 82–106.
33. See Stroumsa 1999: 8–26.
34. Developments in Stroumsa 1999: 44–56.

References

Armstrong, Karen. 2007. *The Great Transformation: The Beginnings of Our Religious Traditions.* New York: Anchor.

Augustine, *Enarrationes in Psalmos*, 56.9, PL vol. 36, col. 666.

Augustine, *Sermo* 5.5, PL vol. 38, col. 57.

Babylonian Talmud, *Berachot* 8a.

Belayche, N. 2001. "Le sacrifice et la théorie du sacrifice pendant la 'réaction païenne': l'empereur Julien." *Revue de l'Histoire des Religions* 218: 455–486.

Bellah, Robert. 2011. *Religion in Human Evolution: From the Paleolithic to the Axial Age*. Cambridge, MA: Belknap Press. http://dx.doi.org/10.4159/harvard.9780674063099.

Bradbury, S. ed. nd trans. 1996. *Severus of Minorca, Letter on the Conversion of the Jews*. Oxford: Oxford University Press.

Brown, P. 1987. ""Brave Old World" (a review of R. Lane Fox's book)." *New York Review of Books* 12 (March): 27.

Dodds, E.R. 1965. *Pagan and Christian in an Age of Anxiety: Some Aspects of Religious Experience from Marcus Aurelius to Constantine*. Cambridge: Cambridge University Press. http://dx.doi.org/10.1017/CBO9780511583582.

Eisenstadt, S.N., ed. 1986. *The Origins and Diversity of Axial Age Civilizations*. Albany: State University of New York Press.

Elior, R. 2004. *The Three Temples: On the Emergence of Jewish Mysticism*. Oxford: Littman Library of Jewish Civilization.

Elsner, J. 1995. *Art and the Roman Viewer: the Transformation of Art from the Pagan World to Christianity*. Cambridge: Cambridge University Press.

Foucault, M. (2001) *L'herméneutique du sujet: cours au Collège de France 1981–1982.* Paris: Seuil/Gallimard.

Fowden, G. 1999. "Religious Communities." In *Late Antiquity: A Guide to the Postclassical World*, edited by G.W. Bowersock, P. Brown and O. Grabar, 82–106. Cambridge, MA: Harvard University Press.

Hadot, P. 2002. *Exercices spirituels et philosophie antique*. Paris: Albin Michel.

Iamblichus, *The Mysteries of Egypt*.

Jaspers, Karl. 1949. *Vom Ursprung und Ziel der Geschichte*. Zürich: Artemis-Verlag.

Julian, *Against the Galileans*.

Lane Fox, R. 1986. *Pagans and Christians*. New York: Viking.

Linder, A. 1987. *The Jews in Roman Imperial Legislation*. Detroit, MI: Wayne State University Press.

Magdalino, P. 1999. "'What we heard in the Lives of the saints we have seen with our own eyes': the Holy Man as literary text in tenth-century Constantinople." In *The Cult of Saints in Late Antiquity and the Middle Ages*, edited by J. Howard-Johnston and P.A. Hayward, 83-114. Oxford: Oxford University Press.

Marrou, H.-I. 1977. *Décadence romaine ou antiquité tardive? III* e *- IV* e *siècle*. Paris: Seuil.

Momigliano, A. 1987. "Religion in Athens, Rome and Jerusalem in the First Century B.C." In *On Pagans, Jews and Christians*. Middletown, CT: Weysleyan University Press.

North, J. 1992. "The Development of Religious Pluralism." In *The Jews among Pagans and Christians in the Roman Empire*, edited by J. Lieu, J. North and T. Rajak, 174–193. London: Routledge.

Porphyry, *On Abstinence*.

Rives, J. 1995. "Human Sacrifice among Pagans and Christians." *Journal of Roman Studies* 85: 65–85. http://dx.doi.org/10.1017/S0075435800074761.

Rutgers, L. (2003) "Justinian's Novella 146, between Jews and Christians." In *Jewish Culture and Society under the Christian Roman Empire*, edited by R. Kalmin and S. Schwartz, 385–407. Leuven: Peeters Publishers.

Scheid, J. (1989) "Religione and societa." In *Storia di Roma*, IV, edited by E. Gabba and A. Schiavone, 631–659. Turin: Einaudi.

Scheid, J. 2001 [1985]. *Religion et piété à Rome*. Paris: Albin Michel.

Smith, W. C. 1993. *What is Scripture? A Comparative Approach*. London: SCM Press.

Stroumsa, G. G. 1999. *Barbarian Philosophy: the Religious Revolution of Early Christianity*.Tübingen Mohr Siebeck.

Stroumsa, G.G. 2001. "John Spencer and the Rooks of Idolatry." *History of Religions* 41(1): 1–23. http://dx.doi.org/10.1086/463657.

Stroumsa, G. G. (2003) "Early Christianity: a Religion of the Book?" In *Homer, the Bible and Beyond: Literary and Religious Canons in the Ancient World*, edited by M. Finkelberg and G. G. Stroumsa, 153–173. Leiden: Brill.

Stroumsa, G. G. (2004) "Cultural Memory in Early Christianity: Clement of Alexandria and the History of Religions," In *Axial Civilizations and World History*, (Jerusalem Studies in Religion and Culture 4), edited by S. N. Eisenstadt, J. P. Arnason and B. Wittrock, 293–315. Leiden: Brill.

Stroumsa, G. G. 2005a. *La fin du sacrifice: Les mutations religieuses de l'Antiquité tardive*. Paris: Odile Jacob.

Stroumsa, G. G. 2005b. *Hidden Wisdom: Esoteric Traditions and the Roots of Christian Mysticism*. Leiden: Brill.

Stroumsa, G. G. 2009. *The End of Sacrifice: Religious Transformations in Late Antiquity*. Chicago, IL: Chicago University Press.

Stroumsa, G. G. 2007. "Arnaldo Momigliano and the History of Religions." In *Arnaldo Momigliano and the Antiquarianism: Foundations of the Modern Cultural Sciences*, edited by Peter N. Miller, 286-311. Toronto: University of Toronto Press.

Sussmann, Y. (2005) "Torah she-be-al-peh peshutah ke-mashma'ah." In *Mehkerei Talmud* 3, 209–384.

Theodosian Codex XVI.10.2.

About the author

Guy Stroumsa is Emeritus Fellowship at University of Oxford. Stroumsa was the first Professor of the Study of the Abrahamic Religions at Oxford University and Professorial Fellow at LMH from 2009 to 2013. Before that he was Martin Buber Professor of Comparative Religions at the Hebrew University of Jerusalem. Prof Stroumsa is a prolific writer with a wide range of expertise in the Abrahamic traditions and has also made important contributions to the Study of Religion in general as a human phenomenon. Among his recent publications we find Le rire du Christ et autres essais sur le christianisme antique 2006 and A New Science: *The Discovery of Religion in the Age of Reason* (2010).

7

The All as *logikē thusia*: The Egyptian Prehistory of a Hermetic Idea

Jørgen Podemann Sørensen

At the end of the Hermetic tractate *Asclepius,* the longest and most elaborate of the extant philosophical Hermetica, Thrice Great Hermes, his son Tat and his pupil Asclepius leave the temple in which their breathtaking dialogue on the *religio mentis* has taken place. The *Logos Teleios,* or "Perfect/Final Discourse" as its original Greek title was, has come to an end, and a philosophical or spiritual illumination has been reached. Almost as a paradox, it is only on leaving the sacred precinct that they engage in ritual activity: they begin to pray to God. Recitation has already started, when Asclepius whispers to Tat, suggesting that, with the consent of Hermes, they should say the prayer *ture addito et pigmentis,* "attended by incense and fragrance." But Hermes himself overhears the suggestion and informs them that to burn incense in this context is the equivalent of sacrilege. God, who is everything or in whom everything is, is in need of nothing, and the highest form of *incensiones* he can be offered are the praises of the mortals.[1]

The same consideration, that god or gods need no nutritional care or worship, is taken up by Sallustius, the *symmachus* of emperor Julian in the struggle for a pagan renaissance, in his delightful little treatise *Peri theōn kai kosmou.*[2] Sallustius is a defender of sacrifice, but wants his readers to understand that sacrifice is no mere feeding of the gods. Sacrifice and other acts of worship are there for the sake of men, he argues, for men need ways to commune with the divine.

If such religious scruples and reconsiderations somehow reflect or represent the end of sacrifice,[3] it is relevant to ask for those traditional,

Keywords: Bear festival, Maat, Hermetism, sacrificial speculation implicit or explicit ideas of sacrifice that had become obsolete or at least problematic. Or – that is a significant third possibility – forgotten. The Hermetic and Neoplatonic texts we have considered seem to take for granted that sacrifice used to be based on the rather naïve idea that gods were in need of certain supplies. In fact, evidence for such ideas could easily be compiled; Babylonian myths relate how mankind was created in order to provide for regular supplies, and several ancient Indian texts state that verily, sacrifice is the food of the gods. On the other hand it is well known from later religious polemics how easy it is to reduce *ad absurdum* any religious idea, and especially religious ideas reconstructed, as it were, from religious practice. New religious ideas are often introduced with the assertion that they should replace or supersede weaker ideas of the past, and the historian should, of course, consider all such assertions as tendentious and insist on examining the ideas of the past on his own.

The proper historical way of exploring traditional ideas of sacrifice (prior to the end or the crisis of sacrifice) is of course to examine each religious tradition specifically. Even the most specific investigation, however, needs a comparative preamble to establish the questionnaire. I shall therefore start by asking in the most general way for the logic of sacrifice in traditional religion, i.e., a set of ideas about sacrifice not yet affected by the processes of *Entmaterialisierung, Spiritualisierung, Sublimierung, Verinnerlichung, Ethisierung* etc. recited by A. Bertholet[4] as characteristic further developments of sacrifice.

Sacrifice is above all a sub-species of ritual. This implies that all general theories of ritual will also have a bearing on sacrifice. What is peculiar to sacrifice is that it employs some material, which is given away, eaten up, burnt or deposed. A theory of sacrifice should therefore above all consider this material and the process it undergoes. While Bertholet and many of his contemporaries, notwithstanding many precious observations, continued to speak of sacrifice and the role of the sacrificial material in terms of sympathetic magic and dynamism, Hubert and Mauss had already in 1898 published a general theory of sacrifice still unsurpassed.[5] Its level of abstraction and its general applicability makes it almost the exemplar of a modern theory in History of religions. Improvements, elaborations and intelligent reformulations[6] have been possible since 1898, but the basic idea still stands: The sacrificial material, made sacred in the manner and the terms of the relevant cultural context, becomes the turning point in an act of exchange and communion between the world of the participants and the other world of gods, ancestors etc., as well as among the participants themselves.

Let us try to elaborate an aspect of this theory by considering a few examples. The famous North Eurasian bear festival, known from Samiætnam in northern Scandinavia and Finland across Siberia and Kamchatka to the northern Japanese island Hokkaido, is well described among the Ainu of Hokkaido. A bear cub was caught and reared, often kept as a pet among the children. When it grew too old for the playground, it was kept in a solid wooden cage till the day of the bear festival or *Iomante*, "Sending back," when it was killed and thus returned to the realm of the bear-gods whence it came. When the men took it out of the cage, they used to address it in the following manner:

> O thou divine one, thou wast sent into the world for us to hunt. O thou precious little divinity, we worship thee; pray hear our prayer. We have nourished thee and brought thee up with a great deal of pain, all because we love thee so. Now, as thou hast grown big, we are about to send thee to thy father and mother. When thou comest to them please speak well of us, and tell them how kind we have been; please come to us again, and we will sacrifice thee.[7]

There is a myth about the Bear-god[8] who falls into the hands of human hunters, participates in their festival and is sent back to his abode in the land of gods, but the ritual text quoted does not refer to it as a primeval exemplar. Rather the festival enacts it as a contemporary sequence of events with the same narrative structure. It is important to note that the former playmate of Ainu children is twice appointed a divine being, and, dramatized as information for the young bear, there follows the postulates as to what will be accomplished in the ritual: The young bear will act as an ambassador of the Ainus among the gods, and the regular exchange between the world of the bear gods and the world of the Ainus will continue.

When the bear had been killed, a meal was cooked on its meat while the head and the skin was taken into a hut and arranged at the fireplace as a participant in the meal. The bear would thus be served with soup, boiled on itself, later supplemented by bundles of dried fish and cakes. The proper *Iomante* or "sending back" was eventually dramatized by moving the head and skin of the bear outside the structure to a more remote altar with exhortations to celebrate a heavenly festival. In this way, the Ainu continue feasting, along with a corresponding, imagined heavenly celebration among the bear-gods.

The bear festival is a very instructive illustration of Hubert and Mauss' theory of sacrifice: The sacrificial animal, the bear, represents the gods among the Ainu and the Ainu among the gods. Even to the point of absurdity, it is the sacrificial material given, the divine receiver of sacrifice, a participant in the ritual among the Ainus and later a participant in the imagined divine celebration. The bear is the turning point or universal condenser in which all the influences and imagined levels of the ritual meet and from which the future has its point of departure.

The Ainu ritual exhibits traditional, yet radical and profound thought about sacrifice. In certain respects it is even more instructive than the theory of Hubert and Mauss. My next example will astonish you less, for it is well known as the product of a highly specialized priesthood. The famous Vedic hymn of *Puruṣa* (RgV. 10, 90) is a late text, and if it was not for the Ainu example just cited, it might be argued that it no longer represent traditional ideas of sacrifice, but rather the result of one of Bertholet's sublimation processes. *Puruṣa* or primeval man is everything that is, has been and will be, and he is also the primeval, exemplar sacrifice, of which all later sacrifices are replicas. In him was the matrix or potential of the whole later world with all its classifications, biological, geographic, cosmic, social, ritual, and when he was sacrificed, all this unfolded itself and became the world we know. Like the Ainu bear, *Puruṣa* combines all the levels and stages of the sacrificial act: He is the sacrificial material, the ritual order of sacrifice, the ritual power and creative potential of the ritual texts and the result of sacrifice: the world, the gods, the rules governing life. The text insists on this universal role of *Puruṣa* even to the point of absurdity, for it concludes: "With the sacrifice the gods sacrificed to the sacrifice." (*Yajñéna yajñám ayajanta devás* – RgV 10, 90, 16). Such a wording could only be the work of a highly specialized priesthood, but behind it is the traditional idea of sacrifice as a universal condenser. Even if dispositions towards *Spiritualisierung* may have crept into the text, its whole logic would not be possible without that traditional idea.

The Christian eucharist or holy communion is not understood in quite the same way by different Christian churches, but there is hardly any doubt that the same traditional, sacrificial logic has influenced both the design and the understanding of the ritual. There is a widespread consensus that the meal somehow denotes the unity and perhaps the solidarity of the congregation or the church. Most churches identify the sacrificial material, bread and wine, as the body and blood of Christ. The body of Christ is, however, also the Church, of which the participants are members. The blood of Christ, on the other hand, associates the ritual with the death of Christ, which some churches think of as the sacrifice to end all sacrifices and the re-union of Christ, whose members the participants are, with his divine father. The sacrificial material is thus identified as Christ, who also denotes the congregation and the church, which performs the ritual, the redemptory events rehearsed in the ritual, and the re-union with God, which is the aim of the ritual. It may be difficult to make theological or Christological sense of this, but sacrificial sense can certainly be made. The sacrificial material is again the universal condenser, in which all levels and influences meet to produce the future.

The *Rituale parvum* of the Roman Catholic Church has a wonderful ultra-short version of the ritual for use outside the church: the communion is administered and addressed as follows:

> O sacrum convivium, in quo Christus sumitur, recolitur memoria passionis eius, mens impletur gratia et futurae gloriae nobis pignus datur.[9]
>
> (O holy common meal, in which Christ is consumed, the memory of his passion recultivated, the mind filled with grace, and a pledge of future glory given us.)

Past, present and future – together with a lot of soteriological issues – are united in this modest ritual. This became possible through the appointment of a sacrificial material as bearer of all these issues and their salvific potential.

We shall deal in a much more elaborate way with our next example, since it is also the background of a Hermetic *Spiritualisierung* and *Verinnerlichung* of sacrifice. We have seen till now, that texts that accompany sacrifice may appoint the sacrificial material to functions and stages in the imagined process performed. The sacrificial material may thus come to denote the means and the end, the giver and the receiver. In the case of the Vedic *Puruṣa* hymn, we have even seen in these functions – as the exemplar sacrificial material – a most universal primeval being denoting everything past, present and future. In the ancient Egyptian sacrifice of Maat, from the New Kingdom (1550–1070 BCE) and well into the first century CE a part of the *Daily Temple Liturgy*, we shall find similar universal claims made in the text that accompanied the rite. The sacrifice of Maat is often depicted in temple reliefs; the king is seen presenting the goddess Maat, sitting in a basket, to a god. Maat is a personification of Maat, the Egyptian concept of cosmic order, or rather the immanent cosmic principle that makes everything exist.[10] Like the *Puruṣa* hymn, the sacrifice of Maat is an expression of the general and central concern of worship and especially sacrifice: to make the world go round by reinvesting the cosmic principle. But while no certain context of ritual action has been shown for the *Puruṣa* hymn, the sacrifice of Maat was actually performed at least once every day, probably in all the major temples of Egypt, during a period of more than 1500 years. We do not know exactly how it was performed; statuettes of Maat have been found, and it is possible that the ritual consisted in the high priest handing over a small statue of the goddess to the god. Equally possible is the idea that the little goddess in the basket shown on the reliefs was there to make the point that the recitation of the ritual text, a long hymn, was a sacrifice.[11] In that case there would be a *logikē thusia,* a sacrifice in words, as early as about 1300 BCE. In order to understand the issue properly, a closer look at the context is necessary.

Since the Maat-sacrifice is an expression of the most central concerns of Egyptian temple ritual – and of royal ideology as well[12] – it is likely that temple reliefs with the king offering Maat often appear outside the proper ritual context of the rite. The one context in which we know that it was performed is the *Daily Temple Liturgy*. This elaborate ritual was performed, as far as can be judged from temple reliefs, in very much the same form in the sanctuaries of all major Egyptian temples from the New Kingdom and well into the Roman period every day. It was followed by the ritual of offerings, in which alimentary offerings were put on tables in the hall of offerings in front of the sanctuary. The text of the *Daily Liturgy* in the great temple of *Amun* at Karnak and a closely corresponding one for his divine consort *Mut* are preserved in two papyri from the 22nd dynasty, now in Berlin.[13] Earlier texts (without the chapter on offering Maat) are preserved, together with stylized pictures of most of the rites in the liturgy, in the temple of Seti I (1306–1290) at Abydos.[14] The following is a résumé of the liturgy as the ritual context of the sacrifice of Maat.

The sacrifice of Maat in the ancient Egyptian daily temple liturgy

Every morning, the high priest or his representative entered the primeval darkness of the sanctuary, struck fire, made ready for the fumigation of the god, burned incense and gradually approached the *naos*, in which the cult statue of the god was locked behind doors. For every single act, a chapter of the liturgy was recited. Thus, to unlock the *naos* involved three acts: cutting the ribbon, breaking the seal and withdrawing the bolt, accompanied by recitation of chapters 7–9. The most critical moment was the opening of the doors of the *naos* (chapter 10); it was an opening of the gates of heaven and earth, and in the immediately following chapters, the priest prostrated himself in front of the god, prayed for his own security in the dangerous encounter and asserted his respect and his legitimate and constructive intentions (chapters 11–17). These chapters serve to establish a liminal period in the ritual, a period in which everything has come down to zero and everything might happen; the priest might fall victim of some mythological battle (chapter 13), or he might change or destroy the god by manipulating with his statue (chapters 14–15).

From this liminal situation, indeed from zero or mythological scratch, the god may now begin to come to life anew. There are hints that the incense burned is the smell and the sweat of the god (chapters 35–36), i.e., that the god is becoming present in the statue, but most important in recreating the god were the hymns (chapter 37–42). The hymns wake up the god and invoke him in all his names and with all his epithets, as if building him up again. "Wake up in peace," is an often recurring phrase in these hymns, for according to chapter 24, the god is "in his rage" (*m nšnj.f*), i.e., still in his liminal, not yet stable condition. Another recurring phrase is "pharaoh has come to you" or, in chapter 42, "I have come to you." The situation is the crucial encounter between a god not yet completely stable in his creative and upholding capacity and a priest acting on behalf of the king, pharaoh, as representing all humanity.

The recreation of the god through the hymn, in an act of sacrificial reciprocity reminiscent of what we have seen in the Ainu bear festival and the *Puruṣasūkta*, is well expressed in some passages of chapter 37:

> Rise! Maat is your daughter; she puts her arms round you; your *ka* is in her.
> Your daughter has formed you, and you have formed your daughter.
> You have become the *ka* of every god.
> You have fostered it; you have given it life.
> You are the one who has created their *kas*.[15]

Maat, the goddess personifying cosmic order or rather the world with its immanent principle of order, is here said to embrace the god; she is his daughter, and his life (*ka*) is in her as it is in every god. The Egyptian creator god does not create beings and things different from himself. He rather reproduces himself into nature, pantheon and kosmos. His *ka* or vital principle is also the vital principle of all the gods, the formative principle in all their doings, and, by implication, the formative, ordering principle of the whole world. That principle is also called Maat, and although basically issued from the god – in the personal aspect as his daughter, in the cosmological aspect as the order he has created – Maat is also said to have formed the god. This makes a certain amount of sense when we consider that the god is ritually in the making; he is being recreated and made ready as creator and upholder of the world. As already suggested, there is, however, also an important reciprocity enacted in this hymn: Maat forms the god and he forms her. As cosmogony or theology this makes no sense. The sense it makes concerns exactly the ritual act of exchange, in which it is pronounced. It is in the ritual encounter, mediated by the hymn, that this exchange becomes possible.

This sacrificial reciprocity or mutual conditionality of Maat and the god is even more explicit in chapter 42, which is not only a hymn, but also the text that accompanies the presentation of Maat. As mentioned already, the ritual scene is well known from Egyptian temples from the New Kingdom to the Roman Period, and the Karnak Ritual for Amun preserves the full and very elaborate text that accompanied it in the daily liturgy. We shall probably never know with absolute certainty what was actually done during the recitation of the hymn that makes out chapter 42. Was a small statuette of the goddess presented to the god? or was the figure of Maat a symbolic expression of alimentary offerings?

Jan Assmann[16] has made a suggestion that goes alone and together with one or both the two other suggestions: The presentation of Maat denotes a sacrifice in words, i.e., a hymn. What is beyond doubt, however, is that the chapter *is* a hymn, and that, very much like chapter 37, it construes the ritual act as giving Maat to the god – or providing the god with Maat. In chapter 42, there are passages that explicitly understand Maat as praise:

> Maat has come in order to be together with you –
> Maat is now everywhere, where you are,
> that you may rely stably on her..
> It is the creatures in the circle of heaven,
> their arms praising you every day.[17]

As we sometimes find it in Jewish and Christian hymns, a heavenly choir joins in with praise when the ritual is enacted. This is in fact a standard feature of ancient Egyptian solar hymns; heavenly baboons, northern and southern divinities are often mentioned in the hymns as transmitters or mediators of the worship.[18] In the Egyptian daily temple liturgy, the ritual is also understood to provide the god with a basis. That basis is Maat, from which the god comes into existence and on which he lives.

Later in the same chapter, the idea that Maat is both ritual praise and at the same time all that the sun encircles, i.e., the whole world, is even more universally viewed as an aspect of the reciprocity or the mutual conditionality of Maat and the god

> When I lift up Maat to you, her arms are right in front of you,
> and your heart is glorious through her.
> When the ends of the world come to you with Maat,
> it is in order to give all that the sun encircles.
> Thoth shall offer up Maat to you –
> his hands are on her glory right in front of you.
> Your *ka* shall belong to you, when Maat praises you,
> your limbs being united with Maat,
> at whose sight you are pleased and rejuvenated.
> The heart of Amon-Re shall live!
> Maat has now appeared in front of him.
> Your daughter Maat is at the bow of the *Sekti*-boat –
> she is the one who belongs in your *naos.*
> When you exist, Maat exists – and *vice versa.*
> When Maat is united to your head,
> she comes into existence in front of you eternally ...[19]

In chapter 37, we noted that the *ka* or life of the god was in Maat, and that his possession of a *ka* was somehow also dependent on Maat. Since the *ka* of the creator god was said to be in every god, it was implied that his relation with Maat is at the very foundation of the god's creative and upholding activity. In the first of the lines just quoted, that relation is the encounter with praise, and the present rite of praise is sacramentally construed as the union of the god with Maat – as a daughter, a member of the crew in the solar boat, a *paredros* in the temple, and at last as the *Uraeus* in his forehead, the symbol of militant royal power that makes cosmic and social order come into existence in front of *Amon-Re*, the king of the gods, eternally.

This important and radical text has taken the full logical consequences of the way it understands the rite: it is about the very existence of the god and the ordered world. When the god exists, Maat exists, but the god is also dependent for his very existence on Maat. One could not want a more clear-cut and explicit expression of the mutual conditionality at the root of all existence. And the sacrificial exchange that makes the world go round takes place in rites of praise during the daily temple liturgy in all Egyptian temples.

The role of the sacrifice of Maat and the surrounding hymns in the daily temple liturgy is thus to make the god and, by implication, the world come into existence. The paradox in calling well established gods into existence was perfectly clear to the ancient authors. Chapter 38, a short, but beautiful hymn to the creator god, puts it in a very salient manner:

> May you come into existence, you lord of everything,
> Atum, who came into existence on the first occasion (i.e. in primeval time)![20]

The sacrifice of Maat with its hymns is thus an act of renewal and re-creation, but, as we have seen, also an encounter that unites creator and creation, worship and object of worship. The subsequent rites of the daily temple liturgy – rites of purification, unction, dressing – serve to establish the god thus recreated in the world. The hymns and the sacrifice of Maat remain the central part and the most decisive one. The long text of chapter 42, "The chapter on offering Maat" is the one that most explicitly applies sacrificial logic to the task carried out by the *Liturgy*. Maat is everything that is given to or done for the god. It is also the cosmic principle immanent in the world, an important creative potential in the god and finally the ordered world created and upheld by the god. At every level or stage of the creative and sacrificial process, Maat is at work as a cause or an energy and eventually as the result.

The philosophy of Maat

This semantic flexibility is characteristic of the concept of Maat. The word embraces a nexus of cause and effect very much like the word "life" in English: Life is both the power of life and the fact that somebody lives (or lived) – or the word may even denote what was accomplished during somebody's life. "Fate" is another word of this kind: both a power or a pattern that governs a life and the result of that government. In Greek, *charis* is both generosity and gratefulness, gift and return: *charis charin gar estin hē tiktous' aei.*[21] And like its Latin equivalent *natura,* Greek *physis* has two sets of meanings: conditioning and contingent, e.g. the nature of things vs. nature as the whole creation.[22] In Scholastic philosophy, the causal nexus embraced by the word was developed into the well-known dichotomy of *natura naturans* ('*idest ipsa summa lex naturae, quae Deus est*'[23]) and *natura naturata,* nature understood as the whole creation. The dichotomy remained important in mediaeval European philosophy and theology and was once more unfolded in the pantheist philosophy of B. de Spinoza. Spinoza's vision of one substance, the cause of itself, viewed *either* under the attribute of spirit *or* under the attribute of extension, was, in a certain sense, able to repatriate the idea of *naturans/naturata.* For the one substance, according to Spinoza, is also *deus sive natura,*[24] and viewed under the attribute of spirit it is the *natura naturans,* under the attribute of extension it is the *natura naturata.* This systematic exposition demonstrated that the causal nexus between *naturans* and *naturata* is not a matter of cause in the exclusive modern sense of an efficient cause, but rather in the Aristotelian sense of a formal cause.

I must apologize for this unbridled excursion into philosophical questions of a very different time. It may perhaps, however, help us to understand the ancient Egyptian concept of Maat. Maat is something, which gods (or men) possess, but also something which gods create and men do. At the same time, Maat is the universal cosmic order, in the sense of both *ordo ordinans* and *ordo ordinatus,* to use Fichte's terms. This semantic flexibility is intrinsic to the concept and makes it a most fitting expression of sacrificial logic. Not only is it able to denote both the substrate and the motive power of the sacrificial process, it is also a concept of that universal order of things which was the central concern of ancient Egyptian temple ritual.

That universal order of things, or Maat, was not seen as a static system, but as an ongoing world process, which temple ritual served to keep going, and to which the individual might also contribute. In the funerary literature, it was relevant to view this process as one of constant regeneration; the central aim of Pyramid Texts, Coffin Texts, The Book of the Dead and other religious texts buried with the dead was in fact to inscribe the deceased person in the regular, regenerative rhythm of nature. In a Coffin Text,[25] the deceased identifies himself as *Neper,* the corn-god, and even as the grain that is sown and must die in order to sprout as new emmer. In this process of regeneration, Maat again has several roles to play:

It is in dying that I live,
I am emmer.
I shall not perish,
for I have entered Maat,
having supported Maat.
I am a possessor of Maat,
for I have issued from Maat ... (CT IV, 169-170)

Maat is the continued existence, he has entered, and it seems that he has qualified himself for access by contributing to Maat; in this way he has accumulated Maat and may also be said to come from a background of Maat. So, once again, Maat is on all stages, as the substrate, the motive power and eventually the result of the process.

In a similar manner, a circulation of Maat may express a relation between man and god. In the tomb of Neferhotep from the 19th dynasty we find the following prayer:

O Re, who has born Maat,
and to whom Maat is sacrificed!
put Maat in my heart,
that I may make her ascend to your *ka*.
I know that you live on her.[26]

Neferhotep views his life in the light of creation and sacrifice and wants to contribute to the interaction of the divine, creative and upholding activity and man's ritual retaliation of it, which keeps the world going. For this purpose he will need Maat, which he will then in turn reinvest in the eternal circulation. That circulation of Maat is vital also for the god, but the text cannot be reduced to the idea that gods are in need of certain supplies. On the contrary, the text is a clue to the much broader idea of a universal circulation, a world process kept going by sacrifice and other ritual activities. That broader idea, which we have also seen in the text recited at the sacrifice of Maat, was, I believe, behind any talk of feeding the gods or of gods in need of supplies.

The philosophy of sacrifice

The more universal ideas expressed in the sacrifice of Maat and related texts did not in any way diminish the amount or frequency of alimentary offerings. It was a much later period that had difficulties with the idea of supplying gods with nourishment and *therapeia*. As we have seen, Sallustius tried to avoid the problem he also felt by taking the apologetic position that sacrifices were really meant for human subjectivity, as a mean term in an act of communion. In this way, sacrifice was still defendable, even recommendable, but in a process of *Spiritualisierung* and *Verinnerlichung.*

The Hermetic position, that ultimately, as an approach to God most high, sacrifice is sacrilege, is much more radical, but also, as we shall see, similar in its appeal to human subjectivity and spiritual life. The interdict of incense at the end of Asclepius is probably the most explicit dissociation from traditional ritual forms in the Hermetic literature, but it is certainly not the only one, and throughout the Corpus, praise is the only form of worship considered productive. It is in fact an important part of quite a number of tractates. Two of them (CH II and XVI) are close to a hymn in composition and phraseology, and other tractates seem to culminate in a hymn.[27] Sacrifice in the traditional sense is probably nowhere in Hermetic literature an option,[28] but never the less important as a metaphor. The variant version of *Asclepius* quoted by Lactantius (cf. note 2) is worth closer inspection: "huius enim sacrificium sola benedictio est" ("praise alone is a sacrifice to him").

The aim of this sentence is of course a negative one, the interdiction of traditional sacrifice in the context, but there is also a positive deduction to make from it: praise was regarded as a functional analogy or even equivalent of sacrifice. In a practical sense, the author of *Asclepius* may have been well beyond the end of sacrifice, but he still believed in sacrificial logic and thought that communion with the divine was possible in praise.

The one tractate that unfolds this sacrificial logic is CH XIII, which is also the best example of a tractate culminating in a hymn. The main theme of the tractate is *palingenesia* or rebirth, i.e., the spiritual breakthrough also called *gnosis.* The tractate is a dialogue between Hermes and his son Tat, who is now ready for the final teaching and the decisive spiritual breakthrough. Tat is rather perplexed to learn that the experience he is going to have is beyond the capacity of the senses and even the thought and the language of men. Ordinary minds, still including that of Tat, are blocked by 12 haunting powers of matter and darkness. These haunting and tormenting powers are vices like *agnoia,* "ignorance," lust, injustice, greed etc.; the human potential to overcome these obstacles to *gnosis* depends on 10 powers, among which are *gnosis, dikaiosynê* and *alêtheia.* The true rebirth or *palingenesia* consists in the 10 powers defeating the 12. Hermes now invokes the 10 powers; in this way he partly teaches and partly performs *palingenesia* on Tat. In fact, the text gradually changes from narrative (or semi-dramatic narrative, as a dialogue is) into performance.[29] This development culminates when Tat, as the crown of his *palingenesia,* wants to learn the secret hymn that Hermes told him that he heard in the eighth heaven. It is this hymn that is called *logikē thusia,*[30] and so is the small hymn which Tat later recites on his own (as well as the hymn in CH I, 31). At last Hermes even encourages Tat to offer up a suitable sacrifice, but insists that it should be "through the word" (*dia tou logou*). The hymn in CH XIII, §§17–20, which is said fully to illuminate the spirit of Tat, is definitely liturgical in style. It addresses first the whole nature of the world, and – reminiscent of the opening of the *naos* in the Egyptian daily temple liturgy (chapter 10) – it starts by opening earth and heavens. From a hymn addressing all nature, it then – elegantly, without further notice – turns into a hymn to the *creator* of all nature, who is also the eye of the *nous*. The union of nature and spirit, and perhaps also creation and *gnosis*, seems almost built into the divinity. Towards the middle part of the hymn, it invokes the 10 powers, which are in the worshipper:

> Powers within me, praise the One and the All!
> Sing along with my will, all powers within me!
> Holy *gnosis*,
> enlightened by you,
> praising the spiritual light (*noētos phōs*) through you,
> I rejoice in the joy (*chara*) of the spirit.
> All powers, praise with me!
> You too, modesty (*enkrateia*), praise for me!
> My righteousness (*dikaiosunē*), praise the righteous (*to dikaion*) through me!
> My generosity (*koinōnia*), praise the All through me!
> Truth (*alētheia*), praise truth (*alētheia*)!
> The good (*to agaton*), praise the good (*to agaton*)!
> Life (*zōē*) and light (*phōs*), from you praise shall go forth to you!
> I thank you, father, the strength of the powers,
> I thank you, God, the power of strength within me!
> Your *logos* praises you through me!
> Accept through me the All in *logos*, a *logikē thusia!*

The powers within Tat – or potentially any performer of this secret hymn: *gnosis, noētos phōs, chara, enkrateia, dikaiosynē, koinōnia, alētheia, to agaton, zōē, phōs* were (according to §§7–10) the powers that would defeat the evils that keep man imprisoned in the non-spiritual world of the senses. In the hymn, the 10 powers are invoked almost as a choir of angels to forward the praise to the ultimate object of worship, but they also denote the human potential of the adept. As the hymn goes on, however, they gradually grow to make up this ultimate object themselves, so that e.g. *alētheia* is urged to praise *alētheia.* The hymn thus enacts a union of man's inner potential and the universal, cosmic conditions to which he must respond. Towards the end of §18 it is betrayed that God is in charge of both the cosmic powers and the powers in man. It is also his word that praises him through the adept, who prays that God will accept the universe in words as a *logikē thusia.* The act carried out by the hymn takes place both within the divinity and within the adept. It is a sacrifice in which human, cosmic, and divine are united, and in almost Upanishadic terms, the following section (§19) speaks of *to pan to en hēmin,* "the All in us," and prays for its salvation and illumination. The manner in which the hymn is seen through the metaphor of a universalized sacrifice is remarkable:

> Thus do the powers within me shout,
> They praise the All, they fulfil your will,
> Your design, which issues from you and returns to you, is the All.[31]
> Accept from all a *logikē thusia*, the All in us –
> Save it, Life! Illuminate it, Light, Spirit, God!

These lines have all the reciprocity and circular logic of the ancient Egyptian sacrifice of Maat, the Ainu Bear Festival and the Vedic *Puruṣasukta.* The hymn is said to be sung by powers within the adept, worshipping the All. By praising the All they fulfil the will of the Father/God, for his design (*boulē*) is one that issues from him and returns to him, and it is also the All. This line of thought may be difficult to follow, but if we recall the ritual logic of the ancient Egyptian sacrifice of Maat, it becomes obvious that this is an act of exchange and union. As we have seen, Maat has the double sense of a creative potential in the god and an immanent order in the world, very much as the *natura naturans* and the *natura naturata* in scholastic philosophy. The sacrifice of Maat is, as we have also seen, an act of exchange in which the god is renewed in his creative and upholding potential by means of the Maat at the disposal of men. It is in sacrifice, and in ritual, that this union of the *natura naturans* and the *natura naturata* makes sense. Their regular union is what makes the world go round; the god forms Maat and she forms him; his *ka,* "life" is in her, and he receives it from her and reproduces it in every god. In the Egyptian text from the daily temple liturgy, Maat tends to be everything on all levels: she is the whole activity of the god, she is with him in the temple, she is everywhere in the world, and she is right here in the ritual act as the hymn (and perhaps as a small figure presented to the god). In this way, the ritual act of sacrifice is made the turning point of everything.

Our Hermetic hymn accomplishes a very similar feat; its performance comes to denote the union of a human microcosm with a divine macrocosm. In the text, "the All" (*to pan*) has very much the role of Maat. The important addition is that this time, it is also "the All in us" that the hymn brings as a *logikē thusia.* I have left this key term untranslated till now, because no single translation can do justice to the idea. "A sacrifice in words" would transmit the idea that a text, that of the hymn, is the most substantial entity consecrated, while "a spiritual sacrifice" would transmit another aspect of the meaning, namely that the sacrifice takes place in a spiritual, not a material sense. Both are relevant and quite to the point, but there is a third component they fail to express: the Stoic concept of *logos.* In the ancient world, the Egyptians were not quite alone in tending to think like Spinoza that there is *one* substance, the cause of itself. The Stoics were also monophysitic thinkers or monists, and their idea of *logos,* which they claimed to have inherited from Heraclitus, was one of an immanent order of nature or *natura naturans,* to use a later term. Without excluding the other two highly relevant meanings, that implication of *logikē* corresponds very much to ancient Egyptian Maat. Stoic *logos,* however, was also a human potential, an order in man, corresponding to the order in nature.[32] The Stoic ideal of *kata physin zēn* or *secundum naturam vivere* has a basis in the idea that a microcosmic structure or process in man corresponds to a macrocosmic structure or process in nature. The Hermetic *religio mentis* obviously shared this basic idea, for what happens when the 10 powers in man praise the 10 powers in the macrocosm, so that e.g. *alētheia* praises *alētheia,* is that this correspondence is enacted. Or, in the words of the hymn itself, that

> "Your *logos* praises you through me;
> Accept through me the All in *logos,* a *logikē thusia.*"

It is almost as if the god addressed and his worshipper are only there to unite *logos* with *logos* or Maat with Maat. Throughout the act of praise, the *logos,* intermittently *naturans* and *naturata,* denotes the human potential, the act itself and the divine order – which we must remember is a process.

What is enacted here is obviously sacrificial logic, adapted to the *religio mentis.* The very moment the *logikē thusia* is accomplished, the hymn turns into a prayer for salvation and illumination. The age-old, traditional logic of sacrifice has become a design for the *unio mystica.*

Conclusion

If the preceding exercises permit a conclusion, it is certainly not that sacrificial logic is a universal truth or a compulsory structure of the human mind that will survive no matter what developments take place around it. I hope to have argued, however, that sacrifice was also in traditional religions a matter of sophisticated thought. It was everywhere an important form of ritual, and even in a small scale society like that of the Ainu, the mere structure of the ritual bears witness to a consistent, abstract and radical thought. Wherever a specialized, educated priesthood had the leisure to philosophize about their doings, like in India or ancient Egypt, sacrificial logic was expressed and elaborated, often in radical terms, in ritual texts. This priestly thinking was often neglected by scholars. Because it was about ritual, it was termed "speculation," but it was as radical and as logically advanced as the celebrated early Greek philosophy. Its aim was, as we have seen in a few specimens, to build up a rhetoric of sacrifice to provide the ritual efficacy of rites and texts.

It was probably as rhetoric that the traditional pattern of thought we have termed "sacrificial logic" was able to survive in a context of "the end of sacrifice" in late antiquity. The novel *religio mentis* had to build up its own religious texts and develop new forms of literature adapted to its practice – like the *Lesemysterium* we have just considered – on the basis of existing patterns of thought and *genres* of text. The philosophy of Maat developed by "speculating" priests could thus – even in a situation of philosophical pluralism and debate – become a leading pattern of thought in a text designed to facilitate the spiritual breakthrough called *gnosis.*

Notes

1. *Ascl. 41,* cf. *CH* II: 352. Cf. Van den Kerchove 2012: 223. Lactantius, *div. int. 6.25.11,* offers a different version: Asclepius asks about *proferri tus et alios odores ad sacrificium dei* ('incense and other fragrances being forwarded as a sacrifice to God') and Hermes asserts that *huius enim sacrificium sola benedictio est* ("praise alone is a sacrifice to him").
2. Sallustius, *de diis et mundo,* Sallustius 1960: 15–16
3. Cf Stroumsa 2009 (French edition 2005, the seminal essay on the general issue) and Petropoulou 2008, who compares Greek, Jewish and Christian ideas of sacrifice. In his contribution to this volume, Christian Bull demonstrates that hermetists did not in general consider traditional sacrifice illegitimate – except, probably, in the very context of a spiritual approach to God most high.
4. Bertholet 1942: 26.
5. Hubert and Mauss 1898: 29–138.
6. cf. notably Leach 1979: 81–93: "The Logic of Sacrifice."
7. Batchelor 1927: 206–11
8. Philippi, 1971: 115–125.
9. *Rituale parvum* 1927: 35–36
10. On this important rite, cf. Frandsen: 1987: 95-108;Teeter 1997; Assmann 1990: 174-200
11. A similar idea, likewise rooted in traditional religion, is found in classical India, where the *Taitiriya Sanhita* (ii.2,7.1–3 – Keith 1914: I, 154)) insists that "the hymn is the food of the gods."
12. Assmann 1989 remains, I believe, the most precise description of the logic of Maat as the key idea in royal ideology.

13. P. Berlin 3055 (The ritual for Amun) and P. Berlin 3014+3053 (The ritual for Mut); French translation in Moret 1902; German translations of the hymns discussed on the following pages in Assmann 1999: 268–281
14. Gardiner 1933–35; German tr. in Roeder 1960: 85–141
15. P. Berlin 3055, 14, 11 – 15, 2
16. Assmann 1969: 154–157
17. P. Berlin 3055, 20, 9 – 21.
18. Cf. Assmann 1969: 207–214; 322–324; Podemann Sørensen 1996: 260–266; Podemann Sørensen 1989: 48–52
19. P. Berlin 3055, 22, 6 - 23, 6.
20. P. Berlin 3055, 16, 9
21. Sophocles, *Ajax* 522; cf. Liddell and Scott 1973: 1978 f.
22. Cf. Liddell and Scott 1973: 1964.
23. Vicentius Bellovacensis 1965 [1372]: IX, 4
24. *Ethica* IV, Praefatio
25. CT IV 169–170.
26. Davies and Davies 1933: I, pl. 17.
27. Cf. Podemann Sørensen 2012: 465–486.
28. Cf. the discussion in Van den Kerchove 2012: 223–234
29. R. Reitzenstein 1927: 52, cf. 64, considered the XIIIth tractate a *Lesemysterium,* i.e. a text performing a ritual like the initiations of the mystery cults on its reader. On the idea of *Lesemysterium,* cf. also Thomassen 2002 and Södergård 2003: 112–120.
30. On the term and the idea of *logikê thusia,* cf. Van den Kerchove 2012: 233, note 36; 281.
31. I take this as a nominal sentence with *to pan* as the predicative: "Your design, from you and to you, (is) the All." For other possibilities, cf. Copenhaver 2000: 194
32. Christensen 1962: 64–73.

Abbreviations

CH:	*Corpus Hermeticum* I-IV, edited by A. D. Nock and A. J. Festugière, Les Belles Lettres 1972.
CT:	*The Egyptian Coffin Texts,* I-VII, edited by A. de Buck,The University of Chicago Press 1935–1961. Translation in Faulkner 1973–1978

P. Berlin 3055:	*Hieratische Papyrus aus den Königlichen Museen zu Berlin,* Erster Band, Leipzig 1901. Transcription and French translation in Moret 1902
Pyr.:	Sethe, Kurt, *Die altägyptischen Pyramidentexte* I-II, Leipzig 1908–1910. English translation in Faulkner 1969
RgV:	*Rigveda*

References

Assmann, Jan. 1969. *Liturgische Lieder an den Sonnengott* (Münchener ägyptologische Studien 19). Berlin: Verlag Bruno Hessling.

Assmann, Jan. 1989. *Maât: l'Égypte pharaonique et l'idée de justice sociale.* Paris: Julliard.

Assmann, Jan. 1990. *Maat: Gerechtigkeit und Unsterblichkeit im alten Ägypten.* Munich: C.H. Beck.

Assmann, Jan. 1999. *Ägyptische Hymnen und Gebete.* Freiburg, Switzerland: Universitätsverlag.

Batchelor, John. 1927. *Ainu Life and Lore.* Tokyo: Kyobunkwan.

Bertholet, Alfred. 1942. *Der Sinn des kultischen Opfers,* (Abhandlungen der Preussischen Akademie der Wissenschaften 1942, Nr. 2). Berlin: Verlag der Akademie der Wissenschaften.

Christensen, Johnny. 1962. *An Essay on the Unity of Stoic Philosophy.* Copenhagen: Munksgaard.

Copenhaver, Brian P. 2000. *Hermetica. The Greek Corpus Hermeticum and the Latin Asclepius in a New English Translation with Notes and introduction.* Cambridge: Cambridge University Press.

Davies, Norman de Garis and Nina M. Davies. 1933. *The Tomb of Neferhotep at Thebes.* New York: Metropolitan Museum of Art.

Faulkner, Raymond O. 1969. *The Ancient Egyptian Pyramid Texts.* Oxford: Clarendon Press.

Frandsen, P. J. 1987. "Trade and Cult." In *The Religion of the Ancient Egyptians. Cognitive Structures and Popular Expressions,* Acta Universitatis Upsaliensis, Boreas 20, edited by Gertie Englund, 95–108. Uppsala: Almqvist & Wiksell International.

Gardiner, A. H., ed. 1933–35. *The Temple of King Sethos I at Abydos, copied by Amice M. Calverley, I-II.* Chicago, IL: The Oriental Institute of the University of Chicago.

Hubert, H., and M. Mauss. 1898. "Essay sur la nature et la fonction du sacrifice." *Année sociologique* 1898, Paris, 29–138. - Repr. in H. Hubert and M. Mauss, *Melanges d'histoire des religions.* Paris 1909, pp. 1–130. English transl. *Sac-*

rifice. Its Nature and Functions. Chicago, IL: University of Chicago Press, Midway Reprint 1981.

Keith, Arthur B. 1914. *The Veda of the Black Yajus School entitled Taittiriya Sanhita* I–II (Harvard Oriental Series 18–19). Cambridge, MA: Harvard University Press.

Leach, Edmund. 1979. *Culture and Communication.* Cambridge, MA: Cambridge University Press.

Liddell, Henry George and Robert Scott. 1973. *A Greek-English Lexicon.* Oxford: Clarendon Press.

Moret, Alexandre 1902. *Le rituel du culte divin journalier en Egypte* (Annales du Musée Guimet Bibliothèque d'étude 14), Paris 1902, repr. Slatkine Reprints 2007.

Petropoulou, Maria-Zoe. 2008. *Animal Sacrifice in Ancient Greek Religion, Judaism, and Christianity, 100 BC to AD 200.* Oxford: Oxford University Press. http://dx.doi.org/10.1093/acprof:oso/9780199218547.001.0001.

Philippi, Donald. 1971. *Songs of Gods, Songs of Humans.* Tokyo: University of Tokyo Press.

Podemann Sørensen, J. 1989. "Ancient Egyptian Religious Thought and the XVIth Hermetic Tractate." In *The Religion of the Ancient egyptians. Cognitive strucures and popular expressions.* Acta Universitatis Upsaliensis, Boreas 20, edited by Gertie Englund, 48–52. Uppsala: Almqvist & Wiksell International.

Podemann Sørensen, J. 1996. "Ritual Art: A Key to the Ancient Egyptian Book of the Dead." In *Dance, Music, Art, and Religion,* Scripta Instituti Donneriani Aboensis XVI, edited by Tore Ahlbäck, 260–266. Åbo, Finland: Donner Institute.

Podemann Sørensen, J. 2012. "The Secret Hymn in Hermetic Texts." In *Mystery and Secrecy in the Nag Hammadi Collection and Other Ancient Literature: Ideas and Practices. Studies for Einar Thomassen at Sixty,* edited by Christian H. Bull, Liv Ingeborg Lied and John D. Turner, 465-486. Leiden: Brill.

Reitzenstein, Richard. 1927. *Die hellenistschen Mysterienreligionen.* Leipzig: Teubner.

Catholic Church. 1927. *Rituale parvum.* Rome: Typis polyglottis Vaticanis

Roeder, Günther. 1960. *Kulte, Orakel und Naturverehrung im alten Ägypten,* Die ägyptische Religion in Texten und Bildern III. Zürich: Artemis.

Sallustius (1960) *Des dieux et du monde.* Edited and translated by G. Rochefort. Paris: Société d'édition "Les Belles lettres", Les Belles Lettres.

Stroumsa, Guy G. 2009. *The End of sacrifice. Religious Transformations in Late Antiquity.* Chicago, IL: University of Chicago Press.

Södergård, J. P. 2003. *The Hermetic Piety of the Mind,* Coniectanea Biblica. New Testament Series 41. Uppsala: Almqvist & Wiksell International.

Teeter, Emily. 1997. *The PresenTation of Maat*. Chicago, IL: Chicago University Press.

Thomassen, Einar. 2002. "Revelation as Book and Book as Revelation." In *The Nag Hammadi Texts in the History of Religion*, Historisk-filosofiske Skrifter 26, edited by S. Giversen, T. Petersen and J. Podemann Sørensen, 35-45. Copenhagen: The Royal Danish Academy of Sciences and Letters.

Van den Kerchove, Anna. 2012. *La Voie d'Hermès: Pratiques rituelles et traités hermetiques*. Leiden: Brill. http://dx.doi.org/10.1163/9789004223653.

Vicentius Bellovacensis (Vincent de Beauvais). 1372 1965. *Speculum doctrinale* IX, 4. Graz: Akademische Druck- u. Verlagsanstalt.

About the author

Jørgen Podemann Sørensen is Associate professor in history of religions, University of Copenhagen, Deparrtment of Cross-cultural and Regional Studies. Podemann-Sørensen was educated as a historian of religions specialized in ancient Egyptian religion at the Universities of Aarhus and Copenhagen (promoted 1979). His primary fields of interest are the religions of Antiquity, especially ancient Egyptian religion and its contribution to the Gnostic and Hermetic currents of Late Antiquity and the comparative study of ritual. He has recently (2013) published a handbook on ancient Egyptian religious literature (with sample translations) and a book on the comparative study of ritual, both in Danish.

8

No End to Sacrifice in Hermetism

Christian H. Bull

Sacrifice was undoubtedly a key institution in the religious framework of the Greco-Roman world. Even if one does not agree with the inordinate importance which has been ascribed to ritual violence and killing in the evolution of human culture by some,[1] it remains a fact that the Greeks and Romans considered the process of consecrating, killing, butchering, and burning animals as the preeminent means to worship and appease their gods.[2] A telling indication of this is the need for suspected Christians to obtain receipts that they had performed libations and sacrifice to the statues of the Emperor during times of persecution. When the Emperors then, from Constantine onwards, gradually outlawed sacrificial cult through a series of regulations,[3] the impact on traditional religiosity throughout the Mediterranean was naturally momentous.

In his *La fin de sacrifice*, recently translated to English, Guy G. Stroumsa posits this ritual transformation as one of the most important ones for the overall transformation of religious structures in Late Antiquity.[4] While actual sacrifice ceased to play a part in the Christian Empire, the language of sacrifice still played a crucial part in the rhetoric concerning the crucifixion of Christ, as well as the deaths of martyrs.[5] The sacrifice of Christ obviated all further need of sacrifice. Stroumsa, as well as others before him, refers to this as a "spiritualization," defined by him as "the shift to a ritual without priests and without blood sacrifices,"[6] which he traces back to the fall of the Jewish temple in Jerusalem in 70 CE, and the subsequent end of Jewish sacrifice. Further predecessors have been found in Greek philosophers critical to animal sacrifice, such

Keywords: Corpus Hermeticum, material sacrifice, Hermetic practice, ancient Egyptian sacrifice as Heraclitus, Theophrastus and later Porphyry.[7] Stroumsa refers to the emphasis in Late Antiquity on *saying* prayers rather than *doing* sacrifices as a modernization, characterized by interiorization and privatization of worship.[8] There is a degree of scholarly prejudice at work here, inherited in part from Christian anti-pagan polemics, that ritual action – and in particular bloody sacrifice – is necessarily inferior to and incompatible with "spirituality." But so long as humans continue to eat meat, there is no a priori reason why public sacrifice should be more barbarous than slaughter in the back of butcher-shops.

An interesting test-case for the supposed polarity between "spirituality" and traditional sacrifice is furnished by Hermetism. The Hermetic treatises purport to have been written in primordial Egypt by the god, or divine sage, Hermes Trismegistus, "the thrice-greatest Hermes."[9] This epithet was assumed by Hermes from his Egyptian counterpart, Thoth, the divine scribe and patron of wisdom and magic. However, the texts are now commonly assumed to have been written in the course of the first three centuries CE, as they were originally written in Greek and contain a mixture of Platonic and Stoic doctrines common in this period. Their real authors are unknown, although the Neoplatonic philosopher Iamblichus claimed that they were written by Egyptian priests well-versed in Greek philosophy (*Myst.* 8.1). Hermetic literature has often been claimed to represent a spiritualization of pagan cult, since Hermes recommends to his son and pupil, Tat, to offer up to the creator-god a *logikē thusia*, translatable as a "rational," "spiritual," or simply "spoken" sacrifice.[10] This expression has parallels in the New Testament, where it is implicitly contrasted with the material sacrifices of the pagans.[11]

Recent scholarship on Hermetism has largely abandoned the formerly dominant view, championed by André-Jean Festugière,[12] that Hermetism was merely a literary phenomenon of philosophical platitudes, which because of its internal disagreements could have no cultic dimension. Impelled by the discovery of Hermetic texts among the Coptic Nag Hammadi codices, mainly Jean-Pierre Mahé (1978–1982, 1991) and Garth Fowden (1986) have ushered in a new consensus that there in all likelihood *did* exist a Hermetic community – though the precise nature of such a community is still debated – and that internal disagreements are largely due to different stages of a spiritual *paideia*.[13] The progression of the Way of Hermes outlined by Mahé and Fowden is one that goes from a world-affirming to a world-denying outlook, where the disciple increasingly withdraws into himself. Concurrently with this, Fowden claims that traditional cult plays a role at the initial stages only, and is to be surpassed at a more spiritually advanced level.[14] Such a stance could be described as "spiritualization" as it is defined by Stroumsa.

In this paper, however, I will aim to show that the overall view on traditional cult, including sacrifice, is positive in the Hermetic texts, and that the reason sacrifice is transformed or downplayed on the more advanced levels has more to do with ontological stratification than any hostility to external *dromena*. This would imply that the drift towards spiritualization is not necessarily the opposite pole of a continued concern with traditional sacrificial cult. In that case, we will need another definition of the "spiritual," which does not place it in opposition to traditional cult. Pierre Hadot, in his *Exercices spirituels et philosophie antique*, employed the term as denoting "not only thought, but the entire psychological makeup of the individual,"[15] and described its corresponding exercises as entailing "a transformation of the worldview and a metamorphosis of the personality."[16] This is certainly in line with the goal of the upper reaches of the Way of Hermes, where the disciple must be divinized in order to comprehend the divine (CH XI, 20). Now, out of the extant Hermetic corpus, there are only two texts which contain explicit references to traditional sacrifice, namely the *Perfect Discourse* and the *Korē Kosmou* (SH XXIII). These are the texts generally admitted to contain the most mythic and cultic information, and are therefore by some considered to be extraneous to Hermetic spirituality.[17] The contrast is certainly marked between these texts and the *Corpus Hermeticum*, especially the first 14 treatises which in some manuscript traditions were transmitted without the last three treatises (CH XVI–XVIII), containing references to traditional Egyptian cult.[18] This strengthens the suspicion that the anthology might have been submitted to Christian censorship at some point during its transmission prior to Michael Psellus in the eleventh century.

We should make a methodological note that recent scholarship on sacrifice has pointed out the need to differentiate between the discourse and practice of sacrifice.[19] Our sources naturally favour the former, and we should be aware that discourses critical to the institutions of sacrifice do not necessarily imply a decline of such practices. Our Hermetic texts naturally reflect the concerns of a literate elite, albeit one of "moyenne culture,"[20] and their view of sacrifice was not necessarily the same as the great majority of people in Late Antiquity.

In addition to showing that the Hermetic discourse of sacrifice presupposes a functioning Egyptian temple-cult, I will in the second part of the paper attempt to show that sacrifice also plays an important role in the claim of Egyptian wisdom to be of primordial age. The institution of sacrifices to the gods is represented as foundational for Egyptian civilization and philosophy, which competed with other "barbarian" cultures to be seen as the most ancient, and therefore also most wise, pious, and divine. As we shall see, this preoccupation with primordial wisdom was a general feature of Post-Hellenistic Philosophy, as has been demonstrated by G. R. Boys-Stones.[21]

Traditional sacrifice in the *Perfect Discourse* and *Korē Kosmou*

The so-called earthly gods of traditional cult are discussed in two passages of the *Perfect Discourse*, a treatise only preserved in a Latin translation called the *Asclepius*, two Coptic fragments from the Nag Hammadi Library, and some Greek testimonies. The first passage we will consider, preserved in Latin and Coptic, states that although statues are indeed made by men – a point of contention in the polemics of idolatry – they are still worthy of worship: just as man is made in god's image, the earthly gods are made in man's image, and thus ensure the divine presence on earth.[22] Indeed, the disasters predicted subsequently, in the famous so-called apocalypse,[23] come as a direct consequence of the gods withdrawing from Egypt. The reason for their departure is the decline of proper worship at the temples. This is worth a little excursus: The Latin expression *religio mentis*, "reverence of mind," which is the form of worship Hermes predicts will be extinguished, is often used to describe Hermetism *in toto*.[24] The passage says: "But, believe you me, a mortal danger will be brought about for the one who dedicates himself to reverence of mind."[25] Unfortunately, the expression is not found in the Coptic parallel, where it only says that "those of this kind" will be in mortal danger, probably referring to the god-fearing Egyptians mentioned earlier.[26] Since the Coptic text is closer to the Greek original, *religio mentis* is most likely simply the Latin translator's embellishment of *eusebeia* – piousness.[27] A. S. Ferguson suspected as much even before the discovery of our Coptic parallel, suggesting *tēs psuchēs eusebeia* – "reverence of the soul."[28] In *Ascl.* 38 we are told that earthly gods consist of a material element – the physical statue – which is imbued with a demon or angel representing the divine element. Now, in the anthropology espoused elsewhere in the text, the ones who attach themselves to the worship of demons achieve a demonic nature, and constitute the second-best class of people after those who attach themselves to the immaterial god (*Ascl.* 5). Thus, those who will be in mortal danger in the eschatology are reverent people, and while the Hermetists certainly saw themselves as the prime representatives of this kind of people, we must also include all those who were devoted to the gods of the traditional Egyptian temples, which is what the passage is about. Elsewhere (SH II B, 2), Hermes states that his philosophy constitutes the peak of reverence, which indicates that a substratum of reverent people who do not practice philosophy is recognized.

In *Ascl.* 37–8 we are told that the discovery of divine nature (*diuina natura*), and the manner in which to bring it down to earth, came after a period of "grave error regarding divine cult and worship" (*cultus religioque diuina*) on the part of the ancestors of Hermes and his disciples.[29] Thus, the art of fabricating images of the gods marks mankind's departure from primal savagery, a theme we shall see developed further in the *Korē Kosmou*. Although these gods take part in matter, they are not devoid of the heavenly element. Hermes tells us the following about the quality of the earthly gods:

> It comes from a mixture of plants, stones and spices, Asclepius, that have in them a natural power of divinity. And this is why those gods are entertained with constant sacrifices (*sacrificiis frequentibus oblectantur*), with hymns, praises and sweet sound in tune with heaven's harmony: so that the heavenly ingredient enticed into the idol by constant communication with heaven may gladly endure its long stay among humankind. Thus does man fashion his gods. (*Ascl.* 38)

It should be noted that this evokes the practices of Egyptian temples rather than Greco-Roman ones, where cult was generally not rendered on a daily basis. Although meat was part of the regular diet of Egyptian gods, ritual killing and slaughtering did not play the central role it did in Greco-Roman cult, mostly taking place in abattoirs adjacent to the temples rather than by the altar.[30] The type of sacrifice is not further specified, but *sacrificium* no doubt renders Greek *thusia*, which most often is used for the consecration, killing, butchering and burning of animals, though it can also refer to other kinds of offerings. The mention of plants, stones and spices could lead one to think of bloodless sacrifices, but these ingredients refer to the nature (*qualitas*) of the earthly god, i.e., the cult statue, not the sacrifice. As the so-called Memphite theology states: "So have the gods entered their bodies – of every kind of wood, every kind of stone, and every kind of frit, everything that grows all over him, in which they have developed. So were gathered to him all the gods and their *ka*s as well, content and combined in the lord of the two lands."[31] These ingredients thus contain a "natural power of divinity," i.e., a sympathetic link with the god meant to inhabit the statue, and it is through sacrifice, hymns and music that the god is induced into its earthly abode and thereupon persuaded to stay. In Egypt the activation of a cult statue was performed by means of an "Opening of the mouth" ritual, where the heart and foreleg of a slaughtered bull was presented to the statue.[32] Thereupon the god was appeased by the daily temple ritual, where meat was burned for it as part of its meal.[33] The animal killed was often conceived of as an enemy of the sun-god Re, giving the slaughter an apotropaic dimension,[34] while the offering represented the Eye of Horus or the goddess Maat, symbolizing the preservation of life and cosmic order.[35] In the end, we cannot be certain if *sacrificium* here refers to animal offerings or not, but can only conclude that such offerings were included in traditional Egyptian temple-cult, which is the type of cult evoked. The important distinction for the Hermetist, however, is between material and immaterial offerings, not bloody and bloodless.

Like humankind earthly gods are part matter, part divine (*Ascl.* 23). In tune with the Hermetic chain of being, in which what is below is like what is above (SH XXIII, 68), the angels or demons entering the statues are representatives or emissaries of the heavenly gods. The hierarchy of being amongst the gods is further explained in CH XVI, 10–18, where the troops of demons are described as overseers of mankind. However, they are not only capable of great benefactions, but can also cause great harm when they're upset (CH XVI, 14; *Ascl.* 24 and 37). They are also the enforcers of fate, and they control all unenlightened people and are adored by them, whereas those who have been enlightened by god are liberated from them (CH XVI, 16). Demons and angels thus represent fate for most people, for good or bad, while the few who are enlightened stand above fate. There is no eschatological notion that the works of fate will someday be dissolved. As Hermes says: "These three, then – Fate, Necessity and Order – are in the very fullest sense the products of god's assent, who governs the world by his own law and divine plan" (*Ascl.* 40). The earthly gods are capable of benefactions, like healing and divination, but also of inflicting calamities such as plague (*Ascl.* 24). "Anger comes easily to earthly and material gods," (*Ascl.* 37) and this implies that they can and must be affected by prayer and sacrifice.[36]

The divine element of earthly gods are thus effluences, or emissaries, of the heavenly gods above, and must be assuaged by sacrifice, hymns and music, in order for them to feel at home during their stay on earth. Sacrifice should therefore be considered an art (*ars*), in company with the arts of hymn-singing and music. These latter are elsewhere described as being sent down by god under the patronage of the choir of Muses, so that earth should not seem devoid of the heavenly harmony (*Ascl.* 9). The arts are in other words gifts from god, or the gods. This is consistent with the role of sacrifice in the *Korē Kosmou* (SH XXIII).

Korē Kosmou is the longest of the Hermetic fragments preserved in the anthology of John of Stobi (5th c. CE), and the title can be variously translated the "maiden of the world" or "pupil of the eye of the world." It is one of five treatises given by Isis to her son Horus, and they are counted as Hermetic because Isis quotes Hermes extensively, and refers to him as her teacher. Here, the "accurate sacrificers" (*akribeis thutai*) are listed as one of the best kinds of rebirth for just souls,[37] along with "righteous kings, genuine philosophers, founders, lawgivers, true diviners, legitimate herbalists, the best prophets of the gods, skilful musicians, and mindful augurs" (SH XXIII, 42). The list implies that sacrifice is a beneficent art on the same level as kingship, philosophy, music, etc. The sacrifice is thus conceived of as a civilizing force, a gift from the gods, and is also counted as such in the aretalogy of Isis and Osiris given towards the end of the treatise:

> It is they who have filled life with life; it is they who have put an end to savage mutual slaughter; it is they who have consecrated enclosures and sacrifices to the ancestral gods (*temenē progonois theois houtoi kai thusias kathierōsan*); it is they who have given laws, nourishment and protection to mortals. (SH XXIII, 65)

The type of sacrifice is not indicated further than that it is performed at the enclosures of the ancestral gods. These are not necessarily human ancestors, since it is Isis who is talking. Heaven is said to be the ancestor (*progonos*) of the souls in §36, while the god Kamephis is said to be the predecessor (*progenesteros*) of all in §32. *Progonos* can be used for gods as founders of a race, as Zeus of the Scythians (Herodotus 4.32), or authors of a craft, as Asclepius of medicine (Plato, *Symp.* 186e). It is thus likely that the ancestral gods are the gods who dwelled in Egypt before mankind and then ascended to the stars, namely Hermes and his kindred gods (*suggeneis theoi*), such as Ptah-Hephaestus (§6). It seems that the institution of sacrifices and temple-enclosures should be seen in connection with the end to "savage mutual slaughter." We may therefore consider Isis and Osiris to be involved in leading mankind out of "grave error concerning divinity," as described in *Ascl.* 37. Here, Isis and Osiris are also described as among the greatest of the earthly gods, along with the namesake ancestors of Hermes and Asclepius.[38] Furthermore, Osiris is almost certainly to be identified with the "great emanation of god" (SH XXIII, 62), put on earth as a judge over mankind to keep them in line and avenge wrongdoings. God granted this emanation in response to a complaint from the elements, that the first generations of mankind were maltreating them. The complaint given by fire is particularly instructive with regards to sacrifice:

> Let those who are shown benefactions learn to give thanks (*eucharistēsai*), so that I, fire, may joyfully serve during libations and sacrifices and send forth fragrant fumes from the sacrificial hearth to you (*hina chairon para loibais para thusiais hupēretēsō to pur, hin euōdeis atmous ap' escharas propempsō soi*). For until now I am being polluted, O Master, and I am forced to consume flesh by the godless audacity of the humans you have created, and they don't permit me to keep to what I was born to do, but debase the incorruptible in an unfitting way (SH XXIII, 56).

This refers to the time of primal savagery, when mankind had not yet discovered divinity, and the earthly cosmos had not yet been "filled with god" (SH XXIII, 60). But how exactly is fire being maltreated, and what is the correct way it wishes to be used? The editors of the text suggested removing the reference to sacrifices (*para thusiais*), which they saw as an unnecessary doublet to the mention of libations (*para loibais*). If so, then fire should only be used during libations,[39] for burning incense and spices.[40] However, the above-mentioned passages (§§42 and 65), extolling the sacrifice and sacrificers, make this an unlikely hypothesis. The blood sacrifice involved burning, of both incense and animal products, so it makes perfect sense to say that fire should serve both at libations *and* sacrifices.[41] Furthermore, we have parallels in the Ptolemaic trilingual decrees of Canopus and Memphis, where Greek *suntelein thusias kai spondas* is rendered with the Egyptian words for whole-burnt offerings and libations.[42] An alternate suggestion by Festugière is that the flesh being consumed godlessly is human flesh, which would mean that the immolation of animal flesh might still be acceptable. This is an attractive hypothesis, since one of the main atrocities committed by early ignorant mankind is described in §53 as killing and burning each other, and then throwing the corpses into the inner shrines of temples, which might imply human sacrifice.[43] The mytheme of rampant cannibalism and human sacrifice in pre-civilized times was common in antiquity, and the critics of the institution of sacrifice were quick to point out its unwholesome antecedents in human sacrifice.[44]

Much again depends on what we make of the word *eschara*, here translated as sacrificial hearth. Again, one could construe this merely as censer, i.e., for incense, as seems to be the case in Plutarch's *On Isis and Osiris* (355a). The word is sometimes basically synonymous to the common *bōmos*-altar, but can also denote the hole often made in altars for burning. *Eschara* can even represent the altar proper, while the *bōmos* was the surrounding structure.[45] Porphyry makes a distinction between several kinds of altars; *bōmos* for the Olympians, *eschara* for chthonian gods and heroes, and finally pits, *bothros* and *megara*, for those of the underworld.[46] At any rate, the *eschara* are universally connected with burnt offerings. A tempting solution here would be to interpret *eschara* as the horned altar, originally from the Syro-Palestine area, but common in Egypt from the time of Petosiris and onwards.[47] This type of altar was placed in front of temples, unlike the more common interior offering-places of Egyptian temples, and could be used both for incense and burnt-offerings.[48] They were also common in later temples of Isis, as can be seen from the famous Herculaneum frescoes, as well as the reconstructed Iseum at Delos.

We should note that the addressee to whom fire wants to send forth fragrant fumes is not the earthly gods, but rather the "monarchic" god (*theos monarchos*), the creator of the souls and the universe. Unlike several other Hermetica, the Korē Kosmou does not distinguish between a transcendent god and a demiurge: here the creator takes main stage, although we have no way of knowing if a further, transcendent principle is presupposed, since the text does not discuss the origin or ontological status of the creator. At any rate, if the complaint of fire means that the creator god did indeed accept burnt-offerings, and not just "rational sacrifices," this would seem to be at odds with certain other Hermetica.

Near the end of the *Asclepius*, in the framing narrative, the value of material sacrifice becomes ambivalent. Leaving the innermost shrine of the temple, the *adytum*, Hermes and his disciples, Asclepius, Tat and Ammon, prepare to render thanks to god:

> In a hushed voice Asclepius asked: "Tat, do you think we should suggest that your father tell them to add frankincense and spices as we pray to god?" When Trismegistus heard him, he was disturbed and said: "A bad omen, Asclepius, very bad. To burn incense and such stuff when you entreat god smacks of sacrilege. For he wants nothing who is himself all things or in whom all things are. Rather let us worship him by giving thanks, for god finds mortal gratitude to be the best incense." (*Ascl.* 41)

Then follows the prayer of thanksgiving, also found in the Papyrus Mimaut (PGM III. 591–609) and the Nag Hammadi library (NHC VI,7), and after the thanksgiving we are told that the interlocutors "went to eat their food which was pure and had no blood in it."[49] Several commentators have used this passage to demonstrate an end of sacrifice in Hermetism.[50] Solutions have varied from seeing the pro-sacrificial statement of §38 as alluding to a prior stage of spiritual progression to be surpassed, to just ignoring it outright.[51] At first glance, the passage *does* seem to contradict *Ascl.* 38, just a few pages prior, but on closer inspection the two are far from mutually exclusive. The sacrifice connected to the idols is explicitly stated to be due to their mixed nature, since the earthly gods possess both a material and a divine element. They have a need for sacrifice and hymns in order to endure their earthly stay. But god himself is or contains all things, and thus lacks nothing.[52] This god is often stated to be wholly immaterial, even if he can be said to be inherent in all material things. Material offerings are thus inappropriate for the immaterial god.

The mistake of Asclepius, then, is not that he has a positive view of material cult, but that he mistakes the nature of the addressee of the thanksgiving. We notice that he does not suggest performing a blood-sacrifice, but rather the burning of spices and frankincense. We are informed that it is sunset when they start praying, and Plutarch supplies us with the information that the Egyptians usually burn the incense *cyphi* to the sun at its setting.[53] The mistake of Asclepius is thus understandable; he believes they are going to hail the sun at its setting, whereas in fact they are about to offer thanks to the god which is above the sun. The prayer of thanksgiving identifies him as "noetic light, life of life,"[54] which would identify him as the mind (*nous*) subsisting in light and life known from the *Poimandres* (CH I), amongst others. Light and life are also called the noetic "essence-principles" (*ousiarchēs*) of the sensible gods Sun and Heaven in *Ascl.* 19,[55] which means that they are the invisible forces governing the visible heavenly gods. We are thus led to suppose that a material sacrifice to the material sun would be justified in the Hermetic system; indeed, in CH XVI, 5–6, the sun is presented as the intermediary between earth and the noetic realm, "sending essence below and raising matter above" (CH XVI, 5). But in order to address the realm beyond the visible heavenly god it is necessary to supply a more refined offering, namely that of gratitude expressed in words as hymns, probably to be identified with the *logikē thusia*, the rational or speech sacrifice. Since the Demiurge is associated with *logos*, and the *logikos* part of the human soul is what is capable of receiving divine *nous*, a sacrifice of *logos* would be ontologically suitable for this deity.[56]

Before proceeding, however, we must ask ourselves if the two texts we have considered are extraneous to the main current of Hermetic thought, or if they represent a stage to be surpassed, as Fowden has suggested. Granted, CH I–XIV contain no overt references to traditional cult, but as we have seen, this could be due to Christian excisions. *The Perfect Discourse* is commonly considered to be posterior to the Greek corpus, but this is mainly due to its compendious nature, presupposing an already existent voluminous Hermetic literature. Indeed, CH IX, 1 refers to a *Perfect Discourse*, to which it is a sequel, and this could very well be our text. As for *Korē Kosmou*, the Hermetic teaching is couched in an Isiac framework, but expressly presents itself as a chain in the tradition of Hermes. But the question of the internal cohesion of the Hermetica unfortunately exceeds the scope of this article. However, an important testimony to the place of traditional Egyptian cult in the Way of Hermes is contained in the *Discourse of the Eighth and the Ninth* (NHC VI,6). Here, the ascent of Tat to the Eighth and Ninth spheres beyond the planets is described, constituting the apex of the spiritual Way of Hermes. At the end of the treatise, Hermes commands Tat to commemorate the discourse by engraving it in hieroglyphs on a stele of turquoise. This is to be placed in the temple of Hermes in Diospolis, i.e., Thebes, during a specific astronomical conjunction. Guardian statues are to be placed beside the stele, and a curse is to be pronounced upon any uninitiated reader, invoking the unbegotten, self-begotten, and begotten god, as well as the elements and the seven essence-principles (NHC VI 61,18–63,32). This latter term is otherwise known only in the *Perfect Discourse*. Even if this passage is a literary fiction, it clearly demonstrates that the author had no intention of diminishing the role of traditional temples and priests, even at the highest level of spiritual progress. Although traditional cult apparently plays no part in the spiritual ascent, it seems to be presupposed as a framework. Likewise, in the *Korē Kosmou*, we find among the benefactions of Isis and Osiris that "the prophet destined to lay his hands upon the gods should never be ignorant of anything that exists, so that philosophy and magic should nourish his soul, while medicine should save his body when anything ails it" (SH XXIII, 68). *Prophētēs* is, of course, the Greek term for the Egyptian high-priest (*ḥm nṯr*), one of whose duties it was to lay his hands upon the god in the daily temple ritual.[57]

Sacrifice and pure philosophy

There is no end to traditional sacrifice in Hermetism then, but it is in fact a crucial part of the attitude of reverence towards the earthly gods, and thus a guarantee for continued divine presence on earth. The lack of attention granted to the material sacrifice in most treatises is rather due to the fact that most Hermetica are more concerned with the upper ontological spectrum of man, cosmos, and god. However, in our two treatises dealing with sacrifice it seems that it plays a crucial part in the origin of civilization, bringing mankind from its bestial state to humanity. Specifically, what is at stake here is the primordial status of Egyptian antiquities, and the prestige of its cultural founders. G. R. Boys-Stones, in his *Post-Hellenistic Philosophy*, has demonstrated a shift in the philosophical thought of the Empire where great age conferred not only prestige on a theology or philosophy, but where its primordiality served as proof of its veracity. According to Boys-Stones (2001), there occurred a decisive shift among the Stoics, around the turn of the Common Era, regarding their view of Hesiod's ages of mankind: Posidonius saw mankind of the golden age as ruled by philosophers who kept the brutes in check, while Cornutus also saw them as formulating universal truths through symbols and riddles. The aim of Stoic allegorical reading was therefore to find traces of this primeval wisdom in ancient myths and poems, an aim that also the Platonists inherited in the increasingly eclectic philosophical milieu of the Empire. Boys-Stones further claims that a main impetus behind Middle-Platonism was the view that Plato had access to this primeval wisdom, and that the truth of doctrines would thus be proved if they could be traced back to Plato.[58] This hypothesis could in turn shed some light on Hermetism.

As we have seen, both the *Korē Kosmou* and the *Asclepius* assign a civilizing function to sacrifice. In the former, we are told that Hermes wrote down the secrets of the universe on stelae and hid them near the secret *adyta* of Osiris even before the souls of mankind had come into existence, in anticipation of them (4–8). The souls were created from the world soul, and at first lived in perfect bliss, before their impertinent curiosity led them to transgress their limits, and they were put into bodies (14–30).[59] The souls saw this as a fall from grace and complained bitterly, whereupon god gave the most worthy of them hope that they would eventually be able to return to heaven (31–42). Among these worthy souls were philosophers, prophets, sacrificers, and kings. Philosophy was thus present among the first generation of embodied souls. This generation now lives a carefree existence, and investigates the mysteries of both nature and the sacred *adyta*, presumably the ones in which Hermes hid his books. But then an earthly spirit of reproach, Momus, complains about the curiosity, arrogance and haughtiness of the humans, and in response Hermes hides divine nature from mankind and institutes the inexorable bonds of necessity (43–48). Strangely, at this point a new creation seems to occur, where chaos is dispersed, and the "dark unity" is separated orderly (*kosmikōs diastasis*) into heaven and earth (49–52). This new creation seems out of place, but perhaps we should see it in parallel with the anthropogony of the *Poimandres*. Here, the heavenly human descends to earth, assumes a material body, and with nature begets seven humans. This first generation of humans lives as hermaphrodites for one cycle (*periodos*), perhaps an astronomical Great Year,[60] before all things are divided into two sexes, so that they can procreate (CH I, 13–19). In both treatises, the dissolving of an original unity is associated with the rule of fate, but it is also providential. In the following age, the *Poimandres* states that there are some who recognize themselves, and arrive at the good, while others follow the path of death. In the *Korē Kosmou*, general war and disorder break out, and this eventually prompts the four elements to denounce the behaviour of mankind to god. In answer to this, a great emanation of god is set to be judge over the humans after death (53–64). This is Osiris, and together with Isis, his sister-wife he also establishes the civilizing institutions which apparently last down to the author's present, including sacrifice (64–70).

Isis and Osiris, it is claimed, thus founded Egyptian civilization by using the wisdom of Hermes (66–68), which was deposited in Egypt at the time when gods reigned. The Egyptian chronography of Manetho included such a period of divine reign, lasting thousands of years before the first mortal dynasties. Indeed, in one of the fragments of Manetho a certain Bydis or Bites is mentioned as the last dynast in the reign of the gods (fr. 1.1). This is probably the same figure as the Bitys mentioned by Iamblichus (*Myst.* 8.5), who reportedly discovered the stelae of Hermes in the temple of the goddess Neith, at Saïs. Bitys reappears as Bitos in Zosimus of Panopolis' *Treatise on the letter Omega*, where he is taken as a witness that Thoth (here: Thouthos) was the first human, and the interpreter of the gods (FH 21). The literary motif of antediluvian stelae of Hermes Trismegistus is also crucial to the (pseudo-) Manethonian preamble to the *Book of Sothis*, preserved by George Syncellus.[61]

The first generation of embodied souls in the *Korē Kosmou*, then, seems to have been ruled over by righteous kings and philosophers, just like Posidonius claimed, before fate was set over them and they became brutish and started killing each other. It is then that the element fire asks god to "initiate the savage state of human life into peace" (*tou biou to agrion muēson eirēnē*). In response Isis and Osiris are sent down to establish laws and regulate sacrifice, among other things.

The *Asclepius* does not include an account going back to creation, but the passage regarding material gods clearly associates the homonymous ancestors of Hermes and Asclepius, as well as Isis and Osiris, with the discoverers of divine nature and the way to fashion gods at a time when "our ancestors," that is the Egyptians, "erred gravely on the theory of divinity." As in the *Korē Kosmou*, the arts of prophecy and casting of lots, medicine and healing, music and hymns are connected with this discovery. Interestingly, in another passage (§§12–14) the arts of music, geometry and arithmetic[62] are subordinated to "pure philosophy," and should only be used to "wonder at the recurrence of the stars" as well as taking measure of creation in order to worship the skill of the creator. Hermes predicts that in the future the sophists will muddle this pure philosophy through pointless speculations. The Hermetic author is thus concerned with preserving a pure philosophy which does not indulge in impertinent curiosity – a crime which made god embody the souls in the *Korē kosmou* – but which is instead deeply committed to reverence of the divine. This attitude is opposed to "loquacity and idle chatter" (CH XIV, 4), and involves turning away from present vulgarity in order to "return to primordial things of old" (CH IV, 9).

Most famously, this attitude is expressed in the introduction to CH XVI, where Asclepius contrasts the "extravagant, flaccid and (as it were) dandified Greek idiom" of the "foolosophy" of the Greeks to the "stately and concise" Egyptian language: Greek has only demonstrative power, while Egyptian carries divine power hidden within itself. All this, of course, is found in a text that was originally composed in Greek, and never translated from Egyptian as it claims. As we can see from these examples, the Hermetica are keen to present themselves as recovered Egyptian primordial wisdom, first written down by the god Hermes on stelae. By echoing Plato, who along with luminaries such as Pythagoras was believed to have studied under the barbarian sages (e.g. Clem. Alex., *Protr.* 15), Hermes actually made it appear as if Plato had copied him. Thus, in this intellectual climate, where the philosophers were eager to reclaim Plato uncluttered by later tradition (and then especially by the

Sceptics), Hermes could do one better, and offer the putative sources of Plato. And the claim was widely believed; the second century Platonist Albinus reportedly held Hermes Trismegistus to be the source of the "ancient account" of Plato's theory of metempsychosis, in *Phaedo* 70c.[63] The Christian Lactantius states more cautiously that: "It may be that Hermes should be counted among the philosophers, even though he was translated to the gods and is honored under the name of Mercury by the Egyptians; perhaps he deserves no more attention than Plato and Pythagoras" (*Div. inst.* 7.4). Elsewhere, however, Lactantius affirms that the Egyptian Hermes agrees with Plato's *Timaeus*, although he is far more ancient than not only Plato, but Pythagoras and the seven sages as well (*De ira* 11.11–12). The implication is clearly that Hermes is their source.[64]

The demand for such sources in the second century is clear from the testimonies of Plutarch and Numenius. Plutarch made use of Books of Hermes allegorizing the ancient gods when writing his *On Isis and Osiris* (375E), while Numenius advocated going back to the "rites, teachings and sacred foundations" of the most illustrious peoples, "Brahmans, Jews, Magi and Egyptians," which are "in agreement with Plato" (fr. 1 a Des Places). And around the time Plutarch was born, in mid first century CE, the Egyptian priest and Stoic philosopher Chairemon made quite an impression in Rome, claiming that the upper echelons of the Egyptian priesthood constituted the "true philosophers" (fr. 10.8).[65] Chairemon likely also made reference to Hermetic sources, though perhaps astrological ones (frs. 9, 17D, 25D).

Iamblichus further confirms that this is indeed how the Hermetica were understood in the treatise *On the mysteries*,[66] written in the guise of an Egyptian high-priest, Abammon, as an answer to a critical letter of Porphyry. According to Polymnia Athanassiadi, Iamblichus can be counted as the foremost proponent of Platonic orthodoxy, and in view of his dependence on Hermes in *On the mysteries*, she suggests that he might have been initiated into a Hermetic group in Egypt.[67] Strikingly, Iamblichus, who was a strong proponent for conformity in the Platonic tradition, defends the lack of doctrinal uniformity in Egyptian theology, stating that this is due to the many sages of old who handed down different accounts of the first principles. All of these were supposedly covered by the Books of Hermes, however, and the plurality down below is resolved in the unity above (*Myst.* 8.1). Thus, what excuses the multitude of opinions is that they all go back to primordial times, were transmitted faithfully, and are essentially in agreement that creation unfolds from unity to multiplicity. At the very outset of the treatise, it is claimed that both Pythagoras and Plato studied the stelae of Hermes, and so had privileged access to this primordial wisdom (*Myst.* 1.1).

A whole book of *On the mysteries* is dedicated to defending Egyptian sacrificial practice as being fully in line with Platonic doctrine. Iamblichus echoes Hermes, that "to offer matter in sacrifices to immaterial deities is alien to them, but it is most proper to all material ones" (*Myst.* 5.14). But whereas the Hermetic material sacrifices aim at propitiating the earthly gods and upholding the cosmic order, they are by Iamblichus seen as pointing the soul of the theurgist upwards. The focus is thus shifted from the community to the individual practitioner. Iamblichus mentions in passing that material sacrifices are necessary for cities and the mass of peoples to achieve the lesser good (*Myst.* 5.15), but his overall preoccupation is the role of material sacrifice as a propaedeutic to the higher immaterial stages of theurgic practice.

Conclusion

As Guy Stroumsa points out, sacrificial ritual could be "transformed from an alliance between the community and its gods into the preparation of a mystical experience," and this drift towards individual salvation is characteristic of the religious change that takes place in Late Antiquity.[68] Thus, according to Ingvild S. Gilhus, "the sacrificial animal was seen less as part of a circle of prosperity, encompassing land and lineage, agricultural production and meat, food and festival, and more as a dynamic element in a personal and religious development based on initiation."[69] In this sense, Iamblichus' idea of sacrifice is closer to that of Philo of Alexandria, where the prime function of sacrifice is not as an offering to deity, but as an act symbolizing the gratitude of the soul towards god (*De spec. leg.* 1.252–3).[70] In our Hermetic treatises, however, the material sacrifice is still used to placate the precarious earthly gods and forms part of the general attitude of reverence, *eusebeia*. Individual ascent, on the other hand, is achieved by means of contemplation, spiritual exercises, and hymns of thanksgiving, called "rational sacrifices," which may be sung in silence. It thus seems that the Hermetic view on material sacrifice is closer to that of traditional Egyptian practice; it was part of the constant obeisance to be performed to the statues in order to appease the indwelling god and thus secure the cosmic order.[71]

Notes

1. Burkert 1972; Girard 1972. Recent scholarship on sacrifice has tended to question the centrality of the killing itself, emphasizing other elements of the ritual (e.g. Smith 2004; Frankfurter 2011). Etymologically, the Latin *sacrificium* means to render something sacred (*sacer facere*), i.e. to transfer an animal, object or even person into the realm of the divine. It is also telling that the word *immolare*, which means to strew salted flour onto an animal, thus making it *sacer*, could be used to describe the whole process of animal

sacrifice. On the Greek side, *thusia* has more to do with burning than the killing itself.

2. Graf 2002: 116f.
3. Beard *et al.* 1998: 2:286–287.
4. Stroumsa 2009: xvi, 56–83.
5. Young 1979; Ferguson 1980: 1162–1165; Thomassen 2006: 148–153.
6. Stroumsa 2009: 64.
7. Young 1979: 24–25.
8. Stroumsa 2009: 62–63, where he goes as far as stating that "[t]he Jews should no doubt pay thanks to Titus... for imposing on them the need to free themselves from sacrifice and its ritual violence." Stroumsa moderated this statement in the course of the conference at Södertörn.
9. The main texts of Hermetism are the seventeen Greek treatises comprising the *Corpus Hermeticum* (= CH), the Greek fragments in the anthology of Stobaeus (= SH), the Latin translation *Asclepius*, and the three Coptic translations found in the Nag Hammadi Library (NHC VI,*6-8*). In addition there are various Greek fragments (= FH), and a collection of Hermetic aphorisms, mainly preserved in Armenian, but with Greek fragments. Cf. Nock and Festugière 1946–1954 for the Greek and Latin texts, Mahé 1978–1982 for the Coptic and Armenian, and Copenhaver 1992 for the English translations of CH and *Ascl.* The translations of *Korē kosmou* (SH XXIII) are my own.
10. CH I, 31; XIII, 18–19, 21; NHC VI 57,19. Cf. Tagliaferro 1984: 1584–1585, on different translations.
11. Rom. 12:1–2; I Pet. 2:5. Also in *Testaments of the twelve patriarchs: Levi* 3.6. Cf. Copenhaver 1992: 122–123. I will not consider the *logikē thusia* in-depth here, since it is treated elsewhere in this volume, in the contribution of Jørgen Podemann Sørensen. See also Podemann Sørensen 2012.
12. Festugière 1944–1954.
13. Mahé 1978–1982, 1991; Fowden 1986.
14. Fowden 1986: 149–150; Van den Kerchove 2012: 222, likewise claims that for Hermetists traditional cult was to be replaced by spiritual exercises and direct contact with the divine.
15. Hadot 1993 [2002]: 21: "non seulement de la pensée, mais de tout le psychisme de l'individu." I tentatively interpret Hadot's use of the obscure *psychism* to imply "psychological makeup."
16. Ibidem: "une transformation de la vision du monde et à une métamorphose de la personnalité."
17. I have treated the related question of "mysteries" in these two texts in Bull 2012.

18. There is no CH XV, due to complications in the history of publication.
19. Knust and Várhelyi 2011; Ullucci 2011.
20. Festugière 1944–1954: 3:2.
21. Boys-Stones 2001.
22. *Ascl.* 23–24 = NHC VI 68,20–70,2.
23. *Ascl.* 24–26 = NHC VI 70,3–74,14.
24. E.g., NF 2:381 n. 216: "une heureuse formule qui pourrait servir à désigner toute la piété hermétique."
25. *Ascl.* 25: *sed, mihi credite, et capitale periculum constituetur in eum, qui se mentis religioni dederit.* Copenhaver 1992: 82, follows Festugière in reading *periculum* as "penalty," but the Coptic parallel gives the Greek loan-word *kindunos*, "danger."
26. NHC VI 72, 35. *prmnnoute*, "the pious person" of ln. 20 is propably intended, though Mahé 1978–1982: vol. 2, 180, supplies "les (spirituels) de cette sorte."
27. This in parallel to an earlier passage, where the Latin gives the more florid *pia mente diuinitatem sedula religione seruasse et omnis eorum sancta ueneratio*, while the Coptic only has *euahise etmntnoute* (NHC VI 70,14; *mntnoute* = *eusebeia* [Crum 1939, 231a]). Cf. also *Ascl.*22 = NHC VI 68,10–12, where the Latin embellishes *ipsos religione et sancta mente ueneratur*, not found in the Coptic.
28. Scott 1924–1936, 4:xii n. 7.
29. Salaman 2007: 21, misreads the passage entirely when he suggests that the fashioning of statues is what constitutes the grave error of the ancestors.
30. Because of this, Frankfurter 2011 questions the utility of the term 'sacrifice' at all in Egyptian religion, and proposes to get rid of the term altogether. In my view, such proposals are seldom very successful, and we should focus our attention on nuancing our terms rather than disposing of them.
31. Allen 1988: 44. Quack 2008: 251, believes that *Ascl.* 38 refers to the Choiak-figures of Osiris, which were made once a year in the month of Choiak, out of earth, gems, herbs and spices. But this is manifestly wrong. The statues of *Ascl.* 38 represent not only Osiris, but all (Egyptian) earthly gods, expressly including Hermes, Asclepius and Isis, and they are worshipped constantly, not once a year.
32. Lorton 1999: 161–162.
33. Dunand and Zivie-Coche 2004: 91–92.
34. Junker 1910: 72; Roeder 2008.
35. Englund 1987: 57.
36. Contra Van den Kerchove 2012: 235.

37. Souls of the dead being described as "just" (*dikaios*) is in line with Egyptian mortuary literature, where the deceased is regularly described as "justified" (*maat ẖrw*, literally "true of voice").

38. Diod. Sic. 1.16 credits Hermes with the discovery of sacrifice, while in §1.20 he establishes the sacrifices and mysteries of Osiris together with Isis. In §1.45, however, Menas is said to have discovered sacrifice.

39. *loibai* rather than the more frequent *spondai* or *choai* (LSJ).

40. Nock and Festugière 1946–1954: 4:45 n. 206.

41. Rather than a doublet, we could emend the text to say *para loibais <kai> para thusias*, or see *para loibais* as apposite to *chairon*, and *para thusias* to *hupēretēsō*: "rejoicing at libations, I will serve during sacrifices."

42. Hieroglyphic: *grr* and *wdn*; Demotic: *gll* and *wtn*. Cf. Dils 1993, 115; Daumas 1952: 239.

43. SH XXIII, 53: "The strong burnt and murdered the powerless, and threw both the living and the dead down into the temples, down into the *aduta*." Cf. the aretalogy from Kyme, ln. 21: "I with my brother Osiris put an end to cannibalism." (Žabkar 1988, 141) Van den Kerchove (2005: 474; 2007: 202–3; 2011: 62–67 and 2012: 234–235) sees the critique as striking all bloody sacrifices. However, Van den Kerchove does not take into account the "accurate sacrificers" extolled in SH XXIII, 42, who can hardly be experts of bloodless sacrifices. Perhaps they are rather to be equated with the Egyptian *moschosphragistai*, "calf-sealers" (cf. Porph., *De abst.* 4.7 = Chairemon fr. 10; Herod. 2.38; Clem. Alex., *Strom.* 6.4.36; Plut., *Is. et Os.* 363A-B; Merkelbach 1968: 12–13). Van den Kerchove alternately suggests that the burning of flesh might be a reference to cremation, abhorrent to the Egyptians (Van den Kerchove 2005, 478–479; 2011, 63–64).

44. See Van den Kerchove 2005: 468 n. 291 for sources to human sacrifice and cannibalism in primeval times; Cf. also Clem. Alex., *Protr.* 3.42.1–45.5, who uses such sources to discredit the institution of sacrifice. Plutarch quotes Manetho that "Typhonian" humans used to be burned alive at Eileithyiaspolis (*Is. et Os.* 380D).

45. Cf. *Scholia in Euripidis Phoenissas* 274; *Der Kleine Pauly*, 2:370a.

46. Porph., *De antro nympharum* 6.

47. Quaegebeur 1993: 331, claims that this altar is often called *bōmos keraouchos*, though I can find no instances of this in either *Thesauros Linguae Graecae*, or *Inscriptiones Graecae*. Petosiris was high-priest of Thoth in Hermopolis towards the end of the Persian domination of Egypt.

48. Quaegebeur 1993: 346, points out that there are iconographic testimonies to smaller, portable horned-altars, but these were not connected to the *grr* sacrifice.

49. NHC VI 65,5–7: *aubōk eunaouōm nteutrophē esouaab emn snof nhēts*. The meal

could be construed to be "holy" or "pure," depending on how one translates *ouaab*. Some see it as a sacramental meal, (e.g., Van den Kerchove 2011, 71) but this is clearly not the case when we consider the remark of Hermes before the prayer, that "it remains for us only to return to the care of the body." (*Ascl.* 40)

50. E.g., Festugière 1944–1954: 1:83: "nous avons la preuve, par un traité hermétique (Asclep. 41), que l'hermétisme répugne explicitement aux actes matériels du culte."

51. Prior stage: Fowden 1986, 149–150; Ignoring: Young 1972, 21–22 and Podemann Sørensen 2012, 467, 471.

52. Similarly, *Trip. Tract.* 69: "For inasmuch as the Father lacks nothing, he returns the glory they give to those who glorify [him]."

53. Plut., *De Is. et Os.* 52. Cf. § 82: "Cyphi is a mixture compounded of sixteen parts...whenever the unguent-makers are mixing these ingredients, sacred writings are read out to them...as most of the ingredients have aromatic powers, they emit a sweet breath and a beneficent exhalation by which the air is changed" (trans. Griffiths 1970).

54. NHC VI 64,23–24: *ō pouoein nnoēton, ō pōnh mpōnh* = *Ascl.* 41: *o lumen maximum solo intellectu sensibile... o uitae uera uita*; PGM III.602 has only *ō tēs anthrōpinēs zōēs* <*zōē*>. This instance of the pair Light-Life is missed by Copenhaver 1992, 103, who otherwise lists CH I, 9, 12, 17, 21, 32; XIII, 9, 18–19; Ascl. 19, 23, 25; Jn 1:4, 8:12; II Tim 1:10.

55. *Ascl.* 19: *caeli uel quicquid est, quod eo nomine conprehenditur,* ousiarchēs *est Iuppiter: per caelum enim Iuppiter omnibus praebet uitam. solis* ousiarchēs *lumen est*. Here Jupiter is the essence-principle who gives life, while in the Coptic text of NHC VI 75,16–17 Zeus and life are identical.

56. Porphyry follows the same gradation, with silent prayer to the supreme god, hymns to the intelligible gods, fumigation of vegetables to the astral gods, but bloody sacrifices only to evil demons; *Abst.* 2.34–36, cf. Young 1979: 24–28; Van den Kerchove 2012: 233 n. 36.

57. Moret 1902, 167; chapter 44 of the ritual is called "Chapitre de mettre ses deux bras sur le dieu."

58. Boys-Stones (2001) has been criticized for exaggerating the dependence of Middle Platonism on supposed primordial wisdom, cf. the review of Harold Tarrant on Bryn Mawr [http://bmcr.brynmawr.edu/2002/2002-02-03.html]. For our purpose, it suffices that the theory was prevalent.

59. On the role of curiosity in *Korē kosmou*, see Betz 1966, 168; Assmann 1999, 54ff. Ferguson, in Scott 1924–1936, 4:453, points out the similarity between Hermes' creation of human bodies here, and the Prometheus myth. We could also point out that the "gifts" of the planets to man in § 28–29 are reminiscent of the Pandora motif.

60. The Great Year was mentioned by Plato, *Tim.* 39d, as the time it takes for all the stars and planets to reset at their original position. It was estimated to be 36,000 years by Hipparchus (Ptol., *Synt.* 7.1–2), and 15,000 years by Macrobius (*Comm. in Somn. Scip.* 11.10–12).

61. I argue for the authenticity of this letter in my doctoral dissertation, Bull 2014: 39–70. To be published in Brill's "Religions in the Graeco-Roman World" book series.

62. We should not consider this passage as outright hostile to the sciences, but rather it is directed against *vain* speculation, i.e., that which does not lead towards god. Justin Martyr (*Dial.* 2) reports that a Pythagorean teacher considered music, astronomy and geometry to be necessary prerequisites for the contemplation of the essential good, and an anonymous compiler of fifteen Hermetic books claimed that Hermes discovered numbers, calculations, geometry, astronomy, astrology, music, and the whole of grammar (Cyr. Alex., *Jul.* 1.548a-c).

63. Pl., *Phaedo* 70 c: *palaios logos*; Tert., *De anima* 28.1: *hinc abeuntes sint illuc et rursus huc veniant et fiant et dehinc ita habeat rursus ex mortuis effici vivos... divinum Albinus existimat, Mercurii forsitan Aegyptii.*

64. Cf. Festugière 1946–1954: 2:49–50.

65. Cf. Van der Horst 1984.

66. This is in fact the title given the work by the renaissance scholar Marsilio Ficino, which has stuck by convention.

67. Athanassiadi 2006: 162–166.

68. Stroumsa 2009: 158

69. Gilhus 2006: 129.

70. A consideration of Philo, who is very important for the history of the spiritualization of sacrifice, would unfortunately exceed the limits of this article. Cf. however Nikiprowetzky 1967.

71. Cf. Englund 1987: 66.

References

Allen, J.P. 1988. *Genesis in Egypt: The Philosophy of Ancient Egyptian Creation Accounts*, Yale Egyptological Seminar. Yale Egyptological Studies 2. New Haven, CT: Yale University Press.

Assmann, Jan. 1999. "Das verschleierte Bild zu Sais-griechische Neugier und ägyptische Andacht." In *Schleier und Schwelle III: Geheimnis und Neugierde*, edited by Aleida Assmann,45-66. Munich: Fink.

Athanassiadi, Polymnia. 2006. *La lutte pour l'orthodoxie dans le platonisme tardif : de Numénius à Damascius*. Paris: Les Belles Lettres.

Beard, Mary, John North and Simon Price. 1998. *Religions of Rome.* 2 vols. Cambridge: Cambridge University Press.

Betz, Hans-Dieter 1966. "Schöpfung und Erlösung im hermetischen Fragment 'Kore kosmu'." *Zeitschrift für Theologie und Kirche* 63: 160-187. Reprinted in *Hellenismus und Urchristentum: Gesammelte Aufsätze I*, Hans Dieter Betz, 1990, 22-51. Tübingen: J. C. B. Mohr (Paul Siebeck).

Boys-Stones, G. R. 2001. *Post-Hellenistic Philosophy: A study of its development from the Stoics to Origen.* Oxford: Oxford University Press.

Bull, Christian H. 2012. "The Notion of Mysteries in the Formation of Hermetic Tradition." In *Mystery and Secrecy in the Nag Hammadi Collection and Other Ancient Literature: Ideas and Practices : Studies For Einar Thomassen at Sixty*, Nag Hammadi and Manichaean Studies 76, edited by Christian H. Bull, Liv Ingeborg Lied and John D. Turner, 399-425. Leiden: Brill.

Bull, Christian H. 2014. "The Tradition of Hermes: The Egyptian Priestly Figure as Teacher of Hellenized Wisdom." Unpublished PhD thesis, The University of Bergen.

Burkert, Walter. 1972. *Homo Necans.* Berlin: Walter de Gruyter.

Copenhaver, Brian P., ed. 1992. *Hermetica.* Cambridge: Cambridge University Press. http://dx.doi.org/10.1017/CBO9781107050075.

Crum, Walter E. 1939. *A Coptic Dictionary*. Oxford: Oxford University Press.

Daumas, François. 1952. *Les Moyens d'expression du grec et de l'égyptien comparés dans les décrets de Canope et de Memphis.* Le Caire: Impr. de l'Institut français d'archéologie orientale.

Dils, Peter. 1993. "Wine for Pouring and Purification in Ancient Egypt." In *Ritual and Sacrifice in the Ancient Near East: Proceedings of the International Conference Organized by the Katholieke Universiteit Leuven from the 17th to the 20th of April 1991*, edited by Jan Quaegebeur, 107–123. Orientalia Lovaniensia analecta, 55. Leuven: Peeters.

Dunand, Françoise, and Christiane Zivie-Coche. 2004. *Gods and Men in Egypt: 3000 BCE to 395 CE.* Translated by David Lorton. Ithaca, NY: Cornell University Press.

Englund, Gertie. 1987. "Gifts to the Gods: a necessity for the preservation of cosmos and life" In *Gifts to the Gods: Proceedings of the Uppsala Symposium 1985*, edited by Tullia Linders and Gullög Nordquist, 57-66. Uppsala: Almqvist & Wiksell.

Ferguson, Everett. 1980. "Spiritual Sacrifice in Early Christianity and its Environment." In *Aufstieg und Niedergang der römischen Welt. II: Principat, 23.2.*, edited by Wolfgang Haase, 1151-1189. Berlin: Walter de Gruyter.

Festugière, André-Jean. 1944-1954. *La révélation d'Hermès Trismégiste*, 4 vols. Paris: Lecoffre.

Fowden, Garth. 1986. *The Egyptian Hermes: A Historical Approach to the Late Pagan Mind*. Princeton, NJ: Princeton University Press.

Frankfurter, David. 2011. "Egyptian Religion and the Problem of the Category 'Sacrifice'." In *Ancient Mediterranean Sacrifice*, edited by Jennifer Wright Knust and Zsuzsanna Várhelyi, 75-93. Oxford: Oxford University Press.

Gilhus, Ingvild Sælid. 2006. *Animals, Gods and Humans: Changing Attitudes to Animals in Greek, Roman and Early Christian Ideas*. London: Routledge.

Girard, René. 1972. *La violence et le sacré*. Paris: Editions Bernard Grasset.

Graf, Fritz. 2002. "What is New about Greek Sacrifice?" In *Kykeon: Studies in Honour of H. S. Versnel*, edited by H. F. J. Horstmanshoff, H. W. Singor, F. T. van Straten and J. H. M. Strubbe, 113-126. Leiden: Brill.

Griffiths, John Gwyn. 1970. *Plutarch: De Iside et Osiride*. Cardiff: University of Wales Press.

Hadot, Pierre. 1993. *Exercices spirituels et philosophie antique*. Paris: Institut d'Études augustiniennes. Revised edition, Paris: Éditions Albin Michel, 2002.

Junker, Hermann. 1910. "Die Schlacht- und Brandopfer und ihre Symbolik im Tempelkult der Spätzeit." *Zeitschrift fur Ägyptische Sprache und Altertumskunde* 48: 247–255.

Knust, Jennifer Wright, and Zsuzsanna Várhelyi, eds. 2011. *Ancient Mediterranean Sacrifice*. Oxford: Oxford University Press. http://dx.doi.org/10.1093/acprof:oso/9780199738960.001.0001.

Lorton, David. 1999. "The Theology of Cult Statues in Ancient Egypt." In *Born in Heaven, Made on Earth: The Making of the Cult Image in the Ancient Near East*, edited by Michael B. Dick, 123-210. Winona Lake, IN: Eisenbrauns.

Mahé, Jean-Pierre. 1978-1982. *Hermès en Haute-Égypte*. 2 vols. Bibliothèque Copte de Nag Hammadi, section "textes" 3 & 7. Laval: Les Presses de l'Université Laval.

Mahé, Jean-Pierre. 1991. "La voie d'immortalité à la lumière des *Hermetica* de Nag Hammadi et de découvertes plus récentes." *Vigiliae Christianae* 45: 347–375.

Merkelbach, Reinhold. 1968. "Ein ägyptischer Priestereid." *Zeitschrift fur Papyrologie und Epigraphik* 2: 7–30.

Moret, Alexandre. 1902. *Le rituel du culte divin journalier en Égypte, d'après les papyrus de Berlin et les textes du temple de Séti 1er, à Abydos*. Paris: Ernest Leroux.

Nikiprowetzky, Valentin. 1967. "La Spiritualisation des sacrifices et le culte sacrificiel au Temple de Jerusalem chez Philon d'Alexandrie." *Semitica* 17: 97–116.

Nock, Arthur D. and André-Jean. Festugière. 1946-1954. *Hermès Trismégiste*. 4 vols. Paris: Les Belles Lettres.

Podemann Sørensen, Jørgen. 2012. "The Secret Hymn in Hermetic Texts." In *Mystery and Secrecy in the Nag Hammadi Collection and Other Ancient Literature: Ideas and Practice. Studies for Einar Thomassen at Sixty*, Nag Hammadi and Manichaean Studies 76, edited by Christian H. Bull, Liv Ingeborg Lied and John D. Turner, 465-486. Leiden: Brill.

Quack, Joachim. 2008. "Spuren ägyptischer Opfertheologie bei Jamblich?" In *Transformations in Sacrificial Practices: From Antiquity to Modern Time: Proceedings of an International Colloquium, Heidelberg, 12-14 July 2006*, edited by Eftychia Stavrianopoulou, Axel Michaels and Claus Ambos, 241-262. Berlin: Lit.

Quaegebeur, J., ed. 1993. "L'autel-à-feu et l'abattoir en Égypte tardive." In *Ritual and Sacrifice in the Ancient Near East: Proceedings of the International Conference Organized by the Katholieke Universiteit Leuven from the 17th to the 20th of April 1991*, edited by Jan Quaegebeur, 329-353. Orientalia Lovaniensia analecta, 55. Leuven: Peeters.

Roeder, Hubert. 2008. "Mundöffnung und rituelle Feindtötung. Die soziomorphe Definition eines altägyptischen Vernichtungsopfers." In *Transformations in Sacrificial Practices: From Antiquity to Modern Time: Proceedings of an International Colloquium, Heidelberg, 12-14 July 2006*, edited by Eftychia Stavrianopoulou, Axel Michaels and Claus Ambos, 19-74. Berlin: Lit.

Salaman, Clement. 2007. *Asclepius: The Perfect Discourse of Hermes Trismegistus*. London: Duckworth.

Scott, Walter. 1924-1936. *Hermetica*. 4 vols. Oxford: Clarendon.

Smith, Jonathan Z. 2004. "The Domestication of Sacrifice." In *Relating Religion: Essays in the Study of Religion*, 145–159. Chicago, IL: University of Chicago Press.

Stroumsa, Guy. 2009. *The End of Sacrifice: Religious Transformations in Late Antiquity*. Chicago, IL: University of Chicago Press.

Tagliaferro, Eleonora. 1984. "Anaimaktos thusia – logikē thusia: Aproposito della critica al sacrificio cruento", In *Sangue e anthropologia nella Liturgia*, edited by Francesco Vattioni, 1573-1595. Edizioni Pia Unione Preziosissimo Sangue.

Thomassen, Einar. 2006. "The Reception of Greco-Roman Religious and Cultic Terminology in Judaism and Christianity, with Special Reference to Sacrificial Terminology." In *Beyond Reception: Mutual Influences between Antique Religion, Judaism, and Early Christianity*, edited by David Brakke, Anders-Christian Jacobsen and Jörg Ulrich, 137-154. Frankfurt am Main: Peter Lang.

Ullucci, Daniel. 2011. *The Christian Rejection of Animal Sacrifice*. Oxford: Oxford University Press. http://dx.doi.org/10.1093/acprof:oso/9780199791705.001.0001.

Van den Kerchove, Anna. 2005. "Pratiques rituelles et traités hermétiques." Paris: EPHE. Section "Science des religions." PhD-thesis.

Van den Kerchove, Anna. 2007. "La voie d'Hermès, la question des sacrifices et les 'cultes orientaux'." In *Religioni in contatto nel mediterraneo antico. Atti del 3° colloquio su "le religioni orientali nel mondo greco e romano," Loveno di Menaggio (Como) 26-28 Maggio 2006*, edited by Corinne Bonnet, Sergio Ribichini and Dirk Steuernagel, 191-204. Rome: Serra Editore.

Van den Kerchove, Anna. 2011. "Les hermétistes et les conceptions traditionnelles des sacrifices." In *L'Oiseau et la poisson: Cohabitations religieuses dans les mondes grec et romain*, edited by Jean-Daniel Dubois and Nicole Belayche, 61-80. Paris: Presses de l'Université Paris Sorbonne.

Van den Kerchove, Anna. 2012. *La voie d'Hermès: Pratiques rituelles et traités hermétiques*, Nag Hammadi and Manichaean Studies, 77. Leiden: Brill. http://dx.doi.org/10.1163/9789004223653.

Van der Horst, Pieter Willem. 1984. *Chaeremon: Egyptian Priest and Stoic Philosopher, The fragments collected and translated*. Leiden: Brill.

Young, Frances M. 1979. *The Use of Sacrificial Ideas in Greek Christian Writers from the New Testament to John Chrysostom*. Cambridge: The Philadelphia Patristic Foundation.

Žabkar, Louis Vico. 1988. *Hymns to Isis in Her Temple at Philae*. Hanover, NH: University Press of New England.

About the author

Christian Bull is a post-doctoral researcher for the project NEWCONT (New Contexts for Old Texts: Unorthodox Texts and Monastic Manuscript Culture in Fourth- and Fifth-Century Egypt) at the University of Oslo, Faculty of Theology. The project is funded by the European Research Council (ERC) under the European Community's Seventh Framework Programme (FP7/2007–2013) / ERC Grant Agreement no. 283741. Bull received his PhD 2014 in religious studies with his thesis "The Tradition of Hermes: The Egyptian Priestly Figure as a Teacher of Hellenized Wisdom." His research interests are ancient religions, Egyptian religions, early Christianity, Gnosticism and theory of the study of religions. He has published on Hermetism, most recently in *Secrecy in the Nag Hammadi Collection and Other Ancient Literature: Ideas and Practices* (2012), co-edited with L. I. Lied and J. D. Turner.

9

Beyond Righteousness and Transgression: Reading the Gospel of Truth and the Gospel of Judas from an Acosmic Perspective

Jörgen Magnusson

Introduction

In 2006 National Geographic Society published a Coptic text on their website: *The Gospel of Judas* (*GospJud*). Since 1982, scholars had known that a document circulated on the black market, a document in which a disciple called Judas seemed to play a central role.[1] The text is part of a codex that suffered immensely in the hands of people not trained in handling ancient documents. In 2000 the church historian and coptologist Bentley Layton discovered that the Judas of the codex was Judas Iscariot. Finally, when the text was published, a group of scholars, who had done fantastic work reconstructing the seriously damaged text published books in which they claimed that this Christian Gnostic gospel revealed a conversation between Judas and Jesus which made evident that the two had made a pact. According to the initial line of interpretation, Judas' task was to help release Jesus from his fleshly prison where his spirit was captive. Moreover, Judas was the favorite disciple, the only one who understood the message of Jesus.[2] From the beginning the view of sacrifice in *GospJud* was related to an evaluation of Judas Iscariot who participated in the sacrificing of Jesus. Far from being the villain of the piece, Judas was held as the hero who helped release Jesus from his fleshly body. According to that view, the crucifixion as well as Judas' role were positive. Soon however, other scholars, myself included, challenged this

Keywords: Gospel of Judas, Gospel of Truth, Gnosticism, early Christianity, myth interpretation. Judas knew Jesus, not because he was the most insightful and good disciple but because he was a demon. Sacrificing Jesus was of no significance to Jesus nor to salvation in general. Rather, it was carried through by people who confused Jesus' spiritual essence with his docetic appearance.[3] This short summary shows the minefields of very theologically marked discourses involved when analyzing *GospJud*. Before making an assertion about the representation of sacrifice in the GospJud, we have to do some ground work. First, we have to address some myth-theoretical considerations. Second, a new perspective on the manner in which so-called Gnostic myths could be used will be introduced, using the example of the *Gospel of Truth* (*GospTruth*) from Nag Hammadi. Then, we are able to analyze *GospJud* from a new perspective and thereby draw a conclusion about the representation of sacrifice in that text.

The quandary of deconstruction

As this paper is part of a cross-disciplinary conference volume, it is appropriate to relate an ongoing debate on Gnosticism among specialists spanning the last 50 years but particularly noteworthy in the last two decades. Before the discovery of the Nag Hammadi texts in 1945, scholars more or less had to build their understanding of Gnosticism on the polemical reports. The reading of the now available primary texts made it clear that many of the stereotypes hitherto connected to Gnosticism were problematic. We will touch upon some of these stereotypes below, but first it is appropriate to describe the most common view that scholars held on Gnosticism 50 years ago.

In 1966, leading scholars gathered in Messina in order to formulate definitions that would take into consideration information from the newly available sources. In their final statement a distinction between Gnosticism and *gnosis* was made:

> In order to avoid an undifferentiated use of the terms gnosis and Gnosticism, it seems to be advisable to identify, by the combined use of the historical and the typological methods, a concrete fact, "Gnosticism," beginning methodologically with a certain group of systems of the Second Century A.D. which everyone agrees are to be designated with this term. In distinction from this, gnosis is regarded as "knowledge of the divine mysteries reserved for an elite."[4]

In the next step, the same scholars went about trying to distinguish common characteristics among the second century sects.

As a working hypothesis the following formulations are proposed:

> I. The Gnosticism of the Second Century sects involves a coherent series of characteristics that can be summarized in the idea of a divine spark in man, deriving from the divine realm, fallen into this

world of fate, birth and death, and needing to be awakened by the divine counterpart of the self in order to be finally reintegrated. Compared with other conceptions of a "devolution" of the divine, this idea is based ontologically on the conception of a downward movement of the divine whose periphery (often called Sophia or Ennoia) had to submit to the fate of entering into a crisis and producing – even if only indirectly – this world, upon which it cannot turn its back, since it is necessary for it to recover the pneuma – a dualistic conception on a monistic background, expressed in a double movement of devolution and reintegration.

II. The type of gnosis involved in Gnosticism is conditioned by the ontological, theological and anthropological foundations indicated above. Not every gnosis is Gnosticism, but only that which involves in this perspective the idea of the divine consubstantiality of the spark that is in need of being awakened and reintegrated. This gnosis of Gnosticism involves the divine identity of the knower (the Gnostic), the known (the divine substance of one's transcendent self), and the means by which one knows (gnosis as an implicit divine faculty is to be awakened and actualized. This gnosis is a revelation-tradition of a different type from the Biblical and Islamic revelation-tradition).[5]

Even though the conference report made it clear that Gnosticism had a close relation to Mandaeism and Manichaeism, scholars of Gnosticism have with a few exceptions excluded these traditions. I would say that the definition of Messina in 1966 was a reaction not only to the increased available material but just as much against the brave conclusions that old comparativists drew from sometimes ill-defined parallels. Nevertheless, scholars of today who deal with "the Second Century sects" have not felt at ease using the Messina definition. Their critique, however, has largely been targeted at stereotypes related to Gnosticism that were not included in the Messina definition.

Frequently these stereotypes are based on a simplified view on the relation between the myth that people believe in and the social behaviour that would be the outcome of that belief. For instance, scholars of earlier generations often held that Gnostics, due to the anti-cosmisity of their myths, would revolt against the cosmic order of the creator god by ignoring ethical norms or revolting against social conventions.[6] In addition, Gnostics were believed to interpret Biblical material in a manner that would reverse the reading of so-called "orthodox" Christians. Furthermore, there was the notion that Gnostics would be uninterested in ethics. They saw themselves as beings that, due to their spiritual nature, did not have to bother themselves with ethics; they would be saved in any case. Ethics was for those who could go astray and thus perish. For the Gnostic the choice lay between libertinism and ascetism.[7] If Gnostics happened to be interested in ethics, it was seen as inconsistent with the views that they were expected to hold.[8]

Today, however, these stereotypes have faded among specialists. On the contrary, if anyone links the Gnostic myths to the moral conduct of the Gnostics, the conclusion is rather that Gnostics maintained at least as high ethical standards as other Ancient Christians or Pagans. Sometimes it has been claimed that their belief in their divine spiritual spark rather encouraged them to understand more and to act more ethically than others.[9] But the main tendency has been to cut the connection between Gnostic myths and ethical conduct. Most of the critique surrounding the use of the term Gnosticism primarily seems to be directed at the stereotypes that actually were not included in the Messina definition. Michael A. Williams has been very successful in demonstrating the weaknesses of, for instance, the above mentioned stereotypes. Nevertheless, he seems to be pessimistic about the probability of getting rid of the stereotypes as long as the label Gnosticism is used. For this reason he has coined the term "Biblical Demiurgical traditions," which has a lot in common with the typological characteristics mentioned in the Messina definition above. He maintains that such a clearly modern redefinition would avoid the deeply rooted stereotypes that many expect to accompany Gnostic texts. Consequently, Williams attempt is to build a category out of typologies deduced from the myths in Biblical Demiurgical traditions. Moreover, he wants to use a category that would not be linked to notions that there was a group that called themselves Gnostics.[10]

Layton[11] and Brakke[12] take the opposite approach and want to start from the group that might have called themselves "the Knowers." Then they describe the myths that the polemical writers say were used by the Knowers. As these myths seems very similar to what one finds in, for instance, the Apocryphon of John, they end up with something very similar to what scholars long have called "classical Gnosticism." Especially for Brakke it is important to stress that the Gnostics were Christians and he sides with Williams regarding the critique of the stereotypes that too often were related to the Gnostics. Birger Pearson was severely criticized by many scholars when he claimed that Gnosticism was a religion of its own, not denying that there were Christian Gnostics as well. Like Brakke, he starts out with the group that designated themselves as "the Knowers." From there Pearson builds up what he calls classical Gnosticism, which he asserts had its origins in Judaism. He then goes on to include Mandaeans and Manichaeans, due to structural similarities with the classical Gnostic myth. Influenced by Williams, Pearson stresses that the stereotypical view on Gnosticism belongs to a past stage of scholarship.[13]

Karen King's ideas are often seen as closely related to Williams, but she has a distinctly different approach. She describes the rhetorical strategies that the polemic writers adopted when they wanted to construct two groups. Their own church descended from Jesus and the apostles, pitted against the other of heretics. According to King, Gnostics were attached to all kinds of heresies and accused for all sorts of evil things.[14] Then she continues by showing that so-called Gnostics ought not to be attached to the stereotypes that often have been connected to them. So far Williams and King have a lot in common. But when King then takes examples of so-called Gnostic texts and shows that they cannot be called Gnostics because they lack the stereotypes that, according to herself, should not be linked to Gnostics, I have difficulties following the logic. Below I quote her assessment of *GospTruth* that we will deal with at length later in this article:

> GospTruth, a writing from the mid-second century thought by many scholars to have been written by "the arch-heretic" Valentinus himself, is an excellent example of a work that defies classification as a "Gnostic" text. This remarkable work exhibits none of the typological traits of Gnosticism. That is, it draws no distinction between the true God and the creator, for the Father of Truth is the source of all that exists. It avows only one ultimate principle of existence, the Father of Truth, who encompasses everything that exists. The Christology is not docetic; Jesus appears as a historical figure who taught, suffered, and died. Nor do we find either a strictly ascetic or a strictly libertine ethic; rather, the text reveals a pragmatic morality of compassion and justice.[15]

I would say that King is right regarding Christology and ethics. But the absence of docetic Christology and ascetic or libertinistic ethics does not make *GospTruth* more or less Gnostic if we stick to the Messina definition. As will be discussed at length below I am of another opinion than King regarding the creator god. The only thing we might conclude is that *GospTruth* could be a Gnostic text without the stereotypes that King wants to do away with.

In 2006 she goes further and claims that the only label that would be appropriate to use for these texts is Christian.[16] Categorizations such as Christian Gnostics or Valentinians would only marginalize these groups in relation to the disparate body of churches that in the second century would soon develop into pre-orthodox Christianities. Thus, King is scrupulous to avoid forcing texts into categories that would conceal the meaning of the individual texts. But this deconstructionist approach leads to reading texts in macro categories. The drawback is that Christian is a category that badly needs to be broken down into subdivisions if it would be of analytical value. Dunderberg (2008) follows King and uses the term Christian, although he still finds Valentinians appropriate for the group he investigates. Recently Jenott has claimed that *GospJud*, the other text that we will focus on, has been misinterpreted because scholars have read it as a Gnostic text. Referring to Williams and King, he calls it Christian.[17]

Conclusion and point of departure

We started out with the definition of Gnosticism from the Messina conference in 1966. At that time the scholars dissociated themselves from a more comparative approach. Mandaeism and Manichaeism were excluded from Gnosticism, as were other trends within Hinduism, Buddhism and other traditions, such as Pythagorean. Instead the second century Christian sects were the starting point for the 1966 historical and typological definition. It is noteworthy that these groups that, according to the Messina definition, would form the beginning of a phenomenon also seem to have become the end of it. Rarely do scholars detect a continuation of the Ancient Gnostic traditions in later periods. This might be due to the difficulty in finding something that would fit the Messina definition in later sources. Those scholars who go further on in history include Manichaeism and Mandaeism in their investigations. Hermetism that earlier was included in the study of Gnosticism, a tradition with a longer history, nowadays is excluded.

Without digging deep into the discussions that preceded the conference in 1966, I suggest that a general tendency to distance themselves from earlier trends in the comparative study of religion was important factor for the authors of the conference report. When Gnosticism is defined narrowly the discussion naturally focuses on relations between different kinds of Christianities. The *Nag Hammadi* texts and *Codex Tchacos,* in which *GospJud* is included, show few of the stereotypes earlier connected to Gnosticism. Although many scholars continue to define Gnosticism on typologies deduced from myths, many have stopped asking what function the myths might have had for those who saw them as sacred narratives. Maybe this is due to the risk of associating oneself with those who constructed the stereotypes and those who later upheld them. Thus, the clear-sightedness brought by scholars such as Williams is very valuable, but it has to be combined with myth-theoretical investigations into the functions of myth. Otherwise the clear-sightedness that has been achieved over the last decades risks being replaced with a theoretical view without nuance.

In this paper I will put forward a proposal for the use of myth in *GospTruth* and then explore how this new perspective could help us analyze the view on ethics and sacrifice in *GospJud.* My aim is to form a hypothesis that could be tested on other material as well. We might be able to use it across religious borders and, in this way, re-establish the comparative study in this field. It goes without saying that this is my first step on a journey that, even with promising results, would have to be tested in many investigations. On a theoretical level I am influenced by fairly general insights from the new comparativism in the history of religions.[18] Too often, typological investigations have been carried through without taking into account how the different types were used in the respective texts. This was one of the drawbacks in old comparativism. I also want to challenge the deconstructive tendency that has taught us to be more careful, but also has undermined the will of explaining relations between different phenomena. As for the discussion above, we have deconstructed categories down to the level of individual texts but ended up with an even more fluid category that is hard to use in analytical work: Christianity. Stating that we deal with nothing other than Christianity rather seems to be a theological statement than a methodological one. Presently I see no reason to invent another term for Gnosticism. The awareness of the problems in earlier investigations has grown rapidly among specialists and in time it will hopefully spread to non-specialists as well. Besides, many still use Gnosticism outside of the restricted sense from 1966. Scholars of Mandaeism, Hinduism, and Buddhism and of New Religious Movements have less negative views on what Gnosticism could have been. That this has had no importance for those criticizing the use of the term Gnosticism shows the problem with the Messina definition: It has narrowed the field to such an extent that it has become an affair of early Christianities only, a field in which myth theoretical questions often are seriously neglected.

Before starting, some words on myth might be appropriate. Many definitions of myth could do for the present purpose, but I have chosen Wendy Doniger's:

> ... a myth is: a narrative in which a group finds, over an extended period of time, a shared meaning in certain questions about human life, to which the various proposed answers are usually unsatisfactory in one way or another. These would be questions such as, Why are we here? What happens to us when we die? Is there a God?[19]

What I especially want to stress here is Doniger's remark that a myth is a story and not an idea. One could, according to Doniger, start out with a metamyth that ideally would consist of subjects and predicates only. Every time when a myth is told, the teller adds something to it. Those additions can tell us something about the context and use of the myth in that specific context. Theoretically we could think of a maximyth that would consist of all those additions to the minimyth, but of course, none of these metamyths have existed. An example of her reasoning is quoted below:

> For example, the hypothesis of an unmarked, neutral experience involving a woman, a man, a garden, a tree, a fruit, a snake, and knowl-

> edge allows us to understand how the Hebrew Bible could tell that story as it does (an evil snake, forbidden fruit, evil woman, disobedient and destructive knowledge), while other interpretations of that story tell it differently... The positive reading of the serpent (though not of the woman) was, however, accepted in the Ophite version of Genesis, in which Yaldabaoth (God) is evil, and the serpent is good. It was further developed by Romantics such as Shelley, who saw a direct parallel between Satan's gift of the fruit and Prometheus' gift of fire – a gift that, like the fruit in Eden, provoked the wrath of the jealous gods and the creation of the first, disastrously seductive woman, Pandora.[20]

According to this reasoning, a myth would not lead to a specific ethical attitude or behaviour; on the contrary, the myth could be interpreted in many ways. However, variations are not limitless. The interpretation must be meaningful for the interpreter, so the context of the interpreter and the ways in which the myth has previously been interpreted will delimit the range of additions to and interpretations of the myth. Therefore, we cannot use the simplified view on myth as earlier scholars often did when they presupposed that Gnostic myths would result in ascetic or libertinistic behaviour. Neither should we overlook the importance of the myth, which seems to be what modern scholars have tended to do when they downplay the importance of making a distinction between non-Gnostic and Gnostic Christian myths.

First, I posit that the myth can be interpreted in many ways but not in an infinite number. The story has to be intelligible. This level is mostly semantic and syntactic. Second, the variations depend on the rules that determine the discourse. By this I mean the manner in which the myth used to be interpreted in particular historical environments. The discourse will normally follow some conventional rules according to the specific context. Of course, I am influenced by Foucault in my reasoning, but for the present purpose we do not need to look deeply into his theories. This second level can be distinguished but probably not isolated from the first level, since semantics and syntactics also are parts of discursive practice. Third, the myth is coloured by a narrower context than that mentioned in my second statement. And here the particularities of the negotiation of power between the teller of the specific version of the myth and the community that decided to preserve it might help us understand in what way they used it. It is on this third level that I assert that many analyses of myths have failed. Too often parts of a myth are taken out of the narration and thus changed into dogmatic statements. In the following analysis I will try to avoid this by paying more attention to the text surface than normally has been the case. Here I am influenced by text linguistic theories. To state it simply, my text linguistic approach is closely related to rhetorical analysis. Thus, I aim at disclosing the strategies that the authors of *GospTruth* and *GospJud* used in order to persuade their audiences.

Beyond anticosmisity

GospTruth is one of the most studied texts from the Nag Hammadi discovery. It is well-preserved in Codex 1. In codex 12 we have a few fragments of what I see as a later version of the text. In this article, however, I will concentrate on parts of *GospTruth* that are not preserved in the fragments. Thus GospTruth always refers to the text of Codex 1. As for the authorship of *GospTruth,* many scholars, among whom I am included, suggest that it stems from Valentinus of Alexandria[21] who led a community in Rome from 138. For us this is of importance as Irenaeus of Lyons reports that Valentinus was building on the Gnostic system when he developed his teaching.[22] In the following analyses I will argue for an interpretation of *GospTruth* in which a special interpretation of the Gnostic myth is criticized and modified. Now it is time to turn to the text analysis. *GospTruth* starts as follows:

The good news of the truth is a joy for those who have received the grace from the Father of the truth, that they might know him through the power of the Word that came forth from that Fullness that is in the Father's thought and mind, this is what they call "the Redeemer" since that is the name of the work that he was to accomplish for the redemption of those who were ignorant of the Father, and since the name of the good news is the revelation of the hope, since it is the discovery for those who are searching for him.[23]

Like the vast majority of scholars I assume that *GospTruth* is a homily. When the speaker steps forward in order to preach, from a text linguistic point of view this corresponds to a marker on the pragmatic level; the community knows that a homily will follow. But the attitude on the part of the community towards the preacher is less obvious. Harold W. Attridge has suggested that *GospTruth* is an exoteric text in which the audience consisted of non-Gnostic Christians who gradually were persuaded to adopt a reinterpreted version of the gospel.[24] Attridge's analysis was an important attempt to see what methods were used to persuade the audience to change their views. But for reasons that will be discussed below, I assume that the audience consisted of people who were acquainted with some sort of Gnostic myth that gradually became reinterpreted.[25] Granting this, those who call the Word their redeemer are the community. Although ignorance of the Father had made itself painfully felt, now the community is said to be in a state of joy as they know the Father. This initial sentence, I suggest, does not function as a prologue to the following main part of the homily[26] as all other scholars have treated it. This observation is more than a quibbling with delimitation in linguistic hyper-technical jargon. Rather, it means that the following sentence that opens with a causal conjunction "because" is subordinated to the first sentence. Following this logic we expect something that was vaguely emphasized in the first sentence to be developed and explained in the second. Moreover, the joy that one should experience is an instruction to the community. Despite the frightening figure of Error, which will evolve in the second sentence that we soon will turn to, one ought to stick to the antidote of fear: the joy that comes with the knowledge of the Father.

> Because[27] the All[28] wandered about searching for[29] the one from whom they had come forth, and yet[30] the All was inside of him, the incomprehensible, inconceivable one who is superior to every thought, thus[31] ignorance of the Father brought anguish and terror, and the anguish grew dense like a fog, so that no one could see,[32] for this reason, Error [33]found strength, worked on its own matter[34] in emptiness[35] since it had not known the truth.[36]

Most likely, the state of searching for the Father had a familiar ring to the community. Once, everybody had been searching for what they now had found. The remark that the All was inside of the Father although they had come forth from him expresses a paradoxical state. The Father contains everything whereas nothing contains him.[37] The bewildered state seems to be caused by the incomprehensive nature of the Father. Out of this confusion anguish and terror emerge. Finally, the perplexity has developed to such degree that no one can see the Father, and because of this, Error finds strength. Although its power is based upon ignorance, Error takes on some kind of real existence. It becomes powerful and works on its own matter. Finally, however, the frightening figure is diminished by the statement that its acts are of no importance since it lacks what the members of the community have: the Truth. The sentence from 17:4a-18a is skilfully designed. It opens with a causal conjunction "because," but we have to wait for the result construction "therefore Error found strength." When Error finally is introduced, the rhetorical function is that it suddenly plays the principal role of the period. As it also takes on mythological characteristics we have two tendencies in the sentence. On the one hand Error is a psychologically based product. It is caused by ignorance and in that regard lacks independent existence. At the same time, Error has many affinities with what we would expect from a demiurge figure in many Gnostic traditions. It works on matter. Its name Error is based on the Coptic word planē. Although I know of no other text in which the Demiurge is called in this way, it is common to describe the Demiurge as somebody who errs, in Coptic *r planaste*. The terminology might have been chosen in order to stress the relationship between the misconception on the part of the All and the existence of Error. Moreover, the state of blindness that those in the fog experience suggests a designation of those holding that the Demiurge is the real God. The following passage illustrates the two mentioned phenomena.

> "Indeed, I am God, beside me there is no one!" When he said this, he sinned against the All.[38] But this speech got up to Incorruptibility. And behold! A voice came forth from Incorruptibility and said: "You are mistaken,[39] Samael" that means "god of the blind[40].[41]

Thus, we encounter a bundle of expressions and themes that would lead listeners who were acquainted with Gnostic myth to see Error as the Demiurge. Its deeds and power are affirmed but, simultaneously, its existence is questioned. Error rather seems to be a product of ignorance on the part of the All. I suggest that the preacher has in mind problems that are related to focusing too much on Error rather than on the Father. If a community with such problems should be persuaded to change its view, it has to be done gradually. The emotional experience of the community has to be affirmed but given a new interpretation. Consequently, the preacher first encourages the community to see themselves as those who rejoice in the grace of knowing the Father. Then, they are told that Error is powerful, albeit a product of their own ignorance. Let us see whether this line of interpretation would make sense when we interpret the following passages.

> Matter came into being[42] in a moulded form,[43] as Error by the power of beauty prepared the substitute for the truth. Now, this was not a humiliation for him, the incomprehensible, inconceivable one. For they were nothing, the anguish, and the oblivion and the moulded form[44] of deceit, whereas the established truth is immutable, imperturbable and impossible to beautify.[45]

First, the work on matter enters actuality and results in a moulded form. This language is a commonplace for many creation stories in antiquity. Here we might add that the initial clause could be alternatively translated as "It happened in a deluding way," which would emphasize the power of Error's deceitful nature, whereas my main translation allows the handicraft on matter and the connection to the creation myths to come into focus. For Coptic listeners and probably to Greek listeners as well, assuming the hypothetical origin of the text, both these clusters of meanings could be grasped simultaneously. It is noteworthy that the modifying preceding statements that Error worked foolishly and does not know the truth are confirmed. It can only create a substitute for truth. In the modifying parts, first of all the Father's superiority to what Error does is emphasized. By no means is Error a threat to the Father.

Second, the dyad of the prior sentence, anguish and terror, is replace by the triad anguish, oblivion and the moulded form of deceit. Oblivion that now takes the place of terror in *GospTruth* is synonymous with ignorance. The captive beauty of matter and its deceitful nature is reaffirmed by the third member of the triad. The triad anguish, oblivion and the moulded form of deceit well summarizes the origin, power and creation of Error. Thus, when we turn to the last part of the sentence, all might and power and reality of Error vanishes. The truth is eternal, firm and impossible to challenge by the most beautiful lie. Once again, the demiurge-myth is not contradicted but reinterpreted. So far the image of Error has been based on a presupposed mythology that the community was acquainted with. Now it is logical that we move from the mythological past to the current state of the community.

> For this reason, ignore[46] Error since it thus [47]has no root!! It came into being in a fog regarding the Father. It exists since it prepares works, and oblivion, and terrors in order to, by them, seduce those of the middle and capture them.[48]

We have reached a meta-communicative level, an explicit instruction on how the receivers should interpret the previous information. The community should not take Error so seriously. The passage indicates that too much focus could have been laid on Error earlier. At the same time the unreal state of Error is expounded upon, and the experience of its presence is affirmed. Error came into being in a fog, probably the one that was mentioned earlier and that basically is a product of ignorance. In this manner, the preacher is able to affirm the reality that people have experienced and at the same time is able to explain that this reality is a product of ignorance. But downplaying Error should not be carried out too fast. Otherwise the community would be more difficult to convince. Thus, the recently quoted passage ends with a description of Error as captivating "those of the middle." The fear may actually have very concrete social consequences. In the following passage, we are informed that the fear that is the result of ignorance does not come from the Father. On the contrary, the Father is opposed to everything that has to do with Error. Next, the persecution and crucifixion of Jesus is taken as an example of how Error can be executed through people, but more importantly, we are told the way such a persecution is turned into a victory for those who know.

> The oblivion that belonged to Error was not revealed. It is not a [thought][49] from the Father. It was not from the Father that oblivion came into being. Now indeed, it was concerning the Father that it came into being. But what comes into being in the Father is the knowledge! The knowledge became revealed in order that oblivion might vanish

> and the Father be known. Since oblivion came into being because the Father was not known, then, when the Father is known, oblivion will not occur again. This the good news of the one for whom they searched revealed to those who were complete through the mercies of the Father, the hidden mystery, Jesus Christ. Through the knowledge he enlightened those who through oblivion were in darkness. He enlightened them, provided a way, and the way is the truth, which he taught them. For this reason, Error grew angry with him, persecuted him, became distressed by him, was defeated by him when they nailed him to a tree, because he became a fruit of the knowledge of the Father![50] Now, it did not perish[51] because it was eaten. On the contrary, to those who ate it, whom he discovered in himself and who discovered him in themselves,[52] it caused them to rejoice in its discovery![53]

The knowledge takes on the key role. It enters history and thereby causes a hostile reaction from those who are rooted in Error. The assault, however, has the opposite effect than Error probably intended; the tree of knowledge appears with a fruit that eternally will be at hand, providing insight, reunion and joy for those who eat it. I assert that we have reached the end of what I call the first chapter of *GospTruth*. It started with the joy in the gospel; then we saw how the Demiurge was described as a terrifying figure. Now the Demiurge is downplayed to the point where it is defeated. Far from being something that the community should pay attention to, the Demiurge and its creation is insignificant.

Why is this analysis important?

On the basis of the above analyses, I want to suggest the following: In *GospTruth* the preacher had to tackle a situation in which people with a fairly literal interpretation of a Gnostic myth had to be persuaded into a psychological understanding of it. Their likely focus, the Demiurge, turned out to be a product of their own imagination. Even though people could kill those who proclaimed the good news, such acts would still result in a triumph for the truth. The physical crucifixion of Jesus made it possible for his disciples to eat the fruit of knowledge.

Thus, the physical violence is not denied. Rather, the preacher emphasizes the transitory nature of the Demiurge's powers. What really matters is the joy that results from the redemption from ignorance. *GospTruth* does not express a positive view of the cosmos that the Demiurge created; it is not a pro-cosmic text. But neither does it express a hostile view of the Demiurge, since such hostility would detract the focus from the joy and knowledge of the Father and, instead, add to the fear that is connected to Error. In this way, *GospTruth* is not an anti-cosmic text either. To revolt against the Demiurge and the laws of retaliation that were related to it would be to increase its importance. Instead one should focus on the Father, and the knowledge of him should be the guide in life. Consequently, it would be equally wrong to follow the cosmic laws as to revolt against them. Sometimes the knowledge would result in actions that would coincide with cosmic conventions; sometimes they would go against them. But that is irrelevant. Ignoring Error and focusing on the Father is typical for what I would call the acosmic perspective. As far as I know, this way of perceiving the myth is my own. To sum up, the myth in itself is not anti-cosmic or pro-cosmic, neither is it acosmic. Rather, it can be used in many different ways, and in this particular case we clearly have an acosmic use of it. In the present article we cannot to any fuller extent discuss the ways the myth is used in ethical discourses.[54] Instead we stop here with the acosmic perspective in mind and turn our attention to *GospJud* in order to see if this acosmic perspective might explain hitherto enigmatic passages of *GospJud*.

Beyond righteousness and transgression

GospjUd is preserved in the so-called Codex Tchacos that is dated to the beginning of the fourth century. But in the second century Irenaeus of Lyons mentions a gospel that may have been the origin to the version in Codex Tchacos.[55] *GospJud* experienced many hardships on its bumpy journey to publication in 2006. The text was seriously damaged, but despite all challenges its restoration was quite successful. In 2009 additional fragments from the original text were presented, and those are included in my analysis of the text. Generally scholars have held that Judas handing over of Jesus to be crucified lacks any salvific meaning in *GospJud*. Recently this view was challenged by Jenott in his doctoral dissertation on that gospel. There he draws upon Aulén's[56] analyses of Christus Victor. Influenced by Aulén, Jenott claims that the crucifixion of Christ in *GospJud* has significance as a salvific drama in which the evil powers of the world are overcome.[57] Acording to Jenott, many scholars have overlooked this perspective due to *stereotypes related to Gnosticism,* for instance, a general belief that "Gnostics rejected ritual in exchange for salvation through esoteric knowledge."[58] In order to form a perspective on these issues, we will analyze the rhetorical processes in *GospJud,* which, as far as I know, have not been closely examined before. Furthermore, we will see if the acosmic perspective could help us solving hitherto enigmatic parts of the text. The text presents a conversation between Jesus and Judas Iscariot before Easter. But before their dialogue starts we also encounter the other disciples.

> When Jesus appeared on Earth, he made signs and great wonders for the salvation of humanity. Even though[59] some walked on the road of righteousness and others in their transgressions, nevertheless the twelve disciples were called. He began to speak about the mysteries

that are above the world, and about what will happen in the end.[60]

Previously, the importance of this passage has been neglected. The 12 disciples belong to two groups, those who follow moral codes and those who transgress them. Nevertheless all of them are called. This remark, I assert, suggests that the moral and immoral conduct of the 12 did not make any difference. Both kinds of behaviour originate from the cosmic sphere. However, we have to consider whether the disciples are a symbol for mankind? As they do not seem to have the chance to be saved, they cannot represent the entire human race. For sure, Jesus made signs and miracles to save at least some parts of humanity, but I doubt that the disciples were included in these parts. Even though the disciples are introduced to the exalted mysteries, they have no capacity to comprehend them. This idea is developed in the following section of the text.

> It happened In Judaea that he one day came to his disciples and found them gathered together, sitting practicing godliness. When he came upon his disciples gathered together, sitting and offering thanks over the bread, he laughed. The disciples said to him "Master, why do you laugh at our offering thanks when we do what is right." He said to them, "Neither am I laughing at you. Nor are you doing this by your own will, but this is the manner in which your god is worshiped." They said to him, "Master, you are Christ the son of our god." Jesus said to them, "How could you know me? Truly I say to you, no race from the people among you will know me." When his disciples heard this they began to be displeased and became angry with him and blasphemed against him in their minds.[61]

Indirectly the disciples are told about another sphere with another God. But the only reaction it provokes is anger and blasphemy. The theme of anger is something that seems to belong to those of the lower realms. This will be of importance for the interpretation of the latter parts of *GospJud* as well. In the following text Jesus continues to provoke the disciples. He challenges them saying that the one who has the power should bring forth "the perfect man" and stand up in front of Jesus. Nobody except Judas could do that. However, he could not look Jesus in his eyes but instead looks down.[62] Despite of this shortcoming Judas knows what the other disciples do not know. He recognizes Jesus and where he has come from.

> Judas said to him, "I know who you are, and from which place you have come. You have come out of the immortal realm of Barbelo, and the name of the one who sent you it is not fitting for me to utter."[63]

Here we come across a reoccurring idea, the favorite disciple. Judas knows what the others do not, and he seems to be the prototype for favorite discipleship, the one who wants to be initiated in the deepest mysteries.[64] From this perspective it is not surprising that Jesus tells Judas to separate himself from the other disciples for deeper initiation in the exalted mysteries. But a gradual change of the scenario is introduced.

> But Jesus knowing that Judas thought about other exalted things said to him, "Separate yourself from the others. I shall tell you about the mysteries of the kingdom, not in order that you will go there,[65] but in order that you will suffer much grief. For someone else will replace you so that the twelve again will be complete in their god.[66]

The established position of the favorite disciple begins to falter. Judas is separated from the other disciples who will replace him with somebody of their own kind. But simultaneously, Judas is not depicted in the way in which we would expect the favorite disciple to be portrayed. The 12 disciples appear as a group that completely lacks knowledge about the mysteries. Judas, for his part, does not reach the level of the favorite disciple but is related to a category of those who know a lot about the mysteries but cannot use the information properly. Judas fails to grasp what Jesus says and asks him when he will be instructed about the great race and the final day. But as he does that, Jesus leaves him.[67] Moreover, the grief that Judas will suffer can be interpreted as a temporal state aimed at developing the "favourite disciple's" spiritual skills. But as we will see at the end of the gospel, this is not the result. I suggest *GospJud* represents a much more skilled rhetoric than hitherto has been acknowledged, as the different stereotypical characters are transformed in the latter parts of the text.

In the next section of the text, the scenario shifts to the 12 disciples. They have had a vision, and they are eager to tell Jesus about it.

> The disciples said to him, "Master, where did you go and what did you do when you had left us?" Jesus said to them, "I went to another great and holy race." His disciples said to him, "Lord, what great race is it that is beyond us and holy, as it is not now in this realm?" But when Jesus heard this he laughed and said to them, "Why do you contemplate on this strong and holy race? Truly, I say to you, no offspring of this realm will see that race, nor will any angelic army of the stars rule over it, nor will any mortal human be able to reach it. Because that race is not from (6-7 letters missing) which has come to be. (Some words missing) The human race that is among you is from mankind. (Two lines that are hard to restore) Another power which you rule (some letters missing)." When the disciples heard that each one were disturbed in their spirit so that they were unable to talk."[68]

Although the disciples are greatly disturbed by his harsh message, another day they tell Jesus about a great vision they have had.

> They told Jesus, "Master, we saw you in a vision. For we saw in a dream the other night." He said, "Why (some letters missing) hidden yours?" They said, "We saw a great building in which there was a great altar. There were twelve men, we would say that they were priests. A name (1 line missing). There was a crowd persevering tenaciously at that altar until the priests were done and had served. And we were tenaciously persevering as well." Jesus said, "What kind of [priests][69] were they?" They said, "Some abstain for two weeks. Others sacrifice their own children, others their wives. As they praise and act humbly towards each other, some sleep with males, others work at slaughtering, and others commit a multitude of sins and injustices. And the men who stand at the altar invoke your name and by all deeds of incompletion that altar is filled." When they had said this they became silent for they were disturbed. Jesus said, "Why are you disturbed? Truly, I say to you, all the priests who stand at the altar invoke my name. And again I say to you, they have inscribed my name on the [altar] for the race of the stars through the race of mankind. And in my name they shamefully have planted fruitless trees." Jesus said to them, "You are those who receive service at the altar you saw, it is the god you serve, and you are the twelve men that you saw. The domestic animals that are led to be sacrificed is the crowd that you lead astray to that altar."[70]

As was mentioned the first time we encountered the disciples, they do not all act the same. Some act in a way that typically would be considered lust, and some in a manner that rather is considered ascetism. In the following passage, the characteristics of righteousness and transgression are retold. Different behaviours among those who were related to the disciples are connected to different epochs. Times of piety are succeeded by times of injustice. But all kinds of behaviours are connected to the rulers of the cosmic sphere. Eventually, the disciples ask Jesus to purify them. This is the culmination of a tendency that has developed through the narration. At the beginning the disciples became angry when Jesus criticized them. Gradually, they have become more disturbed and silent. Now they repent. However, Jesus says that he has come for the sake of the strong and great race and that he cannot take care of everybody.[71] Here we leave the disciples for the last time, as Jesus now begins to teach Judas about the great race. Thus, at the outset the 12 disciples are depicted as hostile persons. At the end, however, they are described as tragic figures rather than as evil ones. They were told about the cosmic sphere, but still gain very little information about the upper realm. At the beginning of the text they were angry. Now, they are humble, but tragically enough cannot receive the esoteric knowledge. However, I posit they have reached a level that in some ways transcends the one that Judas will reach. They understand that their different efforts are irrelevant. In my view, this depiction is developed in a manner that casts a darker shadow over the person who has knowledge but nevertheless lacks insight. Now we will examine what kind of information Judas receives.

> Judas said to him, "Rabbi, what fruit does this race possess?" Jesus said, "The souls of every human race will die. But when they have completed their time in the kingdom and when their spirit separates from them, their bodies will certainly die but their souls will be alive and they will be lifted up."[72]

One could say that this passage opens the second part of *GospJud*. Thus, probably it is no coincidence that we here meet the same theme as we find at the end of the text, the spirit leaving the body in order to ascend to the spiritual realm. Now Judas also wants to share a vision that he hopes that Jesus can interpret for him:

> Judas said, "Master, just as you have listened to all of them, now listen to me as well, because I have had a great vision!" But when Jesus heard this, he laughed and said to him, "Why do you strive that hard, o thirteenth demon? But talk and I will bear with you." Judas said to him, "I saw myself in a vision. The twelve disciples were stoning me, and persecuting me severely. I also came to the place (some letters missing) after you. I saw a building that was too large for my eyes to measure. Some great men surrounded it and it was roofed with greenery, and in the midst of it there was a crowd." (Judas said to him], Master, take me into these persons!" Jesus answered and said to him, "Your star has bewildered you. It is not fitting for a mortal human to enter the building that you saw, since it is a place that is reserved for the holy. The sun and moon will not rule there, nor will the day. But they (the holy) will eternally stand in the realm together with the holy angels." Behold, I have told you the mysteries of the kingdom, and I have instructed you about the error of the stars. (Some letters missing) sent (some letters missing) beyond the twelve realms." Judas said to him, "Master, never will my seed rule the rulers." Jesus answered and said to him, "Come! I will (2 lines hard to restore) but you will groan deeply when you see the kingdom with its entire race." When Judas heard this he said to him, "What is for me in what I have received? Because you have separated me from that race!" Jesus answered and said, "You will become the thirteenth and you will be cursed by the rest of the races. But you will finally rule over them. They will (some letters missing) and you will not ascend to the holy race."[73]

It is interesting to compare Judas' vision with that of the other disciples. In both we see a building, but the placement of the great men and the crowd is reversed, and in Judas' vision there is no altar. Judas' role as the "favorite" disciple is completely reinterpreted. He is a demon that will rule over the 12 cosmic spheres. He possesses more knowledge than the other disciples, but this is of no help as he cannot enter the eternal realm. In this respect his position is the same as that of the Demiurge. Following the acosmic perspective, all realms in the cosmos are linked to grief. Ruler and ruled are linked together in a system that will bring no joy. The text continues with a long retelling of a Gnostic cosmogony. Judas really comes to know the mysteries, but he cannot take part in them. Moreover, towards the end of the text the focus shifts. Judas's problem seems to be that he has knowledge but cannot distinguish cosmic matters from spiritual affairs. Judas and the other disciples will serve the fleshly form of Jesus, confusing matter with spirit.

> Truly I (Jesus) say to you, no hand of mortal human can sin against me. Truly I say to you Judas, those who bring offerings to Saklas (2,5 lines impossible to restore) all evil works. You, Judas will do more than they, for you will bring forth the man that bears me. Already your horn is raised, and your anger is full. Your star has risen and your heart has been grasped.[74]

In a prophetic manner Jesus says that no mortal can sin against him. This statement is linked to the preceding text that deals with those who confuse Jesus real nature with his mortal body. Judas, who initially was the "favorite disciple," now is filled with anger, just as the other disciples at the beginning of the text. Only one small detail has to be added before the Gnostic myth is complete: The prototype for the spiritual race has to ascend.

> Then, the model of the great race of Adam will ascend. Because through the eternal ones the great race came to be before heavens and the Earth and the angels. Behold, I have told you everything. Lift up your eyes and see the cloud and the light which is in it and the stars which surround it. And the star that is the leader of them is your star. And Judas lifted up his eyes and saw the luminous cloud, and he entered into it. Those standing on the ground heard a voice out of the cloud saying, "the great race (some letters missing) image (3,5 lines impossible to restore. And Judas stopped looking at Jesus. And at once a disturbance took place among the Jews.[75]

Based on this long analysis, we are able to assert answers on some hotly debated questions. Judas has received a lot of information, but he is unable to understand what Jesus has told him. No mortal can sin against him. Now Jesus tells that the model of the great race will ascend. I assume that it is Jesus himself who in a prototypical way paves the way for those who are worthy to follow him. But as Judas confuses the mortal body of Jesus with his spiritual essence, he does not recognize that Jesus has ascended. It is hard to determine who it is that enters the cloud. I assume that it is Jesus, but it is also possible that Judas enters and looks down upon the mortal man Jesus. If Jesus' spirit has left him, we may assume that this would be hinted at in the final lines of the gospel. Thus, we turn to these last lines now.

> Then their chief priests murmured because he (Jesus) entered into the guest room for his prayer. And some scribes were there watching closely in order to catch him at prayer, for they were afraid of the people because he was held to be a prophet by them all. And they approached Judas. They said to him, "What are you doing here? You are the disciple of Jesus." But as for him, he answered them according to their will. Then Judas received some coins. He handed him over to them.[76]

As we know that the dialogue between Jesus and Judas was said to take place at Easter, it is not at all far-fetched to see Jesus entering the guest house in order to pray as an allusion to the last supper. Here, I would say, we have an inclusio back to the Eucharist at the opening of the gospel. That Jesus prays and celebrates the Eucharist, to me, is an indication of that he now acts according to the logic of a cosmic man. Judas, despite all information he has received, is unable to distinguish spirit from flesh and hands over Jesus. In this manner we have reached a point where the fleshly Jesus imitates the disciples at the outset of the gospel. This, I would say, repeats what was developed earlier in the text. The godliness that the fleshly Jesus performs is related to the old and lower system. He has become an image of the righteous but tragic figure. Simultaneously, Judas is characterized as a transgressor, who filled with fury, betrays what he thinks is Jesus, not understanding that a man who prays and offers thanks cannot be the spiritual one. At the beginning of *GospJud* Judas knew that Jesus was from the spiritual realm, but at the inclusio, he nevertheless is unable to distinguish matter from spirit.

How to use this analysis

The above presented analysis differs from previous analyses in that it pays more attention to the narration. As the protagonists often undergo transformations through the text, it is not advisable to pick up isolated parts and then choose to analyze them. The disciples, Judas excluded, are symbols for two ways of life, righteousness and transgression. Initially they are hostile to Jesus and question his message about the superior

God from the immortal realm. Nevertheless, they want Jesus's opinion on their vision of the altar. In the vision the two ways of life are exemplified by acts of lust and ascetism. Gradually, however, they understand that there is a realm that transcends cosmos, both regarding the basis for ethical conduct and spiritual insight. They repent, understanding that their cosmically based efforts are futile. But their end is tragic, they are mortal and unable to reach the immortal realm. I assert that the disciples are symbols for non-Gnostics who finally understand that cosmic norms are fruitless, but who, due to their mortal disposition, are bound to mortality.

Judas' end is no less tragic. He starts out being the favorite disciple. But from the beginning, it is clear that something is wrong, he cannot look into Jesus's face. Gradually it is revealed that his insights are due to his demonic character. Although he is instructed about the mysteries, he nevertheless lacks capacity to reach the immortal realm. Instead of, like the other disciples, humbling himself, repenting and accepting his state, he gets angry. Judas ends up in the same condition as the other disciples were at the beginning: wrath. Moreover, at the end Judas fails to distinguish flesh from spirit. He knows that Jesus is the Messiah, Christ. Nevertheless, he believes that he can hand over Jesus. For this reason, from the perspective of his intention, Judas does more evil than others. The priests of the vision of the altar have been described as sacrificing the people as if they were cattle, whereas Judas tries to sacrifice the Messiah.

To sum up, Judas, who should know better, continues to act according to his cosmic disposition, failing to transcend to an acosmic perspective. The other disciples, for their part, also lack capacity to enter the transcendent realm, but nevertheless, humble themselves and affirms the futility of cosmic rituals as the Eucharist, service at the altar and the sacrificing of Jesus.

Putting the pieces together

In this article I have highlighted difficulties in *GospTruth* and in *GospJud* that are solved when we infer an acosmic perspective. This perspective is based upon a special usage of the Gnostic myth. In *GospTruth* it is possible to see the way the acosmic perspective is developed. *GospJud* is different: The reinterpretation of the myth is less obvious, but as parts of *GospJud* become much more intelligible when we infer the acosmic perspective on the text, this approach makes sense. With this said, I do not claim that all texts that share an acosmic perspective are similar in all other respects. For instance, we have seen that the meaning of crucifixion differs widely between these two acosmically oriented texts. In *GospTruth* the crucifixion is of major importance, and it is linked to the Eucharist that is positive. In *GospJud* the crucifixion and Eucharist are insignificant, serving as examples of cosmicly related behaviours only. The analysis of myth has to be combined with a careful study of the rhetorical strategies applied in the text. The myth does not lead to a specific dogmatic position, but it functions as a frame in which many variations can appear. With these examples I hope to reintroduce the study of Gnostic myth, and maybe even to contribute with some ideas of how it can be applied in comparative studies.

And as for the view on sacrifice in the two discussed texts, I posit the following. In *GospTruth* the sacrifice in the form of crucifixion is part of the Christus Victor pattern. Jesus defeats the cosmic powers. In *GospJud*, however, crucifixion, other forms of sacrifice and rituals are of no significance, aside from serving as examples of the foolishness of those who confuse matter and spirit. This discussion was typical in late antiquity, when the tendency to spiritualize sacrifice was common. *GospJud* goes a step farther than *GospTruth.* It might be the case that baptism is important in *GospJud,* but that is still a matter for deeper investigation. But the view of Eucharist and the importance of Jesus's death are strongly called into question.

Notes

1. Krosney, 2006 and Magnusson 2008 for more information about the discovery.
2. For early interpretations see Kasser, Meyer and Wurst 2006 and Pagels and King 2007.
3. For a critique of the earliest view see for instance, De Conick 2007, Robinson 2007, Magnusson 2008, Painchaud 2008 and Thomassen 2008. Recently, Jenott (2011) criticized the opinion that the *GospJud* represents a negative view on sacrifice and of Judas Iscariot.
4. Bianchi 1967 XXVI.
5. Bianchi 1967 XXVI–XXVII.
6. Jonas 1963: 46. According to Jonas 1963: 160, even pagan moral philosophy should have been discarded by the Gnostics.
7. Jonas 1963: 270–276 saw libertinism as the core of Gnosticism, whereas Rudolph 1983: 253–255 rather stressed the ascetic side.
8. Desjardins 1990: 2–3.
9. Pagels 1989: 70–73, Mahe 1998: 35.
10. Williams 1996: 51–53.
11. Layton 1995.
12. Brakke 2010.
13. Pearson 2007: 140, 164–165.

14. King 2003: 20–54.
15. King 2003: 192.
16. King 2006: IX–X.
17. Jenott 2011: 1.
18. Paden 2008 provides a good summary of the state of affairs.
19. Doniger 1996: 112.
20. Doniger 1996: 120.
21. For a detailed discussion of authorship, date of composition, etc. see Magnusson 2006: 13–44.
22. Irenaeus, *Against the Heresies* 1.11.1.
23. All quotations from *GospTruth* are from Nag Hammadi Codex 1. This passage is from 16.31–17.4a. Unless otherwise is indicated, all translations are my own.
24. "The presupposed theology is concealed so that the author may make an appeal to ordinary Christians, inviting them to share the basic insights of Valentinianism." Attridge 1986: 139–140.
25. My general critique of Attridge's argumentation is that it does not carefully enough follow the argumentation of the text. Rather he chooses topics that seem "familiar" and in an interesting manner discusses in what way they become transformed. Such an undertaking must be combined with an analysis of the text surface and the rhetorical strategies that such analysis might disclose. For earlier studies suggesting a more esoteric setting see Säve-Söderbergh 1958 and Segelberg 1959.
26. Even though Grobel 1960 called *GospTruth* a "meditation," the overwhelming majority of scholars have seen it as a homily. Thus, the term *euaggelion* preferably should be taken as a proclamation of the good news, rather than as a definition of genre.
27. *Epidē*: Generally this conjunction is causal rather than temporal in the Nag Hammadi material. The anaphoric and cataphoric uses of it seem to be quite evenly distributed.
28. *ptērf*
29. *Kōte nsa* means search for but wandering about and encircling as well. The Father is described as the one who encircles or contains everything whereas nothing contains him *petktaeit amaeit nim emn petkaeit araf* (*GospTruth* 22:25–27) where the stative of *kōte* is used has influenced my translation. The absurdity in trying to contain the one who contains everything seems to be a backdrop for 17:4a-18a as well.
30. "and yet..." The Coptic conjugation perfect 1 is the main mode of narration in the past tense. Here, however, the straightforward telling of events is

interrupted by the conjunction *auō* followed by the preterit conversion. I assume that it expresses background information, which is the normal use of the preterit, and together with the conjunction, which I treat as emphatic, we reach an expression of surprise. Hence the paradox that the All could come forth from and search for someone that they simultaneously were inside of and who is superior to everything is underscored. This interpretation is a new attempt to reproduce the subtleties of the Coptic carefully construed syntax.

31. The circumstantial has caused scholars many difficulties. My rendering of it is different than that from 2006. I see it as subordinated to the *epidē* "because" in the beginning of the sentence.

32. *Kaase je* is an incorrect construal. Although nobody seems to have commented on it everyone has interpreted it as *je kaas*.

33. *Tplanē* has the connotation of going astray, wandering about.

34. "Matter." The Coptic term is *hylē*.

35. "In emptiness": The Coptic phrase *hnn oupetsoueit* equally well could be translated as "foolishly" or "vainly." Foolishly makes much sense in such a context where it is opposed to truth. However, "in emptiness" stresses the contrast to the Fullness, *pleroma*, that is the quality of the thought and mind of the Father of truth, see 16.31–17.4a.

36. *GospTruth* 17:4b-18a.

37. See *GospTruth* 22:23–27 and the comment in note 29.

38. *Ptērf*

39. *Planaste*

40. *Pnoute pe nbblle* is somewhat tricky. I interpret the initial b in *bblle* as definite article plural. The alternate translation would be "blind God."

41. *The Hypostasis of the Archons* 86:30–87:4.

42. "Matter came into being." *Assōpe* often serves as an opening marker and could be translated as "It happened." Such a treatment accompanied by an analysis of other possible interpretations was argued for by Magnusson, 2006, 74–78. "Matter came into being" or "it happened" both work syntactically well, and the choice does not seriously change the general analysis of the text.

43. "in a moulded form" *hnn ouplasma*. This translation is probably preferable if the prior phrase is translated as in the present text, see the prior note. However, if the choice had been "it happened," I would suggest the rendering "in a deluding way." Influenced by a suggestion of Attridge and MacRae. 1985: 44–45, which they themselves did not adopt, "in a deluding way" was chosen by Magnusson 2006.

44. "Moulded form" *plasma*. See the previous note.

45. *GospTruth* 17.18b-28a.

46. "Ignore" reproduces *katafroni*. Normally it has been rendered with "scorn," "despise" or similar expressions. We have no indication of that the use of this expression differs in Coptic compared with its Greek equivalent, and as the central message of the actual context of *GospTruth* is to downplay the danger of Error and to focus on what brings joy "despise" seems to be a choice that is open to critique. In earlier presentations of this analysis I used "disregard." But as Geoffrey Smith remarked "ignore" is a common rendering of *katafronein* in the Patristic period, Lampe 726a.

47. "since it thus" *teei te the*. I am influenced by Layton 1987: 253 and Orlandi 1992 who translate causally with a simultaneously anaphoric and cataphoric meaning: "..."(cosi) a una pura formula di passaggio, ma come tale é usate in modo scorretto. Infatti il senso richiede qui piuttosto una formula del tipo (perche), se riferita alla frase precedente, o 'dunque,' se riferita alla frase seguente." Orlandi 1992 45.

48. *GospTruth* 17.28–36.

49. The reconstruction is certainly speculative, but, I assert, not unwarranted. First of all we have to reckon with some peculiarities in the Lycopolitan dialect of *GospTruth*. In Sahidic the stative of *eire* normally is *o. In GospTruth that is preserved in the Lycopolitan dialect the stative of* eire *is* oi. The compound construction that in Sahidic would be *o + n* is *oi nnou* in GospTruth. This rare construction is attested in 19.20, 20.38, 23.23 and 29.2 as well. Thus, the final letters on p. 17 cannot be taken as the beginning of a noun. I have chosen to restore the lacuna on the top of p. 18 with *meue* (thought) as we have a resembling expression in 35.15–16: "and it is not with him that the thought of Error resides." The linkage between p. 18 and 35, though without the just described philological reasoning, was earlier suggested by Kragerud 1961: 149.

50. *GospTruth* 18.21b-26a is a long assyndetic construction. The manner of construing the relation between the clauses, of course, is a matter of general interpretation. That the punch line should be at the end is likely, as this is a common phenomenon in Greek and Coptic rhetoric and attested on 19–27–20.6 as well.

51. Most translators have chosen "it did not bring perishability because it was eaten" or other wordings with basically the same meaning. From the grammatical point of view, however, it requires an emendation of the text as *ntafteko* in 18.26b lacks an object and for this reason should be taken ingressively: "it did not enter a state of perishing because it was eaten." My choice to change my mind and to go against other translations is guided both by an inclination to avoid emending and my current opinion that the eternal and unbreakable nature of the Father of truth and of his messenger is the predominant theme on the first pages of *GospTruth. This, however, does not contradict the reality of the suffering on the Part of Jesus. The Saviour dies but resurrects.*

52. I take *nje* in 18.2t9b-30a as a marker of postponed subject *nqi*, with cataphoric as well as anaphoric function.
53. *GospTruth* 17.28b-18.31.
54. This has been done in Magnusson 2012.
55. For a discussion see Kasser, Meyer and Wurst 2006.
56. Aulén 1956.
57. Jenott 2011: 8–9.
58. Jenott 2011: 10.
59. I render the Coptic *men* ... *de*-construction with even though ... nevertheless. This construal has not gotten enough attention previously, and I will argue for its interpretation in the text.
60. *GospJud* 33:6–18.
61. *GospJud* 33:22–34:22.
62. *GospJud* 35:1–14.
63. *GospJud* 35:14–21.
64. For instance the *Gospel of John*, The *Gospel of Mary* and The *Gospel of Thomas*.
65. Earlier the reading was uncertain, making it possible to translate as if it were possible for Judas to reach the kingdom. Now, however, *oukh hina je ekebōk emau* is established.
66. *GospJud* 35:21–36:4.
67. *GospJud* 36:5–10.
68. *GospJud* 36:12–37:8.
69. About six letters are missing. I have followed the majority and restored with *nouēēb* = priests. But if crowd was intended instead we might restore with *pmēēshe*.
70. *GospJud* 37:21–40:2.
71. *GospJud* 41:10–42:15.
72. *GospJud* 43:12–24.
73. *GospJud* 44:15–47:2.
74. *GospJud* 56:9–26.
75. *GospJud* 57:10–58:8.
76. *GospJud* 58:10–26.

References

Attridge, Harold W. 1986. "The Gospel of Truth as an Exoteric Text." In *Nag Hammadi Gnosticism and Early Christianity*, Edited by H. W. Charles & R. Hodgson, 239–255, Peabody, MA: Hendrickson.

Aulén, Gustaf. 1956. *Christus Victor: An Historical Study of the Three Main Types of the Idea of Atonement*. Translated by A. G. Herbert. New York: MacMillan.

Bianchi, Ugo, ed. 1967. *Le origini dello gnosticismo: colloquio di Messina 13-18 aprile 1966*. Leiden: Brill.

Brakke, David. 2010. *The Gnostics. Myth, ritual, and diversity in early Christianity*. Cambridge, MA: Harvard University Press.

De Conick, April D. 2007. *The Thirteenth Apostle,What The Gospel Of Judas Really Says*. New York: Continuum.

Desjardins, Michel R. 1990. *Sin in Valentinianism*. Atlanta, GA: Scholars Press.

Doniger, Wendy. 1996. "Minimyths and Maximyths and Political Points of View." In *Myth and Method*, edited by : Laurie L. Patton and Wendy Doniger, 109–127. Charlottesville: University Press of Virginia.

Dunderberg, Ismo. 2008. *Beyond Gnosticism. Myth, Lifestyle, and Society in the School of Valentinus*. New York: Columbia University Press.

Jenott, Lance. 2011. *The Gospel of Judas. Coptic Text, Translation, and Historical Interpretation of the "Betrayer's Gospel."* Tübingen: Mohr Siebeck.

Jonas, Hans. 1963 [1958]. *The Gnostic Religion: The Message of the Alien God and the Beginnings of Christianity*. Boston, MA: Beacon Press.

Kasser, Rodolphe, Marvin W. Meyer and Gregor Wurst . 2006. "The Gospel of Judas: From Codex Tchacos." Washington, DC: National Geographic.

King, Karen L. 2003. *What is Gnosticism?* Cambridge, MA: Belknap.

King, Karen L. 2006. *The Secret Revelation of John*. Cambridge, MA: Harvard University Press.

Kragerud, Alv. 1961. "En gnostisk teodicé: Om fall och frelse i Evangelium Veritatis". *Norsk Teologisk Tidsskrift* 62: 144-171.

Krosney, Herbert. 2006. *The Lost Gospel: The Quest For The Gospel of Judas Iscariot*. Washington, DC: National Geographic.

Layton, Bentley. 1995. "Prolegomena to the Study of Ancient Gnosticism." In *The Social World of the First Christians: Essays in Honor of Wayne A. Meeks*, edited by Michael L. White and Larry O. Yarbrough, 334–350. Minneapolis: Fortress Press.

Magnusson, Jörgen. 2006. *Rethinking the Gospel of Truth. A Study of its Eastern Valentinian Setting*. Uppsala: Uppsala University Press.

Magnusson, Jörgen. 2008. *Judasevangeliet: Text, budskap och historisk bakgrund.* Lund: Arcus.

Magnusson, Jörgen. 2012. "Bortom Vägs Ände, eller Klarsyntheten som förblindade: En analys av en så kallad akosmisk etik i Sanningens evangelium från Nag Hammadi." *Svensk Exegetisk Årsbok* 77: 225–254.

Mahe, Jean-Pierre. 1998. "Gnostic and Hermetic Ethics." In *Gnosis and hermeticism from Antiquity to Modern Times*, edited by Roelof van den Broek and Wouter J. Hanegraaff, 21-36. Albany: State University of New York Press.

Orlandi, Tito. 1992. *Evangelium Veritatis*. Brescia: Paideia.

Paden, William E. 2008. "Comparison in the Study of Religion." In *New Approaches to the Study of Religion*, Volume 2 Textual, Comparative, Sociological, and Cognitive Approaches, edited by Peter Antes, 77–92. Berlin: Walter de Gruyter.

Pagels, Elaine H. 1989. *Adam, Eve, and the Serpent*. New York: Vintage Books.

Pagels, Elaine H. and Karen L. King. 2007. *Reading Judas:The Gospel of Judas and the Shaping of Christianity*. New York: Viking.

Painchaud, Louis. 2008. "Polemical Aspects of the Gospel of Judas." In *The Gospel of Judas in Context: Proceedings of the First International Conference on the Gospel of Judas, Paris, Sorbonne, October 27th-28th 2006*, edited by Madeleine Scopello, 171–186. Leiden: Brill. http://dx.doi.org/10.1163/ej.9789004167216.i-404.47.

Pearson, Birger A. 2007. *Ancient Gnosticism. Traditions and Literature*. Minneapolis: Fortress Press.

Robinson, James McConkey. 2007. *The Secrets of Judas: The Story of the Misunderstood Disciple and His Lost Gospel.* New York: Harper San Francisco.

Rudolph, Kurt. 1983. *Gnosis: The Nature and History of An Ancient Religion.* Translated and edited by Robert McLachlan Wilson. Edinburgh: T. & T. Clark.

Segelberg, Eric. 1959. "Evangelium Veritatis: A confirmation homily and it's relation to the odes of Solomon." *Orientalia Suecana* 8: 3–42.

Säve-Söderbergh, Torgny. 1958. "Det koptiska 'Evangelium Veritatis'." *Religion och Bibel* 17: 28–40.

Thomassen, Einar. 2008."Judas: Hero or villain? Is Judas Really the Hero of the Gospel of Judas?" In *The Gospel of Judas in Context. Proceedings of the First International Conference on the Gospel of Judas, Paris, Sorbonne, October 27th-28th 2006*, edited by Madeleine Scopello, 157–170. Leiden: Brill.

Williams, Michael A. 1996. *Rethinking "Gnosticism." An Argument For Dismantling A Dubious Category*. Princeton, NJ: Princeton University Press.

About the author

Jörgen Magnusson is Associate professor in the study of religions at Mid Sweden university, department of humanities and of the history of religions at Uppsala University. Magnusson received his PhD in history of religions at Uppsala University 2007. His main focus has been on early Judaism and Christianity, and especially in their Gnostic forms, elucidated, for example, in his dissertation *Rethinking the Gospel of truth: a Study of its Eastern Valentinian* setting 2006. In addition, he has published on the historical Jesus and Manichaeism. He is presently working on a number of analyses of The Gospel of Truth from Nag Hammadi.

10

Sacrificial Subjectivity: Faith and Interiorization of Cultic Practice in the Pauline Letters

Hans Ruin

Introduction

In *Romans* 12.1 St. Paul writes: "I beseech you therefore, brethren, by the mercies of God, that ye present your bodies a living sacrifice (*thusian zōsan*), holy, acceptable unto God." It is immediately clear from the context that Paul is not urging his followers to an actual, concrete sacrificial act. Blood sacrifice in general, and human blood sacrifice in particular, was never a part of Christian ritual or doctrine, despite the fact that martyrdom was recognized as a holy act. On the contrary, Christianity was from the outset distinguished by its aversion against such ancient and "heathen" rituals, eventually epitomized in the later verdict of Constantine II: *Sacrificiorum aboleatur insania* – Let the madness of sacrifices end.[1] In the very next sentence Paul also adds, in a formulation that has puzzled commentators and translators ever since: "This shall be your rational service" (*logikēn latreian*), which is followed by the exhortation "be ye transformed by the renewing of your mind" (*metamorphouste tē anakainosei tou noos*). The "sacrifice" to which the members of the struggling new congregation are called is thus somehow meant to be a spiritual, or spiritualized sacrifice. The remaining part of *Romans* 12 is a summary of the central Christian ethical doctrines and virtues, such as the role of love, joy and hospitality and non-revengefulness.

Keywords: St Paul, faith, sacrificial subjectivity, phenomenology, interiorization

At the same time, it is a basic tenet of Christianity that its initial and founding event is a unique human sacrifice, namely the supposedly sacrificial death of its semi-divine originator, Jesus Christ, whose sacrificial and redemptive death should henceforth serve as a model for a life of self-sacrifice. Or as Paul himself writes to the congregation in Corinth (1 Cor 5.7): "For even Christ our Passover is sacrificed for us" (*to pascha emon etuthe Christos*), and to the Ephesians, that Christ out of love has given himself as sacrifice (*thusian*) for us (Eph 5.2). The memory of this event is cultivated in the ritual of the Eucharist in which the living community symbolically (and in some congregations literally) considers itself to become one and united with the body and blood of Christ, again following a formulation from Paul (1 Cor 10.16f): "The cup of blessing which we bless, is it not the communion (*koinonia*) of the blood of Christ? The bread which we break, is it not the communion of the body of Christ?"[2]

To practice personal sacrifice, to "sacrifice" oneself, and thus to live in what could be called a "sacrificial" mode, is so much a part of what is generally considered a Christian life and thus in accordance with Christian spirituality, that the statement about living sacrifice from *Romans* is not normally noted and recognized in its full historical and genealogical significance. It is simply accepted as an appropriate quasi-metaphorical expression for a basic authentic religious and ethical comportment. Likewise the practice of the Eucharist is so deeply ingrained in Christian everyday life, that its historical and philosophical relation to more ancient sacrificial practices is rarely recognized as such, but simply lived and carried out in a semi-conscious continuation of its ritual and rhetorical presuppositions, in accordance with tradition. Yet the role and meaning of the theme of *sacrifice* (*thusia*) in Paul should not be handled lightly. In identifying it simply as a common way of conveying the attitude of believers in Christ, we lose sight of the historical uniqueness and the significance of this mode of speaking, but also with its role in founding and shaping a new form or mode of spirituality in complex dialogue with its inheritance.

My goal here is to address again the question of the role and meaning of "sacrifice" in the Pauline letters on the basis of the few but important places where it is recalled, in *Romans*, *First Corinthians*, *Ephesians*, *Galatians*, and *Hebrews*.[3] The idea is to explore the metaphor and its legacy, as a means to access the nature of Paul's theological-philosophical teaching, and more specifically the mode or style of "subjectivation" (to speak with Foucault) that is rhetorically shaped and staged in the Pauline Letters. It is an attempt to articulate, from the theoretical standpoint of phenomenology and genealogy, and in dialogue with the analysis by Guy Stroumsa in his *The End of Sacrifice*, the peculiar pathology of Christian spirituality, what I will refer to here as a "sacrificial subjectivity." While taking its lead from Stroumsa's overall interpretative scheme concerning the transformation and internalization of sacrifice during, around, and after the time of Christ, as partly a transformation within Jewish culture itself, the analysis presented here differs when it comes to the specific role and meaning of the Pauline letters. Whereas Paul appears only in the margin of Stroumsa's analysis, and then primarily as the principal spokesman for a *Christian* understanding of a final concrete and redemptive sacrifice, I will here try to read him as a decisive expression of precisely this inner critical transformation of Jewish spiritual culture in the direction of an internalized sacrifice.[4]

It is a notable fact of Pauline scholarship that the theme and role of *sacrifice* was rarely explored as such, and most often simply neglected.[5] Why this is so, also needs to be discussed. It will motivate us to revisit the difficult and contested question of Paul's and Christianity's relation to Judaism. But generally one can note – and I will explore this further in a separate section – that established commentary on Paul in general, and Romans in particular, will naturally be guided by the presupposition that Paul's reference to "living sacrifice" in *Romans* 12 is "simply metaphorical." Support for this is easy to assemble, since he in the very next sentence discharges any expectations that he is speaking of an actual sacrifice in the style of traditional sacrificial blood-rites. From there on, the Christian exegetes can therefore go on to explore "Paul's ethics" in its content, without having to consider the deeper meaning of this "metaphor." I think it is important – in particular against the background of Stroumsa's overall argument – to explore precisely why this "metaphor" is chosen, and furthermore to see how the "metaphoricity" of this metaphor is not as *simple* as it first may seem. Indeed, it is Paul himself who speaks, in the passage quoted above, of the religious initiation as a "metaphorization" of mind (*metamorphouste tē anakainosei tou noos*). Inversely, we will then also see how the "literaticity" of the presumably "literal" sacrifice in the older covenant was perhaps not so literal in the first place. In short, instead of following the movement of the traditional (more or less explicitly) theologically motivated Pauline scholarship, we should let the reference to the "living sacrifice" lead us to a deeper understanding of Paul's relation to his own tradition and the new kind of sacrificial subjectivity for which he is such an eminent exponent, and which ultimately is captured in the core message of his theology, the *sola fide* principle: redemption, or justification, through faith alone (Rom 1.17 passim).

The larger context of the present essay is an attempt to interpret the Pauline letters as an expression of and a response to a sense of *crisis* in the tradition to which he belongs, and thus to see how they shape a subjectivity that in its very ethos is guided by an acute sense of *historicity*. This dimension of my reading will surface briefly towards the end.[6] The initial impetus for my interest in this material came from Heidegger's analysis of temporality and historicity in the Pauline Letters in his 1920/1921 Freiburg course on *The Phenomenology of Religious Life* published first in 1995, and centred partly around an interpretation of *Galatians* and *Thessalonians*.[7] It articulates in an exemplary way the challenge for a philosophical-phenomenological and thus (in a qualified sense) "secular" reading of "confessional" texts. A phenomenology of religious life, Heidegger writes, should not be a theory *about* the religious, conceived of as an object of study in the standard mode of a science of religion, but rather as a way of entering, in understanding, the religious as a type of meaning-fulfillment or *enactment*, in German *Vollzug*. It is not a psychological theory of religious experiences, but an explication of the *meaning* of religion, which therefore does not immediately need to take sides along confessional lines.[8]

Of philosophical relevance for my argument here, is also the book on Paul and *Romans* by Giorgio Agamben, *The Time That Remains* (2000, English translation in 2005). In its focus on the peculiar temporal and historical horizon of the Letters, it was clearly inspired by Heidegger's analysis of kairological temporality in Paul.[9] Yet in opposition to Heidegger, Agamben explicitly situates this supposedly "Christian" sense of kairologial time within the broader context of messianic time, thus affirming Paul's rootedness in Jewish spiritual culture. In this approach he takes his lead in particular from Jacob Taubes and generally from the new hermeneutic framework that has gradually emerged in the more critically reflective and historical mindful branches of Pauline studies in the post-war period that has sought to situate him in the larger context of his Jewish intellectual background.[10]

I

It is thanks to the work of Guy Stroumsa, and before him the later work of Foucault and Pierre Hadot, that we have learned to be more attentive to the nature and significance of the spiritual transformation taking place during late Antiquity, towards new and different modes of "subjectivation." In Foucualt it was epitomized in the expression "care of the self," and in Hadot in the "inner citadel."[11] They were both particularly interested in the different "techniques" whereby people at this stage and time of human history sought to control and shape themselves, resulting in various ascetic practices. It is a time that saw the invention of new forms of subjectivities, the emergence of a new level of "interiority," culminating in the writings of Augustine, where the combination of asceticism, personal piety, remorse, and autobiographical writing forges a synthesis of Jewish-Christian spirituality and Greek and Roman philosophy. By defining the transformations taking place during this time in terms of "the end of sacrifice," Guy Stroumsa has brought out in a more complex way than hitherto the inter-related web of beliefs and practices that constitute the emergence of this new form of spirituality, sensibility or "subjectivation." Under this label he identifies not just a culture of caring for the self, but also a technical transformation in the practices of reading, from the scroll to the codex, and from loud to silent reading, and most importantly in the abandoning of public sacrifices in favour of cults centred around reading, speaking, and prayer, and thus the formation of new religious communities.[12]

A key dimension of Stroumsa's argument concerns Judaism, and its role in this overall transformation of ancient religious and spiritual culture. In earlier studies – notably those of Foucault – the developments within Judaism were left outside the picture. But Stroumsa has shown convincingly that much more attention needs to be paid to the inner transformations of Jewish religious culture if we are to grasp the overall meaning of what takes place during this momentous period in Western culture. Following the final destruction of the temple in 70 AD, the traditional forms of worship, administered by a priestly cast, comes to an end. Yet, following this fateful event, Jewish religion reinvents itself in the form of Rabbinic Judaism, characterized more by the reading of scripture, by personal (ascetic) habits and the maintenance of smaller religious communities, or as he writes: "The Jews seem to be at the origin of each of the transformations I have studied: personal identity, the place of the Book, the abandoning of sacrifices, the development of communities – Judaism seems to have experimented before other religious systems with all these aspects of the 'new' religion that emerges in Late Antiquity."[13] In relation to this transformed rabbinic Judaism, it is rather Christianity that represents and continues the older tradition, especially once it becomes state religion, with its churches, and with its priests who administer its sacrificial blood ritual of the Eucharist.

At the heart of all of these discussions, from Hegel over Nietzsche to Foucault, was always the question of how one should understand the inner convulsion of the ancient cultural identity, with its combination of polytheism and philosophy, to Christianity. How could a small Jewish messianic cult with its idiosyncratic belief in the sacrificial death of its saviour "conquer" the Roman empire? For Nietzsche is was the great "scandal" of history, so much so that he in his *Antichrist*, described it as a "poisoning" of Roman culture brought about precisely by Paul as the "genius of hatred."[14] In relation to the Roman world he depicts the Christians as "vampires and vermin."

Nietzsche's polemic is explicitly meant to serve as a "revaluation" not just in regard to Christianity itself as a historical movement, but also to the subsequent rationalizing interpretations of this phenomenon in

Hegel and his philosophical and theological followers, whose shadow looms large over this entire problematic in the present. For Hegel the breakthrough of Christianity was interpreted in the context of a rational scheme, whereby the spirit discovers itself precisely as interiority. At the end of the *Phenomenology of Spirit*, the death of Christ is elevated to a symbol of a philosophical rational principle, whereby the spirit recognizes itself in the form of a concrete human being, thus also marking the historical birth of self-consciousness in a new and qualified sense.

In both of these diametrically opposed philosophical interpretations of the transformation of ancient spiritual culture, we come across the enigmatic character of Paul and his *Letters*. It is in these documents, that the first decisive steps of Christian theology are taken. It is Paul who first articulates Christ as a break within history and tradition itself. The birth and sacrificial death of Christ marks an event whereby one epoch comes to an end and is replaced by another. Paul is not just an example of this historical break, he is literally the instigator of this very mode of thinking. It is he who defines the moment as a radical crisis within time itself, as the end of one time and the beginning of another, with he and his community living in the in-between, in a time of waiting and apprehension. Despite all his efforts to raise himself in abstract reflection above the concrete events of history, Hegel thus remains fundamentally attached to Luther's interpretation of Pauline theology, as the very break with the old, and thus as the initiator of a new faith. Consequently Hegel was also unable to see and interpret the emergence of Christianity in relation to Judaism in a historically adequate non-confessional, way.

Foucault received his impetus to explore the transformation of ancient spiritual culture partly from Nietzsche's *Genealogy of Morals* and the *Antichrist*. Yet his approach was not primarily critical in Nietzsche's sense, but genealogical. He sought to trace the inner development of the growing asceticism and care for the self in order to render the triumph of Christianity more comprehensible in the context of ancient spiritual and medical practices. In this overall effort he was in the end perhaps closer to Hegel than to Nietzsche, if yet without his implicit confessional commitments to Christianity. Unlike Hegel, he was not theologically conditioned by the Christian neglect of the historical role and significance of Judaism. Still, in his attempt to capture the inner logic of the transformation of ancient spiritual culture, he nevertheless followed a similar itinerary, avoiding the tradition of Judaism in favour of Greek and Roman sources. Throughout his explorations of this period he never confronted the Pauline *Letters*, even though there are indications in the preserved material that he was about to undertake such an interpretation.[15]

In our attempts to understand the kind of transformations with which Stroumsa's study is concerned we should not let ourselves be derailed by the ensuing theological-political rivalries that eventually generate Christian anti-semitism, and that posit Paul as the originator of an entirely new and ultimately non-Jewish religious movement. Instead a philosophical interpretation of the Pauline letters should let itself be guided by the growing body of research that insists not just on the trivial and historically indisputable fact that Paul was Jewish by birth and training, but more so by the fact that his thinking is fundamentally motivated by his understanding of the historical fate and situation of Jewish cultural and religious tradition. In the end, however, it seeks to point beyond the stale and essentializing dichotomy of Jewish and Christian altogether, and to explore what it would mean to read the texts as speaking from within a space where the very nature of what it means to belong to a tradition is precisely what is at stake. This means reading them not primarily from the viewpoint of their legacy as ratified doctrine, but as the poetical-philosophical expressions of a historical subjectivity in the making.

II

The Letters of St Paul, written in Greek and addressed to some of the aspiring communities of "Christians" around the year 60, are among the most influential philosophical-religious documents of the Western world. They constitute the first preserved written piece of Christian theology, where the attempt is first made to expound not just theological meaning of the *teaching* of Christ, but of the historical *event* of the life and death of Christ. Especially through Luther's interpretations of *Romans*, Paul's epistles became the corner stone of a reformed Christian intellectual orientation, while also remaining key texts for Catholic Christianity, not least *Romans*.

To engage in an interpretation of the Pauline Letters is a humbling task in view of the vast amount of scholarship devoted to this relatively small corpus (all in all less than one hundred pages, if we count the authentic letters), by theologians, historians of religion, and philologists over the centuries. Both in regard to the staggering size of research and commentary on Paul, but also and perhaps even more so in regard to the theological *stakes* involved in any reading of his Letters, these texts are notoriously difficult to interpret. Any attempt to reach something like the genuine *meaning* of the texts, implies a wealth of theological, and thus also ethical and political controversies. This is so not least with the problem of *sacrifice*. Any modern (or for that matter, older) theologian will be quick to point out that the most spectacular statement on "sacrifice," the quotation from *Romans* with which we started out, about offering one's "body as a living sacrifice" has nothing to do with older sacrificial practices. On the contrary it is read as taking a clear distance with regard to the supposed blood rites of traditional Judaism. As a good and fairly recent example of this we can consult the celebrated six hundred page commentary to *Romans* by the (Roman-catholic) exegete Joseph Fitzmyer from 1993.[16] In his commentary to the passage in question Fitzmyer simply notes "whereas the Jewish sacrifice implied the slaughter of what was offered, Paul uses the verb figuratively of Christian life and activity."[17] In regard to the subsequent and enigmatic expression that this shall be your "rational service" (*logike latreian*), he translates it as "a cult suited to your rational nature. Or a 'spiritual cult', i.e., worship governed by the logos, as befits a human being with *nous* and *pneuma*, and not merely one making use of irrational animals...," again implying (in a Hegelian echo) the primitiveness of the previous Jewish cult. This refusal to thematize the role and meaning of the sacrificial in Paul seems to be typical of the tradition of theologically motivated commentary. It is also notable that Fitzmyer does not list "sacrifice" in his detailed index.[18]

A theological commentary that takes the role of sacrifice somewhat more seriously is Karl Barth's famous exegetic study *Romans* from 1918. Barth's reading of Romans speaks somewhat in the tone of a Christian existentialism, insisting on the role of choice and action, while placing responsibility ultimately in the hands of divine grace as the primary form of action in creation in which man can take part. It is not an historical or analytical commentary, but carried out more in the style of an extended sermon, exploring the theological-ethical potentials of the text. It is interesting in relation to the remark on "living sacrifice," since Barth explicitly places this it at the outset of his exposition of Paul's ethical thinking.[19] He then develops the thought of sacrifice as a way for the practicing believer to demonstrate a submission to God as the primary task of a Christian. In this sense he goes much further than the standard commentaries, in expounding a kind of personal sacrificial spiritual composure as a centrepiece of Pauline doctrine. Yet, there is no attempt to bring about a more analytical understanding of the genesis and historical possibility of such a sacrificial subjectivity. Instead he operates in proximity to the appeal and force of the original text. Our task here is to take another step and to try to situate the very possibility of such a sacrificial subjectivity within a larger historical-genealogical scheme.

III

Before trying to trace the emergence and form of this new sacrificial spirituality further in the *Letters*, it is important to devote a separate short commentary to how they articulate the role and meaning of the actual sacrifice of Christ, or to be more precise, how they go about to interpret his execution as a sacrificial event. The single most important document for this question is the *Letter to the Hebrews*, which contains two thirds of all the remarks on sacrifice in the Pauline corpus. Its formulations on sacrifice was always the natural focus for a discussion of this theme in Paul and Christianity, not least for Girard who built his theory on the covering up of sacrifice in Christianity partly on this specific text.[20] According to standard contemporary Biblical scholarship it was, however, written not by Paul, but by an unknown educated Jewish-Christian, who was probably affiliated with him, a few decades after his death.

It is in this letter that Christ is presented as a "priest" with an eternal mission, given to him directly from God. He is compared to ordinary priests, who must perform sacrificial rites on a regular basis in order to purify their community and themselves from sin. Unlike them, however, Christ is portrayed as "the perfect and impeccable priest, who rules eternally." He does not need to perform daily blood-sacrifice, for "this he did once, when he offered up himself" (Heb. 7.27). Also: "Neither by the blood of goats and calves, but by his own blood he entered in once into the holy place, having obtained eternal redemption for us" (Heb. 9.12). The same formula of the "once and for all" (*epaphax*) is then repeated several times (e.g. Heb. 10.10). It also describes in some detail how the traditional temple culture was organized, spatially and ritually. All the previous sacrificial gifts and procedures are said to have been only temporary solutions, before the present time that marks a new and better order. With Christ there is a high priest who has sacrificed his own blood, as a "spotless" sacrificial gift to god.

The author then connects Christ's blood-sacrifice to that of Moses, who is said to have initiated the first covenant with blood, for "almost all things are by the law purged with blood" (9.22). Thus the letter establishes a direct theological-liturgical link between the older blood-sacrifices and the event of Christ's death, much more clearly so than in any of the authentic Pauline letters. Through the "final" sacrifice and ultimate gift, that of the blood of Christ, there is supposedly no need for further sacrifice since humanity has been cleansed once and for all. Yet, despite the "finality" of this sacrifice the community must abide by its ethical rules, since the one who sins after this moment is said to deserve no mercy, and to have no further access to cleansing. This is an inner contradiction of the whole message of the letter. The historical event of Christ has once and for all brought about sacrificial cleansing, and yet the community is continuously in peril of becoming impure again, and thus in constant need of re-cleansing. From the viewpoint of the philosophical-ethical problem of sacrifice, and its transformation from outer to inner, this "contradiction" is nevertheless an important clue. The main sacrificial means available to the community after this "final" outer sacrifice is its "faith." The believers must stand by their "faith," so *Hebrews* states. And this faith is then equated with "evidence" (*elegxos*) of things not seen. The importance of the comportment of "faith" (*pistis*) is then supported again with the story of Abraham and his willingness to sacrifice Isaac, followed by a number of glorious deeds performed by the heroes of the old covenant, and their willingness to endure severe personal pain and humiliation. This argument is then followed by a series of ethical rules and regulations, having to do with hospitality and sexuality and generally with the ability to endure.

Towards the very end of the letter the author returns to the image of sacrifice, likening Christ and the community with the sacrificial priest. It is also here that another discursive level around sacrifice appears, indicating not just a final sacrifice but rather a transformation of sacrifice into a model for spiritual existence. The author writes: "By him therefore let us offer the sacrifice of praise to God continually, that is, the fruit of our lips giving thanks to his name. But to do good and to communicate forget not: for with such sacrifices God is well pleased."

This final twist of the letter thus brings out the complex and multilayered nature of sacrifice that we can trace further in the authentic letters, and which is our real interest here. Whereas the manifest level of *Hebrews* confirms – or to be more precise: forges – the orthodox theological-sacrificial interpretation of the event of Christ, as a unique and final blood-sacrifice, which the ensuing community somehow simply have to affirm in order to live redeemed in its wake, its final and concluding formulation points to a more evasive and from our point of view much more interesting dimension of this whole problematic. It indicates how a traditional discourse of cleansing and justification through blood-sacrifice is transformed into a more general model for a new type of spirituality, for which the very act of *praise is understood as a sacrificial action*. This is also what I speak of here as the forming of a "sacrificial subjectivity." The quoted formulations even provide the theological underpinning for such a transformation. Beyond the dogma of orthodox "objectivistic" interpretation of Christ's final sacrifice, they demonstrate the emergence of a sacrificial subjectivity. Precisely because there are no more valid exterior sacrificial rituals, the sacrificial cleansing of life and of the community must take the form of "faith," in the form of the explicit subjection of subjectivity in thought and in action.

The standard interpretation of *Hebrews* – and of Paul – would not go in this direction. Instead it was used throughout the history of Christianity to insist on the principal difference between the so called first and second covenant, where the second implies an end of sacrifice, whereas those who remained faithful to the older tradition still believed in the redemptive force of blood-sacrifice. But from the viewpoint of the interpretation of the *Letters* that we are seeking to develop here, we can see how also in this apocryphal letter from the Pauline school, the early Christian understanding of sacrifice and its transformation receives an important formulation. Sacrifice is over, following the ultimate sacrifice of god himself, and yet sacrifice is now everywhere. Or to be more precise: exterior blood sacrifices are no longer necessary, for the sacrificial altar has been moved to the interior of life. And to be religious is now to live in a permanent sacrificial mode, in sacrificial subjectivity.

IV

Before exploring further how this idea of an inner or internalized sacrifice is developed in Paul, we still need to rehearse critically the basic assumption of doctrinal readings of this whole problematic. Following *Hebrews* it is tempting to conclude that the criticism of the older blood-rites and the "internalization" of sacrifice is an invention of the representatives of the "new" covenant, and one that sets it apart from its tradition, i.e, the supposedly "old" covenant. But, as even such a doctrinal document as *Hebrews* recognizes, this is not the case. On the contrary, the founding myth of the "first" covenant or agreement between God and men, the one between God and Abraham, is based not on Abraham's sacrificial *deeds*, but on his basic comportment which is that of the Hebrew word *emunah*, which in the *Septuagint* was rendered as *pistis*, and in the KJB sometimes "faith" sometimes "believed in," as when first recalled in *Genesis* 15.16: "And he believed in the Lord; and he [i.e, the Lord] counted him for righteousness."

Abraham has *faith* in God, he *relies on* and *trusts* in God – or whichever way we understand the meaning of *emunah* in *Genesis*. The same virtue is celebrated in the story of the sacrifice of Isaac. By being prepared to sacrifice what is most valuable to him Abraham demonstrates that he is loyal to the covenant, and thus righteous and deserving also of its benefits. Finally in *Habakkuk* 2.4 this comportment is celebrated in an expression that will again resonate in Paul (and in Luther), namely that "the just shall live by his faith."[21]

In several of the other texts from the older Jewish literature, notably *Deuteronomy*, we find concrete regulations concerning sacrificial practices, as when it describes how the Lord's people should behave when it conquers new lands, how it should destroy all signs of previous worship, and instead establish the cult of their own lord, through sacrificial practices: "and thither ye shall bring your burnt offerings, and your sacrifices, and your tithes, and heave offerings of your hand, and your vows, and your freewill offerings, and the firstlings of your herds and of your flocks" (Deut. 12.6f). [22]

Yet, these regulations concerning sacrificial practices need to be contrasted with a different and recurring theme throughout several of the books in the "Old" Testament, namely precisely its *critique* of sacrifice, or rather its warnings not to rely on external sacrifice for redemption. In *Psalms* 51.19 we read: "O Lord, open thou my lips; and my mouth shall shew forth thy praise. For thou desirest not sacrifice; else would I give it: thou delightest not in burnt offering. The sacrifices of God are a broken spirit: a broken and a contrite heart, O God thou wilt not despise." In the prophets the same theme resounds again. Isaiah even puts the words in the mouth of God, letting him reject the sacrifices offered to him: "To what purpose is the multitude of your sacrifices unto me? Saith the Lord: I am full of the burnt offerings of rams, and the fat of fed beasts [...] And when ye spread forth your hands, I will hide mine eyes from you: yea, when ye make many prayers, I will not hear: your hands are full of blood. Wash you, make you clean; put away the evil of your doings from before mine eyes; cease to do evil. Learn to do well; seek judgement, relive the oppressed, judge the fatherless, plead for the widow" (Isaiah 1.16f).

The following passage from Jeremiah (7.21) speaks even stronger in the same vein: "Thus saith the Lord of hosts, the God of Israel; Put your burnt offerings unto your sacrifices, and eat flesh. For I spake not unto your fathers, nor commanded them in the day that I brought them out of the land of Egypt, concerning burnt offerings or sacrifices: But this thing commanded I them, saying, Obey my voice, and I will be your God, and ye shall be my people: and walk ye in all the ways that I have commanded you, that it may be well unto you."

These examples suffice to remind us how a tension between outer ritual and inner comportment is clearly recognized and articulated from early on by different writers in the Jewish ethical literature. The proper guidance and orientation of the spirit is captured in the intersection of inner and outer, and also in different dimensions of practical deeds. A properly conducted sacrificial deed (i.e., one that is loyal to tradition) can cease to serve its purpose, as captured poetically by the prophet when describing the refusal of God to receive it. Instead an ordinary deed can take its place, as in the passage also quoted from Isaiah, of how speaking for the fatherless or caring for the widow replaces empty sacrificial practices.[23] It is hard to date more exactly the emergence of this mode of speaking, since the texts have an indeterminate historical origin. But it is clear that the references that explicitly question the meaning and value of concrete sacrifice belong to the later phases of biblical literature, that bear testimony of a gradual emergence of a critical reflection on sacrifice and tradition, and thus of the "law."

It is to these sources, and especially to the prophets, that Paul will connect his discourse. And it is in response and continuation of their ethical pitch that he is able to give voice to that internal criticism of tradition that serves as the true breeding ground for the spirituality or subjectivity that he is trying to articulate. But as the quotations amply demonstrate the critique of sacrifice had already begun earlier. Even more important is that the proper comportment vis-à-vis sacrifice had already begun to be connected to the very nature of what it means to comport oneself ethically. To be *ethical* or *just* is somehow, from early on, connected to an understanding of the genuine nature of sacrifice, both of how to practice it and also how to critically question it. This is at least the general background against which I think we should read the radicalized sacrificial discourse of his *Letters*, to which we now turn for a close reading of a few chosen passages.

V

Traditional sacrificial rituals are carried out by ordained priests in the temple. While these sacrificial practices gradually come to an end, the need for sacrifice does not end, but is transformed and interiorized. But it is not only the case that the sacrificial ritual migrates into new domains, also the very space of sacrifice is transformed and internalized. This is illustrated very graphically in *1st Corinthians*, where Paul asks the question: "What? Know ye not that your body is the temple of the Holy Ghost which is in you, which ye have of God, and ye are not your own?" (1st Cor. 6.19, also 3.17). The image is followed by a series of ethical regulations of how to behave, in particular in sexual matters. The motivating force of the argument is that the body is no longer one's own body, but that it is already inscribed in a larger spiritual-collective context, and thus that there is no other place to go in order to clean it. Instead the temple culture, which was devoted to the cleansing is now internalized. The sacrificial rituals, which were previously carried out in the separate space of the temple, and which were distinct from the individual bodies, are now merged with the everyday practices, sexual and others, so as to constitute the individual personal body as a potentially sacred and sacrificial space.

In a subsequent chapter of *1st Corinthians* Paul comments on the eating of sacrificial meat, which was a problem for the nascent community, namely whether or not one should take part in such meals as a Christian. Here Paul appears inconsistent. On the one hand, he notes that this meat is sacrificed in vain, to a non-existing God, and that therefore it is safe to eat it, as with any other meat (1st Cor. 8.1ff). However, later on he also stressed that they should stay away from idolatry, and that the sacrifices are to idols and demons (*daimonas*). This is also the passage where he speaks for the first and only time about what will eventually develop into the Eucharist, as he writes about the "Lords supper," that it enables a "communion" with the blood and body of Christ. Yet, the main point does not appear to be the actual performance of the ritual, but its metaphorical meaning, its ability to preserve the "memory" of Christ, and thus also to be in communion with him. It is not in order to reinstitute a concrete sacrificial practice that Paul is speaking of the sharing of bread and wine in the memory of Christ.

The transformation of sacrifice that takes place in Paul has to do instead with the way in which the *Letters* consistently speak of the acts of *faith* as in themselves having a sacrificial meaning. In *Philippians* (2.7) he speaks explicitly of the faith of the congregation as a sacrifice to God. This can be compared to a passage in Mark 12.33, which repeats a type of criticism familiar from the earlier biblical literature, of how God prefers devotion to actual sacrifice: "And to love him with all the heart, and with all the understanding, and with all the soul, and with all the strength, and to love *his* neighbour as himself, is more than all whole burnt offerings and sacrifices." Yet, the few formulations in Paul that explicitly address sacrifice in fact go even further in forging what I call here sacrificial subjectivity. The believer is someone who *sacrifices* himself, not primarily as a concrete body but in spirit.

This comportment is grounded in the previous ethical conceptions of the biblical literature, as demonstrated in the key passage from *Galatians* (3.6) where Abraham is presented as righteous by having faith/belief/reliance (*episteusen*) in God. The core meaning of this "faith" is sacrificial. It is a *reliance* defined in relation to sacrifice, as itself a supreme form of sacrifice. In one and the same passage he can thus connect his doctrine to the tradition and question it. In the name of Abraham's faith he denounces the law and the deeds that only follow from the law (to which belong the proclaimed sacrificial rites). The law that ordains sacrifices is no longer valid, for we are living in a time after the law, in a time of "faith," in the redemptive and sacrificial event of Christ. Yet the meaning of this "new" faith in response to the "old" law is still grounded in the possibility once made possible by this older tradition. It is a tradition at once made inoperative and brought to its highest possibility.

The Pauline theological discourse works through such a series of disconnections and reversals. It is made visible not least in his overturning of activity and passivity, and thus of the ancient philosophical matrix of conceiving human subjectivity. In basically all of Greek philosophy up until Paul, the hierarchy of active and passive functions as an organizing matrix for conceptualizing spiritual life. It is through mastery and lordship, and thus in terms of the possibility of *autonomy*, that life understands itself in philosophical discourses.[24] In regard to this way of thinking, Paul's discourse destabilizes inherited patterns when he presents himself in *Romans* as "slave" or "servant" (*doulos*) of Christ.[25] He thus speaks from a position of submission.

The same type of reversal is illustrated in *Romans* 6.18 where he speaks of having become "free from sin" in order to be the "slave of justice" (*edoulothete tei dikaiosyne*), which from a Greek philosophical standpoint would be an absurd formulation. Yet, this is precisely how the Pauline discourse works its effects, down to the rhetorical level, where the transformation or "metaphorization" of mind is accomplished. In *1st Corinthians* 7.22 he speaks of how the free becomes slaves and the slaves become free in their spiritual relation to God, "For he that is called in the Lord, *being* a servant, is the Lord's freeman: likewise also he that is called, *being* free, is Christ's servant."

The same kind of discharging transformation of priorities characterizes his way of speaking about wisdom and folly. This is exemplified throughout the *Letters*, but perhaps most poignantly in *1st Corinthians*, that speaks of how he has come "not with excellency of speech of wisdom" but in "spirit" (2.14), and also in "weakness, and in fear, and in much trembling," and how the teaching will appear precisely as "foolishness" to the Greeks (1.23).

The examples could be multiplied, but what is essential here is to see and analyze how this thinking stages itself as a reversal of values, and how it refuses the legitimacy of the previous order. In the place of activity and reason, it preaches passivity and folly. The deeper dimension of this this poetics or rhetoric of faith can be understood only once we connect it to what we have hitherto explored as sacrificial subjectivity. The central thesis of *Romans* 1.17, and of Pauline theology as such, that "the just shall live by faith," in a righteousness revealed "from faith to faith," is possible to interpret more adequately once we see it as the concentrated exposition of what it means to become oneself a sacrificial deed. Here the very submission of the subject is the act through which the cleansing is made possible, not only of itself, but also of its community. Paul's text becomes more fully legible once we can see how it stages these sacrifices of the self, also on a poetical-rhetorical level. It literally works to destroy or destabilize the forces that maintain the subject in the ethical-rational order, in its power, autonomy, reason and insight, and ultimately the very stability of its tradition. In this way it enacts a poetical sacrifice.

From here we can return again to where we started, to *Romans* 1.12, and its call for a "living sacrifice." It should be clear now that this is not "just a metaphor." It should be read instead as the enactment in language of a transformation of the spirit, as a metaphor to live by, in that it simultaneously performs what it describes. It stages the subject as a sacrificial event, in urging it to become the sacrifice that it depicts. The fact that it describes this activity as a "rational service" (*logike laterian*) should not be taken lightly. In the standard theological-lithurgical interpretation the full significance of this formulation was usually neglected, as somehow saying that the sacrifice is "rational" by following logically upon the new doctrine.[26] But to read it thus is to completely miss its function and effect. Instead we should see it as a "sacrificialization" of reason. The very idea of a "rational" (*logike*) service is a provocation to reason, to the standard conception of reason. In a commentary to this particular passage Bruno Blumenfeld speaks of it as "an excellent example of late Hellenistic taste," that revelled in oxymoronic expressions like "rational worship," or as in *1st Peter* 2.5 that speaks of "spiritual sacrifices" (*pneumatikē thusia*). [27] Yet, these expressions are not just a question of rhetorical or poetical styles and a taste for paradox and oxymoron. I think they can be understood more correctly if we also place them in the larger context of the formation of sacrificial subjectivity, where they can be seen also as the poetical vehicles of a new mode of subjectivation.

VI

Before concluding I want to point to yet another example of Paul's ambiguous reversal-reappraisal of tradition that also contributes to his formation of a sacrificial self, namely the problem of "circumcision."[28] The practice of male circumcision has been documented in many different cultures and religions, from classical Egypt onward. According to Jewish myth it was issued as a command from God to Abraham (Gen. 17.10) in order to seal the covenant: "ye shall circumcise the flesh of your foreskin; and it shall be a token of the covenant betwixt me and you." To be circumcised is to become part of a chosen community, it is a sign cut into the body, to confirm a pact. In the next passage, God declares that whoever is not circumcised in his body shall have his soul "cut off from his people." In this ominous legend the connection is thus established between individual and community, flesh and spirit, sign and pact. The circumcision is a sacrificial act performed on the infant body in order to establish and maintain the community.

Just as in relation to the traditional blood rites, we can see how Paul here forges his message first by connecting to tradition and established practice, then by questioning its legitimacy, and finally by repeating it, but now in the form of an "internalized" and "metaphorized" ritual. This is expressed very clearly in *Romans* where we find the famous line: "For he is not a Jew, which is one outwardly; neither is that circumcision, which is outward in the flesh. But he is a Jew, which is one inwardly; and circumcision is that of the heart, in the spirit, and not in the letter" (Rom. 2.25) The privilege of the special covenant between God, Abraham, and the Jewish people, is here both problematized and expanded. The physical circumcision does not guarantee lawfulness, for in order to take part in the law, and thus in righteousness, one needs to pay tribute not to outer signs but to let one's heart and soul be circumcised.

Later in *Romans* Paul writes that also in the original case of Abraham his justification in the face of God did not come about through his circumcision. "And he received the sign of circumcision, a seal of the righteousness of the faith which he had yet being uncircumcised" (Rom 4:11). Thus we can see how the argument concerning law and faith that we have already studied in its relation to sacrificial ritual is again repeated literally in relation to the practice of circumcision.

All of these themes of course deserve more detailed and separate discussions, but the purpose here was to bring out a more general pattern and logic, to support the general claim, that in Paul and thus in the originator of Christianity, we find an exemplary instance of how Jewish thought and tradition invents itself not through the definitive "end of sacrifice," but through the transformation, metaphorization and finally internalization of external ritual, thus contributing in a historically decisive way to the formation of a new form of spiritual-intellectual comportment that can be designated as a sacrificial subjectivity.

Christianity is one mode, intellectually, poetically and ritually, in which Jewish tradition is transformed and maintained over time. Yet, even such a formulation runs the risk of becoming too simple, as it refers to "tradition" as something whole and integer that continues over time. Through the writings of Paul we should instead also learn to see how "tradition" will always constitute a problem for itself. The problem of *belonging*, what it means to remain loyal and faithful to something, is not exterior to what tradition is. On the contrary, it will always be part of what constitutes it as tradition, namely as a permanently contested memory and sense of obligation.[29] In Paul's writings, composed in a time of extraordinary intellectual and political transformations, this sense of urgency and obligation, and of experienced necessity to define the possibility and legacy of an inheritance, contributes to the shaping of his discourse. The "faith" to which he urges his interlocutors can then be understood as the sign of a *reliance* on the bond that has been broken, and which precisely in this break can be restored again through the personal interiorization of its obligation to sacrifice.

Notes

1. As quoted by Guy Stroumsa in Stroumsa 2009: 57, and also in his contribution to the present volume.
2. Later in 1st *Corinthians* (11.23), he refers to how Christ himself, on the eve of his capture, and after broken the bread, said: "Take, eat: this is my body, which is broken for you: this do in remembrance of me [...] This cup is the new testament in my blood: this do ye, as oft as ye drink *it*, in remembrance of me."
3. *Hebrews* is a special case. It contains most of the literal references to sacrifice, especially concerning the meaning of the sacrificial death of Christ. Yet,

since it was most likely not written by Paul himself but by someone in his circle and at a later date, it cannot be used directly as support of an interpretation of the Pauline conception of sacrifice (as in René Girard, to whom I return later), but will require a separate analysis in the present context.

4. For Stroumsa's comments on Paul, see in particular Stroumsa 2009: 83 passim, where Paul's militant interpretation of the real sacrificial death of Christ is critically compared to the Docetist conception of a laughing Christ.

5. In the *Cambridge Companion to St Paul* from 2003, the word "sacrifice" does not even appear in the index. Surprisingly, considering the magnitude of the scholarship on Paul, there never seems to have been a systematic study of the role and meaning of sacrifice in the *Letters*. In most of the philosophically oriented interpretations of Paul from recent years, the theme of sacrifice is also absent, with the notable exception of Zlavoi Zizek, who in his book *The Puppet and the Dwarf* (Zizek 2006) does address what he describes as the "perverse core of Christianity" partly in terms of the celebration of the death of its figure of worship. It is this emptying out of the central signifier which he, in a Lacanian spirit, reads as a peculiar form of transformation of religious cult and desire. I have left out a more substantial comment on this analysis here, since it does not connect to the more specific problem of *the sacrificial* in Paul, but deals more generally with the theology of the God on the cross.

6. See Ruin 2010 and Ruin 2013.

7 Heidegger 1995.

8. Heidegger 1995, 131. Instead the confessional, as the meaning of *devotion*, is itself among the phenomena to be investigated. Such an explication can also permit the non-understandable to be understandable, precisely by letting-be [*belassen*] its non-understandability. For a more extended discussion of the meaning and challenges of a phenomenology of religion, see my preface to the volume *Ambiguity of the Sacred*, Ruin 2012.

9. The debt to Heidegger in this respect is in fact greater than Agamben recognizes in the footnote that he devotes to Heidegger's published lectures, see Agamben 2005: 33f.

10. Agamben summarizes some of this literature in the introduction of his book, starting with William Davie's book *Paul and Rabbinic Judaism* (1958), emphasizing the work of Taubes (1993), in particular his posthumously published *Die politische Theologie des Paulus* (1993). For this new context of reading Paul in relation to his Jewish context, see also Christer Stendahl (1977), *Paul among Jews and Gentiles* and E. P. Sanders (1977), *Paul and Palestinian Judaism*. A study from the viewpoint of Jewish studies and more post-structuralist thought is Daniel Boyarin (1994), *A Radical Jew: Paul and the Politics of Identity*. For a good summary of recent trends in Pauline scholarship in this regard, see Ben Witherington III's "Contemporary Perspectives on

Paul," in Dunn 2003: 256–269. An extensive presentation of contemporary research on Paul, and on the history of Pauline scholarship is also provided by the Swedish expert on New Testament exegesis, Magnus Zetterholm (2006) in his *Lagen som evangelium?*.

11. See especially Foucault 1984a and 1984b, especially the preface to the former, and also Hadot 1992.

12. See summary of argument on p. 130, in Stroumsa 2009.

13. Stroumsa 2009: 130.

14. "Das Genie im Hass," Nietzsche 1988: 215 (translation from Nietzsche 1968: 154).

15. For an attempt to understand what such a Foucaultian reading of Paul would could have amounted to, see the special issue of *Journal for Cultural and Religious Theory*, Vol 11 1 (2010), devoted to the question of Foucault and Paul, in particular the essay by Valérie Nicolet Anderson 2010 and also my own Ruin 2010.

16. Fitzmyer 1993. He also writes that "...the role that Romans has played in the history of Christianity manifests that it is the most important among the Pauline writings, if not of the entire NT. The Impact that this letter has had on the history of the Christian church is incalculable...," p. xiii. The bibliography lists approximately one thousand titles on *Romans* alone.

17. Fitzmyer 1993: 639.

18. Also in Anders Nygren's commentary to *Romans* from 1943 it simply notes that concerning the passage on the "living sacrifice" it is consistent with what Nygren calls "Paul's ethics," namely that we have been given the responsibility for our lives and for creation in the wake of Gods grace, and that we have to take care of this life here with our living bodies. The more complex, religious-historical background of the problem is left aside, in favour of an actualizing theological Pauline practice. See Nygren 1979: 416f. The same is true of Krister Stendahl's (1993) *Final Account. Paul's Letter to the Romans*, which states on p. 46f that "living sacrifice" was "...a slogan in Jewish terminology. The living sacrifice was a critique of polytheism." He then goes on to discuss *logiken latreian* which he prefers to think of as a "worship offered by mind and heart" from the New English Bible translation, but which, he says, can also be thought of as "spiritual worship."

19. Barth 1940: 415–424.

20. Girard's (1972) understanding of sacrifice, first presented in *La violence et le sacré* sees sacrifice as a fundamental cultural operation, generated out of so called "mimetic rivalry," concentrated and enacted in the scapegoat function. The sacrifice of Christ, or rather the sacrificial interpretation of the ritual murder of Christ (notably as expounded in *Hebrews*), is then interpreted as a covering up of this transcultural matrix, in that it pretends

that the world no longer needs the sacrificial function. For the interpretation of the historical transformation of the meaning of sacrifice around the time of Christ from the perspective of Paul's *Letters* this account, despite its great cultural-political interest, is less relevant. For what Girard can not see from the viewpoint of his theory is precisely the way and extent to which sacrifice is internalised at this point, and made into a dimension of the self.

21. Agamben 2006 (chapter six) has a good discussion about the controversial issue of the relation between *emunah* and *pistis*, that was raised first by Buber, where he argues against Buber's attempt to sharply separate them.

22. In particular in *Leviticus* and *Numbers*, there are abundant advice about how to sacrifice, what part of the animal to burn, which animals were sacrificed and how many, etc. It is also important in this context to note, that whereas the Greek term for sacrifice – *thusia* – is basically the same throughout *Septuagint* and in the New Testament literature, the Hebrew has a number of related terms that were rendered in an undifferented way as *sacrificium/thusia*, notably *ishshe*, *zavach*, *minchah* and *olah*.

23. This formulation also echoed again in Mathew 9.13, where Jesus speaks of how he desires mercy not sacrifice. Already in Psalm 141.2 we find the formulation "Let my prayer be set forth before thee as incense; and the lifting up of my hands as the evening sacrifice."

24. This point is stressed also throughout Foucualt's work on ancient practices of caring for the self.

25. See Agamben 2005:12ff for an extended interpreation of this way of opening the discourse, by affirming his slavishness.

26. Fitzmyer's interpretation of this passage (quoted above) is symptomatic of this common misreading, as he interprets/translates *latreian logiken*: "... as a cult suited to your rational nature. Or a 'spiritual cult', i.e., worship governed by the logos, as befits a human being with nous and pneuma, and not merely one making use of irrational animals..." Fitzmyer 1993: 640.

27. Blumenfeld 2001:379. In conjunction with this he has an excellent discussion of different examples of similar oxymoronic expressions.

28. For a longer analysis of this problem in Paul, and its philosophical reverberations, see Ruin 2013.

29. For a compelling reflection on the problem of sacrifice and the inner dynamics of tradition, I refer to chapter three in Derrida's *Donner la mort*, that also touches upon Paul in a Kierkegaardian reading of the enigma of Abraham's sacrifice, see especially the last paragraphs Derrida 1999.

References

Agamben, Giorgio. 2005. *The Time That Remains: A Commentary on the Letter to the Romans*, translated by P. Dailey. Stanford, CA: Stanford University Press. (Originally published as Il tempo che resta. Un commento alla Lettera ai Romani).

Anderson, Valérie Nicolet. 2010. "Becoming a Subject: The Case of Michel Foucuault and Paul." *Journal for Cultural and Religous Theory* 11(1): 127–141.

Barth, Karl 1940. *Der Römerbrief*. Zollikon: Evangelischer Verlag.

Blumenfeld, Bruno. 2001. *The Political Paul. Justice, Democracy and Kingship in an Hellenistic Framework*. Sheffield: Sheffield Academic Press.

Davie, William. 1958. *Paul and Rabbinic Judaism*. London: S.P.C.K.

Boyarin, Daniel. 1994. *A Radical Jew: Paul and the Politics of Identity*. Berkeley: University of California Press.

Derrida, Jacques. 1999. *Donner la mort*, Paris: Galilée. Transl. by D. Wills, *The Gift of Death*, Chicago, IL: Chicago University Press, 2008.

Dunn, James. 2003. *Cambridge Companion to St Paul*. Cambridge: Cambridge University Press. http://dx.doi.org/10.1017/CCOL0521781558.

Fitzmyer, Joseph. 1993. *Romans*. New York: Doubleday.

Foucault, Michel. 1984a. *Histoire de la sexualité*, vol. 2: *L'usage des plaisirs*, Paris: Gallimard Translation, *The history of sexuality*, vol. 2: *The use of pleasure*, Harmondsworth: Penguin, 1992.

Foucault, Michel. 1984b. *Histoire de la sexualité*, vol. 3: *Le souci de soi*. Paris: Gallimard Translation, *The history of sexuality*, Vol. 3, *The care of the self*, Harmondsworth: Penguin.

Girard, René. 1972. *La violence et le sacré*. Paris: Grasset.

Hadot, Pierre. (1992) *La citadelle intérieure: introduction aux Pensées de Marc Aurèle*, Paris: Fayard. Translation, *The Inner Citadel*, Cambridge, MA: Harvard University Press, 2001.

Heidegger, Martin. 1995. *Phänomenologie des religiösen Lebens*, Gesamtaugabe Bd 60. Frankfurt am Main, Klostermann. Translation, *The Phenomenology of Religious Life* Bloomington: Indiana University Press, 2010.

Nietzsche, Friedrich. 1988. *Der Antikrist*. In *Kritische Studienausgabe* vol 6. Berlin: De Gruyter Translation, *The Anti-Christ*, London: Penguin 1968.

Nygren, Anders. 1979. *Pauli Brev till Romarna*. Stockholm: Verbum.

Ruin, Hans. 2010. "Faith, Grace, and the Destruction of Tradition: A Hermeneutic-Genealogical Reading of the Pauline Letters." *Journal for Cultural and Religious Theory* 11(1): 16–34.

Ruin, Hans. 2013. "Circumsizing the Word: Derrida as Reader of Paul." In *Paul in the Grip of Philosophers*, edited by P. Frick, 71–93. Minneapolis: Fortress Press.

Sanders, E. P. 1977. *Paul and Palestinian Judaism*. London: SCM.

Stendahl, Krister. 1977. *Paul among Jews and Gentiles*. London: SCM.

Stendahl, Krister. 1993. *Final Account: Paul's Letter to the Romans*. Minneapolis: Fortress Press.

Stroumsa, Guy. 2009. *The End of Sacrifice: Religious Transformations in Late Antiquity*. Chicago, IL: Chicago University Press.

Taubes, Jacob. 1993. *Die politische Theologie des Paulus*. Munich: Fink.

Witherington III, Ben 2003. "Contemporary Perspectives on Paul." In *Cambridge Companion to St Paul*, edited by James Dunn, 256–269. Cambridge: Cambridge University Press.

Zetterholm, Magnus. 2006. *Lagen som evangelium? Den nya synen på Paulus och judendomen*. Stockholm: Studentlitteratur.

Zizek, Zlavoi. 2006. *The Puppet and the Dwarf*. Stanford, CA: Stanford University Press.

About the author

Hans Ruin is Professor in Philosophy, Södertörn University, Sweden and director of the research program Time, Memory, Representation. Ruin's areas of research include phenomenology, hermeneutics, deconstruction, theory of history and philosophy of religion. Recent publications are a collection of essays on Heidegger, *Frihet, ändlighet, historicitet. essäer om Heideggers filosofi* (2013) and the co-edited volumes "Ambiguity of the Sacred: Phenomenology, Aesthetics, Politics" (2012). The present text was written with the support of Axel och Margaret Ax:son Johnsons Stiftelse.

REPERCUSSIONS OF SACRIFICE IN WESTERN PHILOSOPHY

11

Philosophical Sacrifice

Marcia Sá Cavalcante Schuback

Contemporary philosophy has developed many reflections about the essence of sacrifice. In a very general sense, these reflections are related to the contemporaneous experience of the sacrifice of being. Sacrifice of being appears as the overwhelming expansion of the meaning of being as thing, as global reification and its many techniques of being. The sacrificial nature of this meaning expansion in which being means nothing but "thing" was seized by Nietzsche and Marx in the 19th century and became the core of the philosophy of sacrifice developed by Georges Bataille. Bataille assumes as starting point for his philosophy of sacrifice that "the principle of sacrifice is destruction"[1]. Accordingly to him, the destruction of sacrifice is however essentially distinguished from annihilation. This sacrificial axiom can be read in his *Theory of Religion*, written 1948, in a moment of historical perplexity facing the threatening reality of annihilation. Bataille's philosophy of sacrifice can be read as a response to this threat. His main thesis is that sacrifice is destructive but not annihilating; it destroys the thing-hood, the value of thing, the reification of the victim, that is, of singular existence. What sacrifice destroys is the logic of utility operating in reification, a logic of reasons, grounds and finalities that speaks in terms of "this is this because of that and for the sake of this" and enables its uses and abuses. Sacrifice destroys the logic of meaning. As this destruction, sacrifice can be considered Bataille's response to omni-reification. It is proposed as the only possibility to bring being back to intimacy, to the immanence between the human and

Keywords: George Bataille, Jean Luc Nancy, phenomenology, existential philosophy, hermeneutics the divine, the human and the world, between the subject and the object[2]. Sacrifice destructs the annihilation of being accomplished by reification, that is, by utilitarian, teleological and instrumental rationality, performing the "return to immanent intimacy," to the affirmation of "intimate life," to the unmeasured violence of the "invisible lightning of life," the most extreme opposition to the reified meaning of being qua "thing." In annihilation, there is only the death of death and hence life without life. Whereas annihilation kills death, sacrifice brings death back into life. With Bataille's own words: "Death reveals life in its plenitude and enables real order to appear in its shadow"[3]. In this sense, Bataille insists that to sacrifice is not to kill but to abandon and to give. What matters in sacrifice is to pass from a stable order, where all consumption of resources is subordinated to the necessity of enduring, to the violence of an unconditional consumption and pure ephemerality[4]. Sacrifice is hence the most extreme opposite to production, thus it sacrifices for nothing, destroying the logic of reasons and therefore the logic of reason as such. In sacrifice the finitude of singular existence is expropriated for the sake of being infinitely appropriated. Sacrifice puts to death what hinders singular finite existence to exist. Sacrifice is proposed here as what cannot be sacrificed for the sake of restoring the value of finite singular existence in total separation of all utility and needs[5]. But would that mean that the intimacy of singular life with the life of life can only be restored through the sacrifice of singular existence? Would that mean that only the sacrifice of finitude restores finitude? Wouldn't this thought of sacrifice be at the end the end of thought and the end of finitude itself? Would not at the end sacrifice perform the infinitization of finitude rather than the finitization of infinitude? These questions are central for the French philosopher Jean-Luc Nancy's own philosophy and for his interpretations and readings of Bataille. In the following reflection I will depart from Nancy's discussions on and in "The Unsacrificeable" for the purpose of contributing to the question about the end of sacrifice and further to the problem of how end and sacrifice are related to each other.

The departing point of Nancy's discussions on Bataille's philosophy of sacrifice is the "end of real sacrifice" and the "closure of its phantom." Nancy has also a thought about "the end of sacrifice" that in very general terms coincide with some central thesis proposed and developed by Guy Stroumsa.[6] Insofar as Nancy's thoughts are concerned with the philosophy of sacrifice and considering how the term and praxis related to the term "philosophy" have a Greek origin, Nancy does not speak about sacrifice in general but about "Western sacrifice." He connects the end of sacrifice with "Western sacrifice" and considers that both Socrates and Christ present a metamorphosis or transfiguration of sacrifice. This, in many senses Nietzschean statement, follows the thought that real or old sacrifice ends through its spiritualization or "sublimation" (to talk with Marx and Freud) and hence by means of being imitated or reproduced for the sake of revealing a new content of truth. The metamorphosis or transfiguration of sacrifice performed by Socrates and Christ is the reproduction of the sacrificial form that through reproduction and preservation voids and avoids its truth for the sake of revealing a new and more universal truth, which is the truth of the universal. Socrates and Christ, Socratic philosophy and Christian religion keep alive the death of the old sacrificial content in the reproduction of old sacrificial forms in order to assure the impactful force of stability of new contents of truth. They build the pillars of what has been called metaphysics and described by Heidegger as onto-theo-logic (super)-structure of Western civilization. Metaphysics can be therefore be defined as philosophical sacrifice.

Nancy describes Western philosophical sacrifice of sacrifice as the articulation of four fundamental traits. Philosophical sacrifice – philosophy qua metaphysics – is for the first *self-sacrifice.* Self-sacrifice can be understood as "the sacrifice of the subject." Socrates suicide presents the self-sacrifice of philosophy. Sacrificing itself, its own body, the body of being and existence, philosophy discovers a life after death, the life of ideas, ideal life. Christ's death on the cross presents the sacrifice of religion. Inflicting death on himself, God in Christ discovers life after death, eternal life. With Socrates and Christ life is sacrificed for the sake of ideal and eternal life, of a life that is more life than life, for a truth that is truer than truth. Because both sacrifices are sacrifices of the body of life and of the world rather than the life and the world of the body, they present a new content of truth in which the truth of life "is itself wholly a sacrifice," a body, a life, a world of sacrifices. "What is involved is a life that would be in and of itself, wholly a sacrifice," "a life of sacrifice alone"[7]. Sacrifice becomes the meaning of life rather than life the meaning of sacrifice. Sacrifice of life is interiorized and inverted into life of sacrifice. The second trait appears is the *unique universality of self-sacrifice.* Self-sacrifice as accomplished by Socrates and Christ is unique and accomplished for all and once for all. Socrates' and Christ's sacrifices are the most exemplary of all possible examples. They universalize the very meaning of sacrifice as a putting-to-death for the sake of a better, ideal, eternal life. This defines however the universality of meaning and the meaning of universality. Sacrifice becomes itself the meaning of meaning as the sacrifice of the singularity of meaning, for the sake of its universality. Singularity is sacrificed in "spirit," to the "spirit," to the universality of the spirit and to the spirit of universality. Sacrifice means putting to death the singular for the sake of the universal (of the common, of the country, of the race, of the whole, of the future, etc.)[8]. Universal sacrifice is sacrifice for the universality of the spirit. Spiritualization is universal sacrifice. The third trait is that the universalization of sacrifice is a claim about the truth of sacrifice as the sacrifice of everything – both the singular and the universal – for truth. *The truth of sacrifice is sacrifice for truth.* The matter is hence not only the sacrifice of the singular and its universalization (or spiritualization) but the sacrifice of the whole life of sacrifice for truth. Nancy recalls a passage from Plato's *Phaedo* in which Socrates said: "As for you, if you will take my advice, you will think very little of Socrates, and much more of the truth" (91b-c). This leads to the fourth trait of Western self-sacrifice, namely the *sublation of sacrifice*, the transcendence of transcendence, that is, the very sacrifice of sacrifice.

For Nancy, the articulation of these four traits in Western philosophical-religious sacrifice – self-sacrifice, universalization of sacrifice, revelation of the spiritual truth of sacrifice, sublation of sacrifice presents "the infinite sacrificial structure of the appropriation of the subject."[9] This "infinite sacrificial structure of the appropriation of the subject" is the essential operation in the Western process of universalization, through interiorization, spiritualization and dialectization of sacrifice. In this sense, Western sacrifice becomes the "westerning of sacrifice."[10] In the interiorization, spiritualization and dialectization of sacrifice that enables the universalization of sacrifice and hence its westerning, sacrifice is reproduced, on one hand, through a "formidable disavowal of itself" in the figure of an "old sacrifice" and on the other, through self-approval "in the form of an infinite process of negativity." Interiorized, spiritualized and dialectized – that is, universalized – sacrifice negates itself as sacrifice for it affirms itself as other than "old" sacrifices. However, in order to do this it has first to "fabricate" the very idea of "old" sacrifices and of the difference between "old" and "modern." In this "fabrication," the end of sacrifice is promulgated insofar as sacrifice is defined as the cruelty of a life without spirit; the cruelty of a life that appropriates otherness by means of self-expropriation (as in anthropophagy) or that communicates with otherness by means of contagion and participation (as in ecstasy). In this sense, sacrifice ends when its definition begins. Definition would be in fact the beginning of the end of sacrifice, self-affirmation through self-negation. One of the main theses of Nancy is that philosophy in its Greek and Western terms, that is, as onto-teo-logic structure is the continuous performance of the sacrifice of sacrifice. This appears most clearly in Bataille's philosophy of sacrifice and his attempts "to think accordingly to sacrifice." To think accordingly to sacrifice means to search a way *back* into the violent intimacy to life of existence cut off by philosophical rationality. Bataille called this search in a paraphrase to Proust's title, "the search after a lost intimacy"[11]. It means a search for a thought *of* radical singularity (which for Bataille means intimacy), beyond interiorization, spiritualization and dialectization, that is, universalization. It means to search philosophy beyond philosophy, a transcendence of transcendence, the sacrifice of philosophical sacrifice. Bataille's philosophy of sacrifice proposes indeed a sacrifice of philosophy, the overcoming of philosophical universalization (operated through interiorization, spiritualization and dialectization) through universalization of universalization. If philosophy is "at the end," that is, in the age of its saturation, the age of global and omni-reification, the age of "planetary technique," annihilation of the "truth of intimate world" (*la vérité du monde intime*),[12] what Bataille proposes is the destruction of this annihilation through a thought accordingly to sacrifice. The main question is how to bring singular existence back to its value of enigma in a world where the only value is the exchange value, the reification of every existence, in which nothing means nothing and thereby the possibility to become whatsoever so that it can be used and abused wherever, whenever, by what and whomsoever. Bataille's proposal of a thought accordingly to sacrifice leaves open the very difficult question about how to perform the sacrifice of philosophical sacrifice? How to give back to singular existence its value of enigma in a world that only knows the laws of ends? Does he mean that the sacrifice of singular existence in global capitalism is already bringing singular existence back to the value of its enigma? Does he mean that omni- and over-reification "at the end" dis-reificates, as a too tight string that would at the end break down and give place to another meaning of being? Would technique, in its global planetary sense, reveal itself as the last secret of sacrifice? At stake is of course a meaning of transformation and overcoming, but of transformation and overcoming from within the without exit of a long history and infinite process of philosophical self-sacrifice. If philosophical self-sacrifice should be understood as the "end" of "old" and "real" sacrifice, this end of sacrifice appears to be an end without end that exposes itself most clearly in attempts, such as Bataille's, to sacrifice philosophical sacrifice and destruct rational annihilation. The more concrete answer given by Bataille is that sacrifice of sacrifice in the sense of a thought accordingly to sacrifice is artistic experience, where another meaning of being appears from within the reification of the meaning of being. In art and not only for Bataille it is made an experience that things are other than things.

Nancy's answer to Bataille moves around the principle question if the destruction of sacrifice is indeed the best means to deny the utilitarian relation between man and life, as Bataille assumes.[13] He considers that the main thought operating here, namely that in sacrifice "the moment of the finite" is transcended for the sake of being infinitely appropriated, fails to seize not the nature and essence of sacrifice but the finitude of the finite itself. The problem lies in the fact that the vocabulary, the ideologies and the philosophies of sacrifice remain in the closure of a violent negation of the violence of the finite, singular existence. Thus, as Nancy, states: "finitude is not a 'moment' in a process or an economy."[14] And further: "A finite existence does not have to let its meaning spring forth through a destructive explosion of its finitude."[15] Finite existence, singularity, is an event, the is-being of its being, and as such what cannot be sacrificed. Finitude is "unsacrificeable." And it is "unsacrificed" because in its is-being it is already offered to the world. It is a "sublime offering"[16] to the world from the world and through the world. To say: "existence is offered" is to say: "existence is sacrificed" or even "existence is sacrifice." In these expressions, the word "sacrifice" is somehow given back to its old meaning of offering and off-spring.

Meant here is the meaning of existence as meaning nothing but its arrival, its taking place and being-thrown into the world. It is not something that offers itself, but pure offering or to recall one verse of the American poet Emily Dickinson: "the web of life woven.[17] Not being what offers itself but the offering itself, it is no longer possible to speak about self-sacrifice. For Nancy, the finitude of existence, that he connects to Heidegger's known formulation in *Being and Time* that "the essence of *Dasein* (= finite existence) lies in its existence,"[18] cannot be understood neither as self-sacrifice nor as sacrifice for nothing, for nothingness or for Otherness, as in Bataille's philosophy of sacrifice. As he says, "it is exactly at this point that both Bataille and Heidegger must be relentlessly corrected."[19] This point, their tendency to remain fascinated with sacrifice, that is, with a meaning of difference as transcending difference, which binds them to the fascination with an absolute outside that would be able to restore a better, truer, more authentic finitude. "Western sacrifice is haunted by an Outside of finitude," Nancy adds.

Nancy alludes to Heidegger's own thoughts on sacrifice referring to a passage from Heidegger's Essay on the "Origin of the Work of Art" form 1935–1936, in which it is said that "essential sacrifice is one of the modes of the putting-to-work that is concentrated in art."[20] Nancy does not articulate his "correction" of Heidegger to this and other passages where Heidegger sketches a philosophy of sacrifice and a "thinking accordingly to sacrifice," in many aspects close to Bataille's. Heidegger even distinguishes between authentic or essential and inauthentic sacrifice,[21] a distinction that is also developed by the Czech phenomenologist Jan Patocka.[22] As Bataille, both Heidegger and Patocka consider that sacrifice is the concrete experience of the ontological and phenomenological difference between Being and beings, between reification of the meaning of Being and the meaning of being as pure is-being, as event, and hence of what in reification cannot be reified. Two main dimensions of this "thinking accordingly to sacrifice" that can be traced among Bataille, Heidegger and Patocka are targets for Nancy's correction. The first is the meaning of finitude, of finite singularity of being itself and the second the very sense of transformation accomplished or performed in and through sacrifice.

Nancy does not propose a sacrifice of sacrifice, and neither the end of sacrifice. His contribution to the question about the end of sacrifice can be rather described as the suspension of sacrifice insofar as he leaves the meaning of sacrifice in suspension, giving it back to the un-known. Socrates' self-sacrifice defined itself as the knowing of not-knowing. Nancy suggests something different: unknowing the known, the loss of the known. Even the current meaning of old or real sacrifice related to "economy" is brought into question. For if the aliments brought to the Gods are more or even less than aliments?[23] Suspending the meaning of sacrifice, he reminds us that the atrocities of contemporary history, the history in which the annihilation and extermination of the universal became universal and total annihilation and extermination, should not be discussed in terms of sacrifice but rather as of the sacrifice of sacrifice. In his sketch for a "correction" of the meaning of finitude and of transformation, of finitude of transformation and of transforming finitude, Nancy proposes rather a shift from a thought accordingly to sacrifice to a thinking accordingly to "the unsacrificeable" truth of existence. This shift is obscure insofar as the "unsacrificeable" truth of existence beholds a negative pre-fixed relation, so to speak, to sacrifice. But maybe at stake here is not a shift from what *must be* sacrificed to what *cannot be* sacrificed, or not even really a shift but the listening to the plural way finitude offers its finite singularity, its "being singular plural" in the word globally concerned with ends without end, with finalities without finality. Philosophical sacrifice, from self-sacrifice to the sacrifice of sacrifice, is concerned with ends to come and coming to ends, committed with a to come, either a world or a singularity to come. Philosophical sacrifice disposes of the end of sacrifice in order to impose the sacrifice for ends. In tension with philosophical sacrifice, Nancy proposes a thought that listens to the subtle differentiation between finality and finitude, between a search for the coming to be and a sensibility for the is-being of being. No sacrifice, but openness for the offering of "the present as element of nearness."[24] Instead of philosophical sacrifice, Nancy insists upon the urgency for a thought of "sublime offering," of the sublime of the offering of the singular, that rather than impose, proposes and presents the present – the nearby – as an offering. In the offering, he says, the given is in fact not given; the given is open, the given of the open, the exposure to the given open.

Notes

1. Bataille 1973: 58.
2. Bataille 1973: 59.
3. Bataille 1973: 64.
4. Bataille 1973: 66.
5. Bataille 1973: 67
6. Stroumsa 2009.
7. Nancy 1991: 22
8. Hegel's discussions about "patriotic sacrifice" summarize this unique universalization of self-sacrifice, as can be read in a passage from The Encyclopedia quoted by Nancy: "country and fatherland then appear as the power by which the particular independence of individuals and their absorption in the external existence of possession and in natural life is convicted of its own nullity – as the power which procures the maintenance of the general substance by the patriotic sacrifice on the part of these individuals of this natural and particular existence – so making nugatory the nugatories that confronts it.," "Dieser Zustand ziegt die Substanz des Staates in ihrer zur abstrakten Negativität fortgehenden Individualität, als die Macht, in welcher die besondere Selbständigkeit der Einzelnen und der Zustand ihres Versenktseins in das äußerliche Dasein des Besitzes und in das natürliche Leben sich als ein *Nichtiges* fühlt und welche die Erhaltung der allgemeinen Substanz durch die in der Gesinnung derselben geschehende Aufopferung dieses natürlichen und besonderen Daseins, die Vereitelung des dagegen Eitlen vermittelt (Hegel 1970: §546).
9. Nancy 1991: 25
10. Nancy 1991: 34
11. Bataille 1967: 95.
12. Bataille 1967: 95
13. Bataille 1967: 94
14. Nancy 1991: 35.
15. Nancy 1991: 35.
16. For a more extensive discussion of the sublime as offering, see Nancy 1988: 37–75.
17. Emily Dickinson, T*he Complete Poems*, (Johnson 1960), by such and such an offering/ to Mr. So and So - the web of life woven/So martyrs album show," p. 23, poem 38.
18. Heidegger 1962: §9.
19. Nancy 1991: 36
20. Heidegger.

21. For a discussion about Heidegger's thoughts on sacrifice, see Trawny 2010), especially 208–218.

22. Cf. my article. "Sacrifice and Salvation: Jan Patocka's Reading of Heidegger on the Question of Technology," in Chvatik and Abrams 2011:23–37, where Heidegger's concept of sacrifice is compared with Jan Patocka's thoughts on authentic sacrifice.

23. Nancy 1991: 35

24. Nancy 2012: 63.00

References

Bataille, Georges. 1973. *Théorie de la religion*. Paris: Gallimard.

Bataille, Georges. 1967. *La part maudite*. Paris: Les editions de Minuit.

Chvatik, I., and E. Abrams, eds. 2011. *Jan Patocka and the Heritage of Phenomenology*. London: Springer.

Johnson, Thomas H, ed. 1960. *The Complete Poems of Emily Dickinson*. Boston, MA: Little Brown & Co.

Hegel, G.W.F. 1970. *Enzyclopädie der philosophiscehen Wissenschaften III, Werke 10*. Frankfurt am Main: Suhrkamp.

Heidegger, Martin. 1962. *Being and Time*. Translated by John Macquarrie and Edward Robinson. New York: Harper.

Nancy, Jean-Luc. 1991. *The Unsacrificeable" in Litterature and the Ethical Question*, Yale French Studies, no 79. New Haven, CT: Yale University Press.

Nancy, Jean-Luc. 1988. "L'Offrande sublime." In *Du Sublime*, edited by Jean-François Courtine, 37-75. Paris: Belin.

Nancy, Jean-Luc. 2012. *L'Équivalence des catastrophes (Après Fukushima)*. Paris: Galilée.

Stroumsa, Guy. 2009. *The End of Sacrifice: Religious Transformations in Late Antiquity*. Chicago, IL: Chicago University Press.

Trawny, Peter. 2010. *Heidegger und Hölderlin oder der Europäische Morgen*. Würzburg: Königshausen & Neumann.

About the author

Marcia Sá Cavalcante Schuback is Professor of Philosphy at Södertörn University, Sweden. Cavalcante Schuback has been Associate Professor at the Universidade Federal do Rio de Janeiro (UFRJ) in Brazil. Her field of research is continental philosophy, with focus on phenomenology, hermeneutics, German Idealism, and hermeneutical readings of ancient philosophy. Her latest monographs are *Att tänka i skisser: essäer om bildens filosofi & filosofins bilder* (2011), *Being with the without* (2013) and *Dis-orientations. Philosophy, Literature and the Lost Grounds of Modernity* (2015).

Index

References to notes are entered as, for example, 159n.

A

abstract action 34–40
Achsenzeit (Axial Age) 64–66, 67–68, 77–80, 99–105
acosmic perspective 180–181, 185, 187–188
adhvaryu 47, 48, 53
Aeschylus 91–92
Agamben, Giorgio 200, 214n, 216n
agency 45–58, 60n–61n
Agni (god) 23, 24, 29–30
Agnihotra 27–30
Ainu 8, 124–126
akousmata 4
Albinus 156
altars 150, 160n
animal sacrifice 4, 5, 6, 8, 15–19, 27, 47, 99, 124–126, 157n–158n, 209, 216n
apotheosis 91
Armstrong, Karen 100
asceticism 4, 69, 88, 169–170, 171, 188n, 202
Asclepius 123, 134, 138n, 146–148, 151–153, 155–156, 159n, 161n
askēsis 106
Assmann, Jan 87, 102, 130, 138n
astronomy/astrology 75–77, 162n
Aśvamedha 15–19, 26, 27, 47
ātman 46–47, 51–58
Attridge, Harold W. 175, 189n
Augustine of Hippo, Saint 106, 109, 116, 200
Aulén, Gustaf 180
Axial Age 64–66, 67–68, 77–80, 99–105
axial age 8
Ayer, A. J. 69

B

bandhu (connection) 16–19, 21–22, 23, 28–31
Barth, Karl 204
Basham, A. L. 76, 79
Bataille, Georges 9, 221–222, 224–225
bear sacrifice 8, 124–126
Bell, Catherine 35, 36
Bellah, Robert 8, 100, 101–102, 103, 104
Berger, Peter 115
Bertholet, Alfred 124, 126
Bible 9, 107, 108, 109–111, 197–213, 214n–215n. *see also* religions of the Book
blood sacrifice 1, 63, 110–114, 126–127, 143–144, 147–148, 150,

www.ingramcontent.com/pod-product-compliance
Lightning Source LLC
Chambersburg PA
CBHW061011280326
41935CB00009B/919
* 9 7 8 1 7 8 1 7 9 1 2 5 7 *